The MIDI IMPLEMENTATION BOOK

by
STEVE DE FURIA and
JOE SCACCIAFERRO

Produced by John Cerullo
Art Direction by John Flannery

Produced and Published by
Third Earth Publishing Inc.
Pompton Lakes, N.J.

Distributed Exclusively by Hal Leonard Books.

ISBN 0-88188-558-4

Contents

Introduction

One of the main problems that the designers of the MIDI specification had to face *was to make the definition* wide enough to embrace the vast range of features that synthesizers, drum machines, etc. *might* include. And I emphasize the word "might" because it is an operative point about MIDI: There are no "MIDI Police" to insist that all possible MIDI features be present on a given machine. And of course, some MIDI commands have no direct meaning on a given unit, such as After Touch on a drum machine. So we have a specification that has very wide possibilities and very specific implementations.

The MIDI Implementation Chart was an attempt on the part of the Japanese manufacturers (members of the Japanese MIDI Standards Committee, or JMSC) to provide, in a unified way, information concerning the way that MIDI is implemented on a synthesizer, drum machine, sequencer, accessory box, or indeed, any unit that has MIDI connector. What commands does the unit send; what commands does it respond to? Does it send Velocity with its notes? What does it do with Program Change commands outside of its normal range? How about range of Note Commands? Systems Exclusive? Song Position Pointer? What Modes does it go into?

The Implementation Chart was born to display all of the information, and immediately was adopted by the MIDI Manufacturers Association, who represent all non-JMSC manufacturers. But a couple of problems developed:

1) Getting a copy of the Imp Chart was sometimes quite difficult. In a minority of cases, it was printed in the owner's manual, but generally had to be obtained by contacting the manufacturer. And usually, the manufacturer had no normal distribution channels for this information.

2) A great deal of the equipment on the market had no Imp Charts at all — many manufacturers had never gotten around to it. Until Ferro Technology formally requested access to this data from MMA, that body had no "official" stance on the subject. That has now changed.

3) Even if you did have a good collection of Imp Charts, organizing them was a frustrating job. I have a drawer full of them and yet have no idea of exactly what I have.

At last, with the Ferro Technology "MIDI Implementation Book," we have an extensive set of Imp Charts in one organized place.

It is an old axiom that knowledge is power. I've always felt that if I couldn't have knowledge, I would settle for information. With that in mind, this book should be a powerful addition to any MIDI user's book collection.

Jim Cooper
President, MMA and J.L. Cooper Electronics

Authors' Notes

Acknowledgements

Collection of the data for these books was an enormous task. We would like to thank the MIDI Manufacturers Association, the Japanese MIDI Standards Commitee, and the International MIDI Association, as well as the engineers and designers from the many manufacturers who contributed to this effort. In particular we would like to thank Jim Cooper, Chris Meyer, Jim Mothersbaugh, Paul M. Young, Jerry Kovarsky, Dan Ramsauer, Mark Koenig, and the staff at Triple S Electronics for their assistance and support.

About The Conventions Used In The Book

Every effort has been made to ensure that the information in these charts is accurate and up to date. A substantial number of the charts in this reference were created from data transferred directly from MIDI implementation charts supplied by the manufacturers. Some of the instruments in this book have never had implementation charts supplied as part of their factory documentation. In those cases we compiled the charts ourselves by carefully researching the existing documentation and when necessary, bench-testing the device in question.

However, the MIDI implementation chart, as defined in the MIDI 1.0 Detailed Specification document, is not a rigidly specified format. As a result, there are considerable inconsistencies in the way any two manufacturers (sometimes even one manufacturer) may notate the same data on different charts. In order to maximize the usefulness of this reference, we felt it important to present implementation data in as consistant a manner as possible.

Therefore, we have adopted several conventions and applied them to every chart. All of these conventions are consistent with the guidelines recommended in the Detailed MIDI Specification, and whenever possible, they follow the format used on the majority of the charts used to compile this book. In the charts in this book for instance, "O" always means "yes" and "X" always means "no." We refer to the four MIDI modes as Mode1, Mode 2, Mode 3, and Mode 4, and mode messages are given as OMNI ON, OMNI OFF, POLY, and MONO. All numbers used in these charts are decimal unless specified otherwise. A complete description of the conventions used for these charts is provided in *The MIDI Resource Book.*

For the sake of clarity, we have removed redundant data. For example, there is no need to list the range of recognized Note Numbers twice if the "Recognized" and "True Voice" values are the same. This applies to "Recognized" and "True #" ranges of Program Change messages as well. In such situations, the range is given once as the "Recognized" range.

The section of the chart used to list transmitted and recognized mode messages was a problem area. The problem seems to be caused by confusing MIDI *modes* with MIDI mode *messages.* For the record, there are six mode messages defined by the MIDI specification. Of these six, four are used to convey actual MIDI "mode" information. As mentioned above, these four mode messages are listed on our charts as OMNI ON, OMNI OFF, POLY, and MONO.

On our source charts, it was common to find transmitted or recognized mode messages listed erroneously. A typical entry for "transmitted/recognized mode messages" might be "Modes 1, 3, 4." Although this does describe valid MIDI modes, it does not describe any actual mode *messages,* making it impossible to say what the device in question actually transmits or recognizes.

In such situations, we took it upon ourselves to research other available documentation, call the designers, and (in some cases) actually bench test the unit in order to obtain the correct information for the chart. If we were unable to obtain the actual messages used by the device, we marked the section "unavailable at printing," rather than re-use the erroneous information given in the original source chart.

S. De Furia and J. Scacciaferro
Fall '86

How To Use
The MIDI Reference Books

Within the Ferro Music Technology Series, *The MIDI Resource Book, The MIDI Implementation Book,* and *The MIDI System Exclusive Book* form a series within a series. If you are involved with MIDI as an engineer or computer programmer, then you are undoubtedly already familiar with reference and resource books. You'll find these three books form a long overdue, and invaluable, desk reference set.

If your involvement with MIDI is based on a more practical user's point of view, then the concept (and usefulness) of such a reference work might be new to you. So we thought a few words on what these books are, and how to get the most from them, might be helpful here.

The tools and techniques we use to create, produce, and perform music incorporate increasingly more MIDI concepts into both their design and operation. Therefore, the musician who can understand and exploit MIDI concepts can take best advantage of the tools made available via this technology. The MIDI Reference Series is designed to help you to both understand MIDI technology and put that understanding to practical use.

The MIDI Resource Book is your source of information about MIDI concepts, standard conventions, and specifications. Use this book to learn what MIDI means and how it works. When you understand the information in this book you'll know how MIDI concepts can be applied to any application, and you will be able get the most from the data in the other two books.

Use *The MIDI Implementation Book* and *The MIDI System Exclusive Book* to learn the practical details of how MIDI has been utilized in a particular device, and how it can be used effectively with other units in a MIDI system. You'll find these books can be invaluable if you want to know how well one MIDI instrument can control (or be controlled by) another, or when you're looking for a device to solve a particular interfacing problem. If you're shopping for a new addition to your MIDI system, you'll find that comparing implementations and system exclusive functions of similar instruments can help you make an informed choice as to which instrument best fits your needs.

Of Course, as MIDI and related products evolve, Ferro Technologies will release updated versions of these books.

The MIDI Resource Book

This book is the core to our "series within a series." It contains up-to-date MIDI specifications and standards documentation. In it you'll find MMA and JMSC documentation for

> The Complete MIDI 1.0 Specification
> The MIDI Sample Dump Standard
> Manufacturer's Published System Exclusive Formats

We have provided supplemental sections to each of the above documents that contain further explanations, reference charts, and more. For example, the sections on *How to Read and Use MIDI Implementation Charts* and *Interpreting System Exclusive Codes* will give you the keys to unlocking any instrument's full MIDI potential.

This is a true engineering reference. All of the information is logically organized and cross-referenced to provide quick and easy access to any MIDI specification related details.

The MIDI Resource Book also contains a complete directory of MIDI related references and resources. In it, you'll find listings of

> MIDI Manufacturers
> MIDI Organizations
> Electronic Bulletin Boards
> Related Books and Publications

The MIDI Implementation Book

In this book, there are over 200 complete Implementation Charts from over 30 makers of MIDI devices. These charts (collected with assistance of the MMA, JMSC, IMA, and many independent MIDI manufacturers) represent virtually every type of MIDI product on the market today. We've provided a unique *double-listing system* that allows you to locate any Implementation Chart within the book by two different methods. Use the ***Product Listing*** when you want to locate a specific product and the ***Application Listing*** when you are looking for a device that meets particular MIDI criteria, or if you want to compare MIDI implementations of similar devices.

The ✤ symbol is our cross-reference symbol. When you see it in entries in either Listing, it indicates that System Exclusive data and/or detailed programming data for that device can be found in ***The MIDI System Exclusive Book.***

The MIDI System Exclusive Book

System Exclusive codes are used to perform instrument specific functions and operations that don't fall under the realm of Voice, Mode, Common, and Real Time MIDI messages defined by the MIDI specification. This book contains the complete listing of all system exclusive codes registered with the MMA. It also contains any additional programming information, such as parameter tables and bit-maps, made available by the manufacturers for a given product (or products).

The data in this book is organized with the same double-listing system used in ***The MIDI Implementation Book.*** You can locate information by manufacturer/product with ***Product Listing,*** or use the ***Application Listing*** to locate devices by functional description.

The ✤ symbol indicates that an Implementation Chart for that device can be found in ***The MIDI Implementation Book.***

About The Double-Listing System

The double-listing system used in *The MIDI Implementation Book* and *The MIDI System Exclusive Book* allows you to locate information by two methods. The *Product Listing* lets you find data quickly when you need information for a specific product. The *Application Listing* allows you to locate data for devices designed for specific applications.

Product Listing

The *Product Listing* is an alphabetized list of manufacturers. Each manufacturer's products are in-turn listed in alphabetical order. To find a specific device, find the manufacturer and then locate the device you're looking for in the product list.

Each item in the list shows the *Model, Version, and Description* fields as they appear in the actual implementation chart and the page number where the data can be found. Many of the items will also have this symbol ✣. It indicates that data for the product is contained in both *The MIDI Implementation Book* and *The MIDI System Exclusive Book*. You can tell at a glance if additional data is available without having to flip through a second book.

Application Listing

The *Application Listing* organizes the products into twenty-four general applications as follows:

Digital Synthesizers	**Interfaces**
Hybrid Synthesizers	**MIDI Data Routing Units**
Samplers	**Synchronization Devices**
Pianos	**MIDI Control Devices**
Preset Instruments	**Channel Converters**
Organs	**CV Converters**
Accordians	**Lighting Controllers**
Performance Controllers	**Data Storage**
Sequencers	**Data Display**
Drum Machines	**Software**
Audio Processors	**Modifications**

Where appropriate, the products listed within each application are further categorized according to *TYPE , ONBOARD CONTROLLER,* or *COMPUTER INTERFACE.*

TYPE is used to further qualify products within a particular application. For example, **Audio Processors** is subdivided into the following types of devices: *Effects, Reverbs, Mixers, Mutes,* and *Volume Controls.*

ONBOARD CONTROLLER is used to indicate the type of controller builtin to performance instruments. You can see which instruments use *Guitar, Percussion,* or *Keyboard* controllers to generate MIDI Note On/Off messages. Instruments that can only be controlled remotely by another device, are indicated with the word *Slave* . In addition, instruments with built-in sequencers are indicated with the word *Sequencer.*

COMPUTER/INTERFACE lists the type of computer and or interface required by software products.

Within the categories *TYPE, ON-BOARD CONTROLLER,* and *COMPUTER/ INTERFACE.,* they are listed alphabetically by manufacturer. Each item in the *Application Listing* shows the *Manufacturer, Model,* and *Version* fields as they appear on the Implementation Chart and appropriate *TYPE, ON-BOARD CONTROLLER,* or *COMPUTER/INTERFACE* notes. The ✣ symbol is used to indicate that data for an item is contained in both books. The page number shows where the data can be found in this book.

Application Listing

Digital Synthesizers

PAGE		MODEL	VERSION	ON-BOARD MIDI CONTROLLER	
22	Casio	CZ-5000 ✤	—	Keyboard	Sequencer
23	Fairlight	CMI Series III	3.10	Keyboard	Sequencer
24	Kurzweil	Kurzweil 250	3.1	Keyboard	Sequencer
25	New England Digital	Synclavier	0.9	Keyboard	Sequencer
26	PPG	Wave 2.2 / 2.3 ✤	6.0	Keyboard	Sequencer
26		EVU ✤	3.0	Keyboard	Sequencer
27	Casio	CZ-1	—	Keyboard	
28		CZ-101 ✤	—	Keyboard	
29		CZ-3000 ✤	—	Keyboard	
30	Yamaha	DX5 ✤	—	Keyboard	
31		DX7 ✤	—	Keyboard	
32		DX9 ✤	—	Keyboard	
33		DX21 ✤	1.2	Keyboard	
34		DX27 ✤	1.0	Keyboard	
35		DX100 ✤	1.0	Keyboard	
36	Kurzweil	K150 Expander	1.2	Slave	
37	Yamaha	TF1 ✤	1.0	Slave	
38		TX7 ✤	1.0	Slave	

Hybrid Synthesizers

PAGE		MODEL	VERSION	ON-BOARD MIDI CONTROLLER	
39	Roland	GR-77B ✤	1.0	Bass Guitar	
40		GR-700 ✤	1.2	Guitar	
41	Ensoniq	ESQ 1 ✤	1.0	Keyboard	Sequencer
42	Fender	Chroma Polaris ✤	3	Keyboard	Sequencer
43	Korg	POLY-800 + MDK ✤	—	Keyboard	Sequencer
44	Korg	POLY-800 MK2 ✤	1.0	Keyboard	Sequencer
45	Roland	JX-3P ✤	1.0	Keyboard	Sequencer
46		JX-3P ✤	2.1	Keyboard	Sequencer
47		JX-10 ✤	1.01	Keyboard	Sequencer
48		JX-10 ✤	1.00	Keyboard	Sequencer
49	Sequential	Max ✤	0.3	Keyboard	Sequencer
50		Multi Trak ✤	—	Keyboard	Sequencer
51		Prophet 10 ✤	—	Keyboard	Sequencer
52		Six Trak ✤	—	Keyboard	Sequencer
53		T-8 ✤	3.7	Keyboard	Sequencer
54	Siel	DK-80 ✤	0	Keyboard	Sequencer
55	Akai	AX-60	1.0	Keyboard	
56		AX-73	1.0	Keyboard	
57	Korg	DW-6000 ✤	1.0	Keyboard	
58		DW-8000 ✤	1.0	Keyboard	
59		POLY-61M	1.0	Keyboard	
60	Oberheim	OB-8 ✤	—	Keyboard	
61		Matrix 6 ✤	2	Keyboard	
62		Matrix 12 ✤	1.4	Keyboard	
63	Roland	JP-6 ✤	4	Keyboard	
64		JP-6 ✤	6	Keyboard	
65		JU-1 ✤	1.0	Keyboard	
66		JU-1 ✤	1.1	Keyboard	
67		JU-2 ✤	1.0	Keyboard	
68		JU-2 ✤	1.1	Keyboard	
69		JX-8P ✤	1.0	Keyboard	
70		JUNO-106 ✤	1.0	Keyboard	
71	Sequential	Prophet 5 ✤	10.2	Keyboard	
72		Prophet 600 ✤	6.07	Keyboard	
73		Prophet VS ✤	—	Keyboard	
74	Siel	DK 600	8	Keyboard	
75		DK 700 ✤	—	Keyboard	

Hybrid Synthesizers (continued)

PAGE		MODEL	VERSION	ON-BOARD MIDI CONTROLLER
76	Hohner	MR 250	1.0	Slave
77	Siel	EX-600	0	Slave
78	Akai	VX-90	1.0	Slave
79	Korg	EX-800 ❖	1.0	Slave
80		EX-8000 ❖	1.0	Slave
81	Roland	MKS-7 ❖	1.0	Slave
82		MKS-7 ❖	1.0	Slave
83		MKS-7 ❖	1.0	Slave
84		MKS-7 ❖	1.0	Slave
85		MKS-80 ❖	1.0	Slave
61	Oberheim	6R ❖	2	Slave
62		Xpander ❖	1.4	Slave

Samplers

PAGE		MODEL	VERSION	ON-BOARD MIDI CONTROLLER	
86	Emu	Emulator II	—	Keyboard	Sequencer
87	Ensoniq	Mirage	3.2	keyboard	Sequencer
88		Mirage ❖	2.0	keyboard	Sequencer
89	Emu	E-Max ❖	—	Keyboard	
90	Sequential	Prophet 2000 ❖	—	Keyboard	
91	Akai	S-612 ❖	—	Slave	
92		S900 ❖	1.2	Slave	

Pianos

PAGE		MODEL	VERSION	ON-BOARD MIDI CONTROLLER	
93	Kurzweil	Ensemble Grande	—	Keyboard	Sequencer
94	Technics	SX-PX1M	—	Keyboard	Sequencer
95	Ensoniq	SDP-1	1.0	Keyboard	
96	Roland	EP-50 ❖	1.0	Keyboard	
97		HP-100 ❖	1.0	Keyboard	
98		HP-300 ❖	1.0	Keyboard	
99		HP-350 ❖	1.0	Keyboard	
100		HP-400 ❖	1.0	Keyboard	
101		HP-450 ❖	1.0	Keyboard	
102		HP-5500,5600 ❖	1.0	Keyboard	
103		RD-1000 ❖	1.0	Keyboard	
104	Yamaha	PF70 ❖	1.0	Keyboard	
105		PF80 ❖	1.0	Keyboard	
106	Roland	MKS-10 ❖	1.0	Slave	
107		MKS-20 ❖	1.0	Slave	

Preset Instruments

PAGE		MODEL	VERSION	ON-BOARD MIDI CONTROLLER	
108	Casio	CT-6000	—	Keyboard	Sequencer
109		CT-6500 ❖	—	Keyboard	Sequencer
110	Siel	MK 1000	1.0	Keyboard	Sequencer
111	Casio	CZ-230S ❖	—	Keyboard	
112	Siel	MK-610 / MK-890	1.0	Keyboard	
113	Hohner	PK 150	—	Keyboard	
114	360 Systems	MIDI Bass	—	Slave	
115	Hohner	PK 250 ❖	7.0	Slave	
116	Roland	EM-101 ❖	1.0	Slave	
117		MKS-30 ❖	1.0	Slave	

Organs

PAGE		MODEL	VERSION
118	Hohner	D 160	—
119		D 180	—
120		GP 180/D 180	7.2
121	Technics	SX-EX50(L)	—
122		SX-EX60	—

Accordians

PAGE		MODEL	VERSION
123	Hohner	Atlantic	—
124		Fortuna	—
125		Morino	—
126		Tango	—
127		VOX 5	—

MIDI Performance Controllers

PAGE		MODEL	VERSION	TYPE	
128	Roland	PAD-8	1.0	Percussion Pads	
129	Korg	MPK-130	1.0	Foot Pedals	
130	Ibanez	MC1	1.1	Guitar	Pitch / MIDI
131	K-Muse	Photon	1.0	Guitar	Digital
132		Photon	2.0	Guitar	Digital
133	Synthaxe	Controller	1	Guitar	Digital
134	Casio	AZ-1	—	Keyboard	Strap-on
135	Korg	RK-100	1.0	Keyboard	Strap-on
136	Lync Systems	LN-1	1.02A	Keyboard	Strap-on
137	Roland	AXIS-1 ✤	1.0	Keyboard	Strap-on
138	Yamaha	KX5	—	Keyboard	Strap-on
139	Akai	MX-73	1.0	Keyboard	
140	Kurzweil	MIDIBOARD	1.1	Keyboard	
141	Mimetics	Soundscape	1	Keyboard	
142	Oberheim	XK ✤	1.0	Keyboard	
143	Roland	MKB-200 ✤	1.0	Keyboard	
144		MKB-300, 1000 ✤	—	Keyboard	
145	Yamaha	KX88	1.0	Keyboard	

Sequencers

PAGE		MODEL	VERSION
146	Casio	SZ-1	1
147	Korg	MP-100	1.0
148	Korg	SQD-1 ✤	1.0
149	Linn	Linn 9000	—
149		Linn Sequencer	—
150	Roland	MCP-PC8 ✤	1.00
151		MRC-PC98	1.00
152		MRC-PC8,FM7, X1 ✤	1.00
153		MSQ-100 ✤	1.0
154		MSQ-700 ✤	1.41
155		PR-800 ✤	1.0
156	Yamaha	QX1 ✤	1.0
157		QX7 ✤	1.0
158		QX21 ✤	1.0

Drum Machines

PAGE		MODEL	VERSION
159	Casio	RZ-1 ✤	1
160	J L Cooper	Sound Chest II ✤	—
161	Korg	MR-16	1.0
162	Oberheim	DX ✤	—
163	Roland	TR-505 ✤	1.1
164		TR-505 ✤	1.2
165		TR-707	1.0
166		TR-727 ✤	1.0
167		TR-909 ✤	1.2
168	Yamaha	RX11 ✤	—
169		RX21L ✤	1.0
170	Emu	Drumulator	—
171		SP12 ✤	—
172	Sequential	Drum Traks ✤	0.5 / 0.4
173		Tom ✤	—
174	Siel	MDP 40	1.0

Audio Processors

PAGE		MODEL	VERSION	TYPE
175	Alesis	MIDIFex	—	Effect
176	ART	DR1 ✤	1.2	Effect
177	Korg	DVP-1 ✤	1.0	Effect
178		SDD-2000 ✤	1.0	Effect
179	Lexicon	PCM 70	1.00	Effect
180	Roland	SDE-2500	1.0	Effect
181	Yamaha	SPX90	1.0	Effect
182	Alesis	MIDIVerb	—	Reverb
183	Ibanez	SDR1000 ✤	1.0	Reverb
184	Roland	SRV-2000	1.0	Reverb
185	Yamaha	REV7	1.0	Reverb
186	Akai	MPX-820 ✤	1.01	Mixer
187	J L Cooper	MIDI Mute	—	Mute
188		Expression Plus	—	Volume Control

Interfaces

PAGE		MODEL	VERSION	TYPE
189	Clarity	MIDI / XLV	1.00	224XL
189	Hinton	MIDIC / AMS DMX	—	AMS DMX 15-80s
190		MIDIC / Rev 1	—	Rev 1
190	J L Cooper	QMI	—	Quantec QM1
191	Passport	MH-01M	1.0	Macintosh
191		MH-01X	1.0 - 1.1	IBM PC
192		MH-01A / MH-02A	1.0	Apple II
192		MH-01C / MH-02C	1.0	Commodore
193	Roland	MD-8 ✤	4	MIDI / DCB
193	Roland	MD-8 ✤	5	MIDI / DCB
194	Siel	MCI ✤	—	Z80, 6502, 6510 CPUs

MIDI Data Routing Units

PAGE		MODEL	VERSION	TYPE
194	360 Systems	MIDI Merge +	—	Merger
195	J L Cooper	Blender	—	Merger
195	360 Systems	MIDI Patcher +	—	Switcher
196	J L Cooper	MSB 1	—	Switcher
196		MSB 16 / 20 ✤	—	Switcher

Synchronization Devices

PAGE		MODEL	VERSION	TYPE
197	J L Cooper	MIDI Sync II	—	Clock / MIDI
197		MIDI Sync I	—	MIDI / Clock
198	Korg	KMS-30	1.0	MIDI / Clock
198	Fostex	4050	—	MIDI / SMPTE
199	Roland	SBX-10 ✣	1.0	MIDI / SMPTE
199		SBX-80	—	MIDI / SMPTE

MIDI Control Devices

PAGE		MODEL	VERSION	TYPE
200	Axxess Unlimited	Mapper	—	Processing Unit
200	Alesis	MPX	—	Program Change Unit
201	J L Cooper	MIDI Link ✣	—	Program Change Unit
201	Roland	PG-300 ✣	1.0	JU-1, JU-2 Programmer
202	Voyce	LX-4	—	Control Unit
202	Yamaha	MCS2	1.0	Control Unit

Channel Converters

PAGE		MODEL	VERSION	TYPE
203	J L Cooper	Channelizer	—	Channel Converter
203		Channel Filter	—	Channel Filter
204	Roland	MPU-103 ✣	1.0	Filter / Converter

Control Voltage Converters

PAGE		MODEL	VERSION	
204	J L Cooper	CV Out	—	MIDI / CV
205		MIDI Interface	—	MIDI / CV
205		CV In	—	CV / MIDI
206		MIDI Wind Driver	—	CV / MIDI
206	Roland	MPU-101 ✣	1.0	MIDI / CV
207		OP-8M ✣	1.2	CV-MIDI

Lighting Controllers

PAGE		MODEL	VERSION	TYPE
207	IDP	IDP 612	1.00	
208	J L Cooper	MLC-1	—	

Data Storage

PAGE		MODEL	VERSION
208	J L Cooper	MIDI Disk	—
209	Korg	MEX-8000 ✣	1.0

Data Display

PAGE		MODEL	VERSION
209	Roland	MKS-900 ✣	1.0

Software

Modifications

Product Listing

MODEL	VERSION	DESCRIPTION	

Korg (continued)

Kurzweil

Lexicon

Linn

Lync Systems

Mimetics

New England Digital

Oberheim

Passport

MODEL	VERSION	DESCRIPTION	

PPG

MODEL	VERSION	DESCRIPTION	

Sequential

Siel

Southworth Music

Synthaxe

Technics

Voyce

Yamaha

Manufacturer
Casio
[Digital PD Synthesizer/Sequencer]

Model
CZ-5000
Version —   Date —

Function		Transmitted	Recognized	Remarks
CHANNEL	Default	1	1	
	Changed	1 — 16	1 — 16	
MODE	Default	Mode 3	Mode 3	Honors Modes 3, 4
	Messages	X	X	
	Altered			
NOTE NUMBER		36 — 96	0 — 127	
	True Voice		36 — 96	
VELOCITY	Note On	X	X	
	Note Off	X 9nH (v=0)		
TOUCH	Key's	X	X	
	Chan's	X	X	
PITCH BENDER		O	O	8 bit resolution
CONTROL CHANGE	mod 1	O	O	
	portamento time	X	O	
	5	X	O	
	master tune 6	O	O	
	sustain 64	O	O	
	portamento 65			
PROGRAM CHANGE		0 — 63	0 — 63	0 — 31 preset
	True #			32 — 63 memory
SYSTEM EXCLUSIVE		O	O	Timbre data, sequencer
SYSTEM COMMON	Song Pos	X	X	
	Song Sel	X	X	
	Tune	X	X	
SYSTEM REAL TIME	Clock	O	O	when MIDI mode enabled
	Messages	O	O	
AUX	Local Control	X	O	
	All Notes Off	X	X	
	Active Sense	X	X	
	Reset	X	X	

NOTES:

Mode 1 : OMNI ON, POLY   Mode 2 : OMNI ON, MONO   O : Yes
Mode 3 : OMNI OFF, POLY   Mode 4: OMNI OFF, MONO   X : No

Manufacturer
Fairlight CMI
[Computer Music Instrument]

Model
SERIES III
Version 3.10   Date 9/5/86

Function		Transmitted	Recognized	Remarks
CHANNEL	Default	MIDI not transmitted	chan #= instrument #	any CMI instrument can
	Changed	1 — 16	1 — 16	TX or RX on any channels
MODE	Default	MIDI not transmitted	MODE 3	Honors Modes 1 — 4
	Messages	X	X	
	Altered			
NOTE NUMBER		29-101	0 — 127	pitch wraps around when
	True Voice			sample rate is exceeded
VELOCITY	Note On	O	O	note 1
	Note Off	X	O	
TOUCH	Key's	X	X	
	Chan's	X	X	
PITCH BENDER		O	O	note 2
CONTROL CHANGE	0—63	O	O	any MIDI controller can be patched to
	64—95	O	O	any CMI parameter
PROGRAM CHANGE		X	X	
	True #			
SYSTEM EXCLUSIVE		X	X	
SYSTEM COMMON	Song Pos	X	X	
	Song Sel	X	X	
	Tune	X	x	
SYSTEM REAL TIME	Clock	X	X	
	Messages	X	X	
AUX	Local Control	X	X	
	All Notes Off	O	O (123 — 127)	
	Active Sense	X	X	
	Reset	X	X	

NOTES: NOTE 1: Keyboard sends note-on velocity in 16 steps: V=7, 15, 23, 31...127)
        NOTE 2: Pitch bender has eight bit resolution - 0—127 semitone variable range

Mode 1 : OMNI ON, POLY   Mode 2 : OMNI ON, MONO   O : Yes
Mode 3 : OMNI OFF, POLY   Mode 4: OMNI OFF, MONO   X : No

Manufacturer	Model
Kurzweil	**Kurzweil 250**
[Sampling Keyboard]	Version 3.1 Date 7/7/86

Function		Transmitted	Recognized	Remarks
CHANNEL	Default	1	1	
	Changed	1 — 16	1 — 16	
MODE	Default	Mode1	Mode 3	
	Messages	X	OMNI ON/OFF	
	Altered			
NOTE NUMBER		21 — 108	0 — 127	kbd range: A0—C8
	True Voice		21 — 108	
VELOCITY	Note On	O	O	
	Note Off	X 9nH(v=0)	X	
TOUCH	Key's	X	X	
	Chan's	X	X	
PITCH BENDER		OX	OX	
CONTROL CHANGE	Slider 1	OX	OX	control assignments are programmable (0-31, 64-95)
	Slider 2	OX	OX	
	Slider 3	OX	OX	
	Left Lever	OX	OX	
	Right Lever	OX	OX	
	Pedal 1	OX	OX	
	Pedal 2	OX	OX	
	R Pedal	OX	OX	
	L Pedal	OX	OX	
PROGRAM CHANGE		0 — 127	0 — 127	
	True #		1 — 64 250 — 313	
SYSTEM EXCLUSIVE		X	X	
SYSTEM COMMON	Song Pos	O	O	
	Song Sel	O	O	
	Tune	X	X	
SYSTEM REAL TIME	Clock	O	O	
	Messages	O	O	
AUX	Local Control	O	O	
	All Notes Off	O	O	
	Active Sense	X	X	
	Reset	X	X	
NOTES:				

Mode 1 : OMNI ON, POLY   Mode 2 : OMNI ON, MONO   O : Yes
Mode 3 : OMNI OFF, POLY   Mode 4: OMNI OFF, MONO   X : No

Manufacturer
New England Digital
[Synclavier Digital Music System]

Model
Synclavier MIDI Option
Version 0.9   Date 10/31/85

Function		Transmitted	Recognized	Remarks
CHANNEL	Default	1 — 16*	1 — 16	*see note 1
	Changed	1 — 16 *	1 — 16	
MODE	Default	Mode 1	Mode1	
	Messages	X	OMNI ON/OFF, POLY, MONO	
	Altered			
NOTE NUMBER		24 — 108	0 — 127	
	True Voice			
VELOCITY	Note On	O	O **	** see note 2
	Note Off	X 9nH (v=0)	X **	
TOUCH	Key's	O *	O**	*see note 1
	Chan's	O *	O**	**see note 2
PITCH BENDER		O	O **	see note 2
CONTROL CHANGE	mod 1	O	O**	** note 2
	breath 2	0	O**	
	pedal-2 4	O	O**	
	sustain 64	O	O**	
	portamento 65	O	O**	
PROGRAM CHANGE		X	X	
	True #			
SYSTEM EXCLUSIVE		X	X	
SYSTEM COMMON	Song Pos	X	X	
	Song Sel	X	X	
	Tune	X	X	
SYSTEM REAL TIME	Clock	X	X	
	Messages	X	X	
AUX	Local Control	X	X	
	All Notes Off	O	O	
	Active Sense	X	X	
	Reset	X	X	

NOTES: NOTE 1: information stored with sequence

NOTE 2: 7 bit resolution
information recorded by Memory Recorder

Mode 1 : OMNI ON, POLY   Mode 2 : OMNI ON, MONO   O : Yes
Mode 3 : OMNI OFF, POLY   Mode 4: OMNI OFF, MONO   X : No

Digital Synthesizers

Manufacturer	Model
PPG	**Wave 2.2/2.3 EVU**
[Computer Music System]	Version Wave 6.0/EVU 3.0 Date 4/4/86

Function		Transmitted	Recognized	Remarks
CHANNEL	Default	1	1	
	Changed	1 — 16	1 — 16	
MODE	Default	Mode 3	Mode 3	
	Messages	X	MONO, POLY	
	Altered			
NOTE NUMBER		36 — 96	1 — 127	
	True Voice		21—102	
VELOCITY	Note On	X	O	
	Note Off	X	X	
TOUCH	Key's	X	X	
	Chan's	X	O	
PITCH BENDER		O	O	
CONTROL CHANGE	mod 1	O	O	
	WAVES 2	X	O	
	cutoff 4	X	O	
	volume 7	X	O	
	release 8	X	O	
	sustain 64, 66, 67	X	O	
PROGRAM CHANGE		0 — 99	0 — 99	
	True #			
SYSTEM EXCLUSIVE		X	O	
SYSTEM COMMON	Song Pos	X	X	
	Song Sel	X	X	
	Tune	X	X	
SYSTEM REAL TIME	Clock	X	X	
	Messages	X	X	
AUX	Local Control	X	X	
	All Notes Off	O (123,125-127)	O (123, 125-127)	
	Active Sense	X	X	
	Reset	X	X	

NOTES:

Mode 1 : OMNI ON, POLY	Mode 2 : OMNI ON, MONO	O : Yes
Mode 3 : OMNI OFF, POLY	Mode 4: OMNI OFF, MONO	X : No

Manufacturer	Model
Casio	CZ-1
[Digital PD Synthesizer]	Version — Date —

Function		Transmitted	Recognized	Remarks
CHANNEL	Default	1 — 16	1 — 16	memorized
	Changed	1 — 16	1 — 16	
MODE	Default	Mode 3	Mode 3,4	
	Messages	X	POLY, MONO (M=1)	
	Altered			
NOTE		36 — 96	0 — 127	
NUMBER	True Voice		20 — 108	
VELOCITY	Note On	O	O	
	Note Off	X 9nH (v=0)	O	
TOUCH	Key's	X	X	
	Chan's	O	O	
PITCH BENDER		O	O	see note 1
CONTROL	mod 1	O	O	
CHANGE	portamento time	X	O	
	5	X	O	
	main volume 7	O	O	
	sustain 64	O	O	
	portamento 65			
PROGRAM		0 — 63	0 — 63	Tone/operation memory
CHANGE	True #			
SYSTEM EXCLUSIVE		O	O	see note 2
SYSTEM	Song Pos	X	X	
COMMON	Song Sel	X	X	
	Tune	X	X	
SYSTEM	Clock	X	X	
REAL TIME	Messages	X	X	
AUX	Local Control	X	O	
	All Notes Off	X	X	
	Active Sense	X	X	
	Reset	X	X	

NOTES: NOTE 1: 8 bit resolution. 0-12 semitones.

NOTE 2: Tone data, operation memory data, other.

Mode 1 : OMNI ON, POLY	Mode 2 : OMNI ON, MONO	O : Yes
Mode 3 : OMNI OFF, POLY	Mode 4: OMNI OFF, MONO	X : No

Manufacturer		Model	
Casio		**CZ-101**	
[Digital PD Synthesizer]		Version —	Date —

Function		Transmitted	Recognized	Remarks
CHANNEL	Default	1	1	
	Changed	1 — 16	1 — 16	
MODE	Default	Mode 3	Mode 3	
	Messages	X	POLY, MONO	
	Altered		Mode 1 —>3, Mode 2—>4	
NOTE NUMBER		36 — 84	0 — 127	
	True Voice		36 — 96	
VELOCITY	Note On	X	X	
	Note Off	X 9nH (v=0)	X	
TOUCH	Key's	X	X	
	Chan's	X	X	
PITCH BENDER		O	O	8 bit resolution
CONTROL CHANGE	vibrato ON/OFF 1	O	O	
	portamento time 5	X	O	
		X	O	
	master tune 6	O	O	
	portamento 65			
PROGRAM CHANGE		0—79	0—79	see note 1
	True #		0—15, 32—47, 64—79	
SYSTEM EXCLUSIVE		O	O	TONE DATA
SYSTEM COMMON	Song Pos	X	X	
	Song Sel	X	X	
	Tune	X	X	
SYSTEM REAL TIME	Clock	X	X	
	Messages	X	X	
AUX	Local Control	X	O	
	All Notes Off	X	X	
	Active Sense	X	X	
	Reset	X	X	

NOTES: NOTE 1: 0-15 PRESET memories, 32-47 INTERNAL memories, 64-79 CARTRIDGE memories

Mode 1 : OMNI ON, POLY	Mode 2 : OMNI ON, MONO	O : Yes
Mode 3 : OMNI OFF, POLY	Mode 4: OMNI OFF, MONO	X : No

Manufacturer		Model	
Casio		**CZ-3000**	
[Digital PD Synthesizer]		Version —	Date —

Function		Transmitted	Recognized	Remarks
CHANNEL	Default	1	1	
	Changed	1 — 16	1 — 16	
MODE	Default	Mode 3	Mode 3	honors Modes 3, 4
	Messages	X	X	
	Altered			
NOTE		36 — 96	0 — 127	
NUMBER	True Voice		36 — 96	
VELOCITY	Note On	X	X	
	Note Off	X 9nH (v=0)	X	
TOUCH	Key's	X	X	
	Chan's	X	X	
PITCH BENDER		O	O	see note 1
CONTROL	mod 1	O	O	
CHANGE	portamento time	X	O	
	5	X	O	
	master tune 6	O	O	
	sustain 64	O	O	
	portamento 65			
PROGRAM		0 — 63	0 — 63	0 — 31 preset
CHANGE	True #			32 — 63 memory
SYSTEM EXCLUSIVE		O	O	Timbre data, etc.
SYSTEM	Song Pos	X	X	
COMMON	Song Sel	X	X	
	Tune	X	X	
SYSTEM	Clock	O	O	when MIDI mode enabled
REAL TIME	Messages	O	O	
AUX	Local Control	X	O	
	All Notes Off	X	X	
	Active Sense	X	X	
	Reset	X	X	

NOTES: NOTE 1: 8 bit resolution. 0-12 semitones.

Mode 1 : OMNI ON, POLY	Mode 2 : OMNI ON, MONO	O : Yes
Mode 3 : OMNI OFF, POLY	Mode 4: OMNI OFF, MONO	X : No

Manufacturer	Model
Yamaha	**DX5**
[Digital Programmable Algorithm Synthesizer]	Version — Date —

Function		Transmitted	Recognized	Remarks
CHANNEL	Default	1	1	
	Changed	1-16	1-16	
MODE	Default	Mode 3	Mode 3	
	Messages		OMNI ON/OFF, POLY, MONO	
	Altered			
NOTE NUMBER		28-103	0-127	
	True Voice			
VELOCITY	Note On	O	O	
	Note Off	X	X	
TOUCH	Key's	X	X	
	Chan's	O	O	
PITCH BENDER		O	O	
CONTROL CHANGE	mod 1	O	O	
	breath 2	O	O	
	P.Time 4	O	O	
	data entry 6	O	O	
	volume 7	X	O	
	sustain 64	O	O	
	portamento 65	O	O	
	+/- 96/97	O	O	
PROGRAM CHANGE		0-63	0-127	
	True #		1-32 (bank A,B)	
SYSTEM EXCLUSIVE		O	O	data dump, parameters
SYSTEM COMMON	Song Pos	X	X	
	Song Sel	X	X	
	Tune	X	X	
SYSTEM REAL TIME	Clock	X	X	
	Messages	X	X	
AUX	Local Control	X	X	
	All Notes Off	X	O	
	Active Sense	X	O	
	Reset	X	X	

NOTES:

Mode 1 : OMNI ON, POLY	Mode 2 : OMNI ON, MONO	O : Yes
Mode 3 : OMNI OFF, POLY	Mode 4: OMNI OFF, MONO	X : No

Manufacturer	Model	
Yamaha	**DX7**	31
[Digital Programmable Algorithm Synthesizer]	Version —	Date —

Function		Transmitted	Recognized	Remarks
CHANNEL	Default	1	1	
	Changed	X	1-16	
MODE	Default	Mode 3	Mode 3	
	Messages	X	OMNI ON, POLY, MONO	
	Altered			
NOTE NUMBER		36-96	0-127	
	True Voice			
VELOCITY	Note On	O	O	
	Note Off	X 9nH (v=0)	X	
TOUCH	Key's	X	X	older DX7s used control 3 for this message
	Chan's	O	O	
PITCH BENDER		O	O	
CONTROL CHANGE	mod 1	O	O	
	breath 2	O	O	
	foot control 4	O	O	
	data entry 6	O	O	
	sustain 64	O	O	
	portamento 65	O	O	
	+/- 96/97	O	O	
PROGRAM CHANGE		0-63	0-127	
	True #		1-32	
SYSTEM EXCLUSIVE		O	O	data dumps, parameters
SYSTEM COMMON	Song Pos	X	X	
	Song Sel	X	X	
	Tune	X	X	
SYSTEM REAL TIME	Clock	X	X	
	Messages	X	X	
AUX	Local Control	X	X	
	All Notes Off	X	O	
	Active Sense	O	O	
	Reset	X	X	
NOTES:				

Mode 1 : OMNI ON, POLY   Mode 2 : OMNI ON, MONO   O : Yes
Mode 3 : OMNI OFF, POLY   Mode 4: OMNI OFF, MONO   X : No

Manufacturer	Model
Yamaha	**DX9**
[Digital Programmable Algorithm Synthesizer]	Version — Date —

Function		Transmitted	Recognized	Remarks
CHANNEL	Default	1	1	
	Changed	X	1-16	
MODE	Default	Mode 3	Mode 3	
	Messages	X	POLY, MONO	
	Altered			
NOTE NUMBER		36-96	0-127	
	True Voice			
VELOCITY	Note On	X	X	
	Note Off	X 9n 0vh	X	
TOUCH	Key's	X	X	
	Chan's	X	X	
PITCH BENDER		O	O	
CONTROL CHANGE	mod 1	O	O	
	breath 2	O	O	
	data entry 6	O	O	
	sustain 64	O	O	
	portamento 65	O	O	
	+/- 96/97	O	O	
PROGRAM CHANGE		0-19	0-127	
	True #		1-20	
SYSTEM EXCLUSIVE		O	O	data dumps, parameters
SYSTEM COMMON	Song Pos	X	X	
	Song Sel	X	X	
	Tune	X	X	
SYSTEM REAL TIME	Clock	X	X	
	Messages	X	X	
AUX	Local Control	X	X	
	All Notes Off	X	O	
	Active Sense	O	O	
	Reset	X	X	
NOTES:				

Mode 1 : OMNI ON, POLY	Mode 2 : OMNI ON, MONO	O : Yes
Mode 3 : OMNI OFF, POLY	Mode 4: OMNI OFF, MONO	X : No

Manufacturer	Model
Yamaha	**DX21**
[Digital Programmable Algorithm Synthesizer]	Version 1.2 Date 3/9/85

Function		Transmitted	Recognized	Remarks
CHANNEL	Default	1 — 16	1 — 16	memorized
	Changed	1 — 16	1 — 16	
MODE	Default	Mode 3	Mode 1, 2, 3, 4	memorized
	Messages	X	POLY, MONO (M=1)	
	Altered			
NOTE NUMBER		36 — 96	0 — 127	
	True Voice			
VELOCITY	Note On	X	O	
	Note Off	X	X	
TOUCH	Key's	X	X	
	Chan's	X	X	
PITCH BENDER		O	O	see note 3
CONTROL CHANGE	mod 1	O	O	note 1
	breath 2	O	O	
	port time 5	X	O	
	data entry 6	O	X	
	volume 7	O	O	
	sustain 64	O	O	
	portamento 65	O	X	
	+1/-1 96/97	O	X	
PROGRAM CHANGE		0 — 31	0 — 127	
	True #		0 — 31	
SYSTEM EXCLUSIVE		O	O	note 2
SYSTEM COMMON	Song Pos	X	X	
	Song Sel	X	X	
	Tune	X	X	
SYSTEM REAL TIME	Clock	X	X	
	Messages	X	X	
AUX	Local Control	X	X	
	All Notes Off	X	O (123,126,127)	
	Active Sense	O	O	
	Reset	X	X	

NOTES: All MIDI communications are enabled if MIDI switch is on.

NOTE 1: transmit/receive if CH informatiopn switch is on.
NOTE 2: transmit/receive if system information switch is on.
NOTE 3: 7 bit resolution 0-12 semitones.

Mode 1 : OMNI ON, POLY	Mode 2 : OMNI ON, MONO	O : Yes
Mode 3 : OMNI OFF, POLY	Mode 4: OMNI OFF, MONO	X : No

Manufacturer		Model	
Yamaha		**DX27**	
[Digital Programmable Algorithm Synthesizer]		Version 1.0	Date 5/10/85

Function		Transmitted	Recognized	Remarks
CHANNEL	Default	1 — 16	1 — 16	memorized
	Changed	1 — 16	1 — 16	
MODE	Default	Mode 3	Mode 1, 2, 3, 4	memorized
	Messages	X	POLY, MONO (M=1)	
	Altered			
NOTE NUMBER		36 — 96	0 — 127	
	True Voice		13 — 108	
VELOCITY	Note On	X	O	
	Note Off	X 9nH (v=0)		
TOUCH	Key's	X	X	
	Chan's	X	X	
PITCH BENDER		O	O	see note 4
CONTROL CHANGE	mod 1	O	O	note 1
	breath 2	O	O	
	port time 5	X	O	* 7 = data entry in play mode
	data entry 6	O	X	
	volume 7	O	O *	
	sustain 64	O	O	
	portamento 65	O	O	
	+1/-1 96/97	O	X	
PROGRAM CHANGE		0 — 119*	0 — 127**	*see note 2
	True #		0 — 119	** see note 1
SYSTEM EXCLUSIVE		O	O	note 3
SYSTEM COMMON	Song Pos	X	X	
	Song Sel	X	X	
	Tune	X	X	
SYSTEM REAL TIME	Clock	X	X	
	Messages	X	X	
AUX	Local Control	X	X	
	All Notes Off	X	O (123,126,127)	
	Active Sense	X	O	
	Reset	X	X	

NOTES: All MIDI Communications are enabled if MIDI switch is on.

NOTE 1: transmit/receive if CH information switch is on.
NOTE 2: transmit if CH information switch is on and system information switch is off.
NOTE 3: transmit/receive if system information switch is on.
NOTE 4: 7 bit resolution 0-12 semitones.

Mode 1 : OMNI ON, POLY	Mode 2 : OMNI ON, MONO	O : Yes
Mode 3 : OMNI OFF, POLY	Mode 4: OMNI OFF, MONO	X : No

Manufacturer		Model	
Yamaha		**DX100**	
[Digital Programmable Algorithm Synthesizer]		Version 1.0	Date 5/10/85

Function		Transmitted	Recognized	Remarks
CHANNEL	Default	1 — 16	1 — 16	memorized
	Changed	1 — 16	1 — 16	
MODE	Default	Mode 3	Mode 1, 2, 3, 4	memorized
	Messages	X	POLY, MONO (M=1)	
	Altered			
NOTE NUMBER		36 — 84	0 — 127	
	True Voice		13 — 108	
VELOCITY	Note On	X	O	
	Note Off	X 9nH (v=0)	X	
TOUCH	Key's	X	X	
	Chan's	X	X	
PITCH BENDER		O	O	see note 4
CONTROL CHANGE	mod 1	O	O	note 1
	breath 2	O	O	
	port time 5	X	O	* 7 = data entry in play mode
	data entry 6	O	X	
	volume 7	O	O *	
	sustain 64	O	O	
	portamento 65	O	O	
	+1/-1 96/9	O	X	
PROGRAM CHANGE		0 — 119 note 2	0 — 127 *	* see note 1
	True #		0 — 119	
SYSTEM EXCLUSIVE		O	O	note 3
SYSTEM COMMON	Song Pos	X	X	
	Song Sel	X	X	
	Tune	X	X	
SYSTEM REAL TIME	Clock	X	X	
	Messages	X	X	
AUX	Local Control	X	X	
	All Notes Off	X	O(123,126,127)	
	Active Sense	O	O	
	Reset	X	X	

NOTES: All MIDI communications are enabled if MIDI switch is on.

NOTE 1: transmit/receive if CH information switch is on.
NOTE 2: transmit if CH information switch is on and system information switch is off.
NOTE 3: transmit/receive if system information switch is on.
NOTE 4: 7 bit resolution0-12 semitones.

Mode 1 : OMNI ON, POLY	Mode 2 : OMNI ON, MONO	O : Yes
Mode 3 : OMNI OFF, POLY	Mode 4: OMNI OFF, MONO	X : No

Manufacturer	Model
Kurzweil	**Kurzweil150 Expander**
[Rack Mount Digital Synthesizer]	Version 1.2 Date 7/7/86

Function		Transmitted	Recognized	Remarks
CHANNEL	Default	N/A	1	
	Changed		1 — 16	
MODE	Default	N/A	Mode 1	
	Messages		OMNI ON/OFF	
	Altered			
NOTE NUMBER		N/A	0 — 127	key range: C0—C9
	True Voice		12 — 120	
VELOCITY	Note On	N/A	O	
	Note Off		X	
TOUCH	Key's	N/A	O	
	Chan's		O	
PITCH BENDER		N/A	O	
CONTROL CHANGE	1-31	N/A	O	control assignments are programmable
	64-95		O	
PROGRAM CHANGE		N/A	0 — 127	see note
	True #		1 — 128	
SYSTEM EXCLUSIVE		N/A	O	
SYSTEM COMMON	Song Pos	N/A	X	
	Song Sel		X	
	Tune		X	
SYSTEM REAL TIME	Clock	N/A	X	
	Messages		X	
AUX	Local Control	N/A	X	
	All Notes Off		O	
	Active Sense		X	
	Reset		O	

NOTES: N/A: Not Applicable

NOTE 1: program numbers may be mapped thru a 128 element list

Mode 1 : OMNI ON, POLY	Mode 2 : OMNI ON, MONO	O : Yes
Mode 3 : OMNI OFF, POLY	Mode 4: OMNI OFF, MONO	X : No

Manufacturer	Model
Yamaha	**TF1**
[FM Tone Generator]	Version 1.0 Date 6/16/86

Function		Transmitted	Recognized	Remarks
CHANNEL	Default	1	1—16*	* memorized
	Changed	X	1—16*	
MODE	Default	Mode 3	Mode 1-4	memorized
	Messages	X	OMNI ON/OFF, POLY, MONO	MONO (M=1)
	Altered			
NOTE NUMBER		X	0—127	
	True Voice			
VELOCITY	Note On	X	O	
	Note Off	X	X	
TOUCH	Key's	X	X	
	Chan's	X	O	
PITCH BENDER		X	O	
CONTROL CHANGE	mod 1	X	O	
	breath 2	X	O	
	foot controller 4	X	O	
	portamento time 5	X	O	
		X	O	
	data entry 6	X	O	
	volume 7	X	O	
	sustain 64	X	O	
	portamento 65	X	O	
	+1/-1 96/97			
PROGRAM CHANGE		X	0—127	
	True #		0—31	
SYSTEM EXCLUSIVE		O	O	voice parameters
SYSTEM COMMON	Song Pos	X	X	
	Song Sel	X	X	
	Tune	X	X	
SYSTEM REAL TIME	Clock	X	X	
	Messages	X	X	
AUX	Local Control	X	X	
	All Notes Off	X	X	
	Active Sense	X	O	
	Reset	X	X	
NOTES:				

Mode 1 : OMNI ON, POLY   Mode 2 : OMNI ON, MONO   O : Yes
Mode 3 : OMNI OFF, POLY   Mode 4: OMNI OFF, MONO   X : No

Digital Synthesizers

Manufacturer	Model
Yamaha	**TX7**
[FM Expander]	Version 1.0 Date 11/10/84

Function		Transmitted	Recognized	Remarks
CHANNEL	Default	X	1 — 16	memorized
	Changed	X	1 — 16	memorized
MODE	Default	X	Mode 1- 4	memorized
	Messages	X	OMNI ON/OFF, POLY, MONO	MONO (M=1)
	Altered			
NOTE NUMBER		X	0 — 127	
	True Voice			
VELOCITY	Note On	X	O	
	Note Off	X	X	
TOUCH	Key's	X	X	
	Chan's	X	O	
PITCH BENDER		X	O	
CONTROL CHANGE	mod 1	X	O	
	breath 2	X	O	
	foot controller 4	X	O	
	portamento time	X	O	
	5	X	O	
	data entry 6	X	O	
	volume 7	X	O	
	sustain 64	X	O	
	portamento 65	X	O	
	+1/-1 96/97			
PROGRAM CHANGE		X	0-127	
	True #		0 — 31	
SYSTEM EXCLUSIVE		O	O	Voice parameters
SYSTEM COMMON	Song Pos	X	X	
	Song Sel	X	X	
	Tune	X	X	
SYSTEM REAL TIME	Clock	X	X	
	Messages	X	X	
AUX	Local Control	X	X	
	All Notes Off	X	X	
	Active Sense	X	O	
	Reset	X	X	

NOTES:

Mode 1 : OMNI ON, POLY   Mode 2 : OMNI ON, MONO   O : Yes
Mode 3 : OMNI OFF, POLY   Mode 4: OMNI OFF, MONO   X : No

FERRO TECHNOLOGIES

Manufacturer	Model
Roland	**GR-77B**
[Bass Guitar Synthesizer]	Version 1.0 Date 9/9/85

Function		Transmitted	Recognized	Remarks
CHANNEL	Default	1 — 16	N/A	memorized
	Changed	1 — 16		
MODE	Default	Mode 3	N/A	
	Messages	OMNI ON/OFF, POLY ON		
	Altered			
NOTE NUMBER		21 — 71	N/A	
	True Voice			
VELOCITY	Note On	O	N/A	
	Note Off	X 9nH (v=0)		
TOUCH	Key's	X	N/A	
	Chan's	X		
PITCH BENDER		OX	N/A	see note 2
CONTROL CHANGE	mod 1	OX	N/A	see notes
	volume 7	OX		
	hold 64	OX		
PROGRAM CHANGE		0 — 95	N/A	
	True #			
SYSTEM EXCLUSIVE		X	N/A	see notes
SYSTEM COMMON	Song Pos	X	N/A	
	Song Sel	X		
	Tune	X		
SYSTEM REAL TIME	Clock	X	N/A	
	Messages	X		
AUX	Local Control	X	N/A	
	All Notes Off	O 123-125,127		
	Active Sense	X		
	Reset	X		

NOTES: N/A: Not Applicable

Note 1: Bender, Program Change, and Control Change messages can be set and memorized to O or X manually in MIDI EDIT mode.

Note 2: When powered up, OMNI OFF, POLY ON are sent in default channel.

Mode 1 : OMNI ON, POLY	Mode 2 : OMNI ON, MONO	O : Yes
Mode 3 : OMNI OFF, POLY	Mode 4: OMNI OFF, MONO	X : No

Hybrid Synthesizers

Manufacturer
Roland
[Guitar Synthesizer]

Model
GR-700
Version 1.2   Date 12/13/83

Function		Transmitted	Recognized	Remarks
CHANNEL	Default	1	N/A	Transmitter only
	Changed	X		
MODE	Default	Mode 3	N/A	F-3 only
	Messages	OMNI OFF, POLY		
	Altered			
NOTE NUMBER		35-96	N/A	
	True Voice			
VELOCITY	Note On	O	N/A	
	Note Off	X 9nH (v=0)		
TOUCH	Key's	X	N/A	
	Chan's	X		
PITCH BENDER		X	N/A	
CONTROL CHANGE	hold 64	O	N/A	F-1 only
PROGRAM CHANGE		O	0—127	F-2 only (see note)
	True #			
SYSTEM EXCLUSIVE		X	N/A	
SYSTEM COMMON	Song Pos	X	N/A	
	Song Sel	X		
	Tune	X		
SYSTEM REAL TIME	Clock	X	N/A	
	Messages	X		
AUX	Local Control	X	N/A	
	All Notes Off	O (123)		
	Active Sense	X		
	Reset	X		

NOTES: N/A: Not Applicable

No mode messages are sent unless GR-700 is set to F-3. (Power up while pressing STRING 3 switch).   When set to F-3, OMNI OFF, POLY is sent out over channel 1.

GR-700 is a transmitter only.

Mode 1 : OMNI ON, POLY   Mode 2 : OMNI ON, MONO   O : Yes
Mode 3 : OMNI OFF, POLY   Mode 4: OMNI OFF, MONO   X : No

Manufacturer	Model
ENSONIQ	ESQ 1
[Digital Waveform Synthesizer]	Version 1.0 Date 5/1/86

Function		Transmitted	Recognized	Remarks
CHANNEL	Default	1	1	
	Changed	1 — 16	1 — 16	
MODE	Default	Mode 1,2,3,4,*	Mode 1,2,3,4,*	*memorized
	Messages	X	OMNI ON/OFF, MONO	
	Altered		OMNI OFF -> MULTI	
NOTE NUMBER		21 — 108	21 — 108	
	True Voice			
VELOCITY	Note On	O	O	
	Note Off	O	O	
TOUCH	Key's	O	O	Transmitted only if recorded
	Chan's	O	O	
PITCH BENDER		O	O	
CONTROL CHANGE	mod 1	O	O	1—31 are programmable
	breath 2	O	O	
	foot pedal 4	O	O	
	data entry 6	O	O	
	volume 7	O	O	
	+1/-1 96/97	O	O	
	p. select low 98	O	O	
	p. select high 99	O	O	
PROGRAM CHANGE		0 — 119	0 — 119	
	True #			
SYSTEM EXCLUSIVE		O	O	
SYSTEM COMMON	Song Pos	O	O	
	Song Sel	O	O	
	Tune	X	X	
SYSTEM REAL TIME	Clock	O	O	
	Messages	Start, Stop, Cont	Start, Stop, Cont	
AUX	Local Control	X	X	
	All Notes Off	X	O	Only Mode Change
	Active Sense	X	X	
	Reset	X	X	

NOTES: Global Controllers in MIDI MONO mode

Mode 1 : OMNI ON, POLY   Mode 2 : OMNI ON, MONO   O : Yes
Mode 3 : OMNI OFF, POLY   Mode 4: OMNI OFF, MONO   X : No

Manufacturer		Model		
Fender		**Chroma Polaris**		
[Polyphonic Synthesizer]		Version 3	Date —	

Function		Transmitted	Recognized	Remarks
CHANNEL	Default	1 — 16	1 — 16	see note 1
	Changed	1 — 16	1 — 16	memorized
MODE	Default	Mode 1	Mode 1	see note 2
	Messages		OMNI ON/OFF, POLY, MONO	
	Altered			
NOTE NUMBER		24 — 96	9 — 120	
	True Voice			
VELOCITY	Note On	O	O	see note 3
	Note Off	X 90H (v=0)	O	
TOUCH	Key's	X	O	pressure interpreted as pedal moves
	Chan's	O	O	
PITCH BENDER		O	O	
CONTROL CHANGE	perf. volume 0	X	O	this is a partial lisiting, see note 4 and 5
	mod 1	O	O	
	volume 2	O	O	
	sweep rate 4	O	O	
	env attack 13	O	O	
	ocs1 vibrato 24	O	O	
	ocs2 vibrato 25	O	O	
	vcf cutoff 103	O	O	
	sustain 64	O	O	
PROGRAM CHANGE		O	0-127	see note 5
	True #			
SYSTEM EXCLUSIVE		O	O	ID = 8
SYSTEM COMMON	Song Pos	X	X	
	Song Sel	X	X	
	Tune	X	O	
SYSTEM REAL TIME	Clock	O	O	only when MIDI clock and metronome are enabled
	Messages	Start, Stop	Start, Stop	
AUX	Local Control	O	O	
	All Notes Off	O	O	
	Active Sense	X	X	
	Reset	X	O	

NOTES: 1. Basic channel = b, Link on = b+1, sequencer on = b+2. There is a Soft Switch to recognize channels b+3 through b+7 (MIDI Extra Channels)
2. Mode commands received on any recognized channel affect all recognized channels.
3. Sequencer remmbers note off with velocity & will retransmitt them
4. See owner's manual for complete list of control change messages transmitted/recognized.
5. Transmission of Control Change and Program Change messages is selectable from front panel.

Mode 1 : OMNI ON, POLY	Mode 2 : OMNI ON, MONO	O : Yes
Mode 3 : OMNI OFF, POLY	Mode 4: OMNI OFF, MONO	X : No

Manufacturer		Model	
Korg		**POLY-800 + MDK**	
[8 Voice Polyphonic Synthesizer]		Version — Date 7/1/84	

Function		Transmitted	Recognized	Remarks
CHANNEL	Default	1, 2*	1 — 16 **	* note 1
	Changed	X	1 — 16	**memorized
MODE	Default	Mode 1	Mode 1	
	Messages	OMNI ON/OFF, POLY	OMNI ON/OFF	
	Altered		Mode 4 —> 3, Mode 2 —> 1	
NOTE		36 — 84	0 — 127	
NUMBER	True Voice		36 — 84	
VELOCITY	Note On	X	X	
	Note Off	X	X	
TOUCH	Key's	X	X	
	Chan's	X	X	
PITCH BENDER		O	O	
CONTROL	DCO mod 1	O	O	
CHANGE	VCF mod 2	O	O	
PROGRAM		O	1 — 64	
CHANGE	True #			
SYSTEM EXCLUSIVE		O	O	
SYSTEM	Song Pos	X	X	
COMMON	Song Sel	X	X	
	Tune	X	X	
SYSTEM	Clock	O	O	
REAL TIME	Messages	O	O	
AUX	Local Control	X	X	
	All Notes Off	X	X	
	Active Sense	X	X	
	Reset	X	X	

NOTES: NOTE: 1 Keyboard transmits on channel 1, sequencer transmits on channel 2

Mode 1 : OMNI ON, POLY	Mode 2 : OMNI ON, MONO	O : Yes
Mode 3 : OMNI OFF, POLY	Mode 4: OMNI OFF, MONO	X : No

Manufacturer	Model
Korg	**POLY-800 MK2**
[8 Voice Polyphonic Synthesizer]	Version 1.0 Date 7/14/86

Function		Transmitted	Recognized	Remarks
CHANNEL	Default	1 — 16*	1 — 16*	* memorized
	Changed	1 — 16	1 — 16	(see notes)
MODE	Default	Mode 1	Mode 1	
	Messages	X	OMNI ON/OFF	
	Altered			
NOTE		36 — 84	0 — 127	
NUMBER	True Voice		36 — 84	
VELOCITY	Note On	X	X	
	Note Off	X	X	
TOUCH	Key's	X	X	
	Chan's	X	X	
PITCH BENDER		O	O	
CONTROL	DCO mod 1	O	O	
CHANGE	VCF mod 2	O	O	
PROGRAM		0 — 63	0 — 127	*set by parameter 88
CHANGE	True #		0 — 63*	
SYSTEM EXCLUSIVE		O	O	data dump/load
SYSTEM	Song Pos	X	X	
COMMON	Song Sel	X	X	
	Tune	X	X	
SYSTEM	Clock	O	O	set by parameter 86
REAL TIME	Messages	O	O	
AUX	Local Control	X	X	
	All Notes Off	X	X	
	Active Sense	X	X	
	Reset	X	X	

NOTES: Sequencer always transmits on channel 2.

Mode 1 : OMNI ON, POLY	Mode 2 : OMNI ON, MONO	O : Yes
Mode 3 : OMNI OFF, POLY	Mode 4: OMNI OFF, MONO	X : No

Manufacturer	Model
Roland	**JX-3P**
[6—Voice Synthesizer]	Version 1.0 Date 4/20/84

Function		Transmitted	Recognized	Remarks
CHANNEL	Default	1	1	old MIDI
	Changed	X	X	
MODE	Default	Mode 1	Mode 1	
	Messages	POLY	OMNI ON, POLY	
	Altered			
NOTE NUMBER		36-96	0 — 127	
	True Voice		36 — 96	
VELOCITY	Note On	X	X	
	Note Off	X 90H (v=0)	X	
TOUCH	Key's	X	X	
	Chan's	X	X	
PITCH BENDER		OX	OX	see note
CONTROL CHANGE	64 hold	OX	OX	
PROGRAM CHANGE		0—63	0—127	transmit/ receive can be set on power up
	True #		0 — 63	
SYSTEM EXCLUSIVE		X	X	
SYSTEM COMMON	Song Pos	X	X	
	Song Sel	X	X	
	Tune	X	X	
SYSTEM REAL TIME	Clock	X	X	
	Messages	X	X	
AUX	Local Control	X	X	
	All Notes Off	O (127)	O (125, 127)	
	Active Sense	X	X	
	Reset	X	O	
NOTES:	9 bit resolution 2, 4, 7 semitones			

Mode 1 : OMNI ON, POLY	Mode 2 : OMNI ON, MONO	O : Yes
Mode 3 : OMNI OFF, POLY	Mode 4: OMNI OFF, MONO	X : No

Hybrid Synthesizers

Manufacturer
Roland
[6—Voice Synthesizer]

Model
JX-3P
Version 2.1   Date 7/9/84

Function		Transmitted	Recognized	Remarks
CHANNEL	Default	1	1	
	Changed	X	X	
MODE	Default	Mode 3	Mode 3	
	Messages	OMNI OFF, POLY	OMNI ON/OFF, POLY	
	Altered			
NOTE NUMBER		36 — 96	0 — 127	
	True Voice		36 — 96	
VELOCITY	Note On	X	X	
	Note Off	X 90H (v=0)	X	
TOUCH	Key's	X	X	
	Chan's	X	X	
PITCH BENDER		OX	OX	see note 2
CONTROL CHANGE	hold 64	OX	OX	
PROGRAM CHANGE		0—63	0—127	transmit/receive can be set at power up
	True #		0— 63	
SYSTEM EXCLUSIVE		X	X	
SYSTEM COMMON	Song Pos	X	X	
	Song Sel	X	X	
	Tune	X	X	
SYSTEM REAL TIME	Clock	X	X	
	Messages	X	X	
AUX	Local Control	X	X	
	All Notes Off	O (123)	O (123—127)	
	Active Sense	X	X	
	Reset	X	X	

NOTES: Note 1: When powered—up, OMNI OFF, POLY ON are sent in channel 1.

Note 2: 9 bit resolution 2, 4, 7 semitones

Mode 1 : OMNI ON, POLY	Mode 2 : OMNI ON, MONO	O : Yes
Mode 3 : OMNI OFF, POLY	Mode 4: OMNI OFF, MONO	X : No

| Manufacturer **Roland** [12 Voice Polyphonic Synthesizer] | | Model **JX-10** Version 1.01 Date 2/21/86 | | |

Function		Transmitted	Recognized	Remarks
CHANNEL	Default	1 — 16	1 — 16	memorized
	Changed	1 — 16	1 — 16	see note 1
MODE	Default	Mode 3	Mode 3	
	Messages	OMNI OFF, POLY	X	
	Altered			
NOTE NUMBER		28 — 103	0 — 127	
	True Voice		21 — 108	
VELOCITY	Note On	O	O	
	Note Off	X 9nH (v=0)	X	
TOUCH	Key's	X	X	memorized
	Chan's	O	OX	
PITCH BENDER		OX	OX	memorized (see note 2)
CONTROL CHANGE	mod 1	OX	OX	memorized
	portamento time	O	O	
	5	OX	OX	
	volume 7	OX	OX	
	hold 64	OX	OX	
	portamento65			
PROGRAM CHANGE		0 — 127	0 — 127	memorized (see note 3)
	True #			
SYSTEM EXCLUSIVE		OX	OX	memorized
SYSTEM COMMON	Song Pos	X	X	
	Song Sel	X	X	
	Tune	X	X	
SYSTEM REAL TIME	Clock	O	X	when sequencer cartridge is set
	Messages	O	X	
AUX	Local Control	X	O*	* default ON
	All Notes Off	O	O (123 — 127)	
	Active Sense	X	X	
	Reset	X	X	

NOTES: NOTE 1: Independent channel assignment for UP and LO
NOTE 2: Bender resolution is 8 bits. Range is 2, 3, 4, or 7 semitones.

NOTE 3: 0 — 99 as TONE #s (100 — 127 ignored if received.)
0 — 127 as PATCH #s
0 — 127 as optional program Prog # (transmitted only)

See each implementation notes for details.

Mode 1 : OMNI ON, POLY   Mode 2 : OMNI ON, MONO   O : Yes
Mode 3 : OMNI OFF, POLY   Mode 4: OMNI OFF, MONO   X : No

Manufacturer

Roland

[12 Voice Polyphonic Synthesizer]

Model

JX-10

Version 1.00   Date 2/19/86

Function		Transmitted	Recognized	Remarks
CHANNEL	Default	1 — 16	1 — 16	memorized
	Changed	1 — 16	1 — 16	see note 1
MODE	Default	Mode 3	Mode 3	
	Messages	OMNI OFF, POLY	X	
	Altered			
NOTE NUMBER		28 — 103	0 — 127	
	True Voice		21 — 108	
VELOCITY	Note On	O	O	
	Note Off	X 9nH (v=0)	X	
TOUCH	Key's	X	X	memorized
	Chan's	O	OX	
PITCH BENDER		OX	OX	memirized (see note 2)
CONTROL CHANGE	mod 1	OX	OX	memorized
	portamento time	O	O	
	5	OX	OX	
	volume 7	OX	OX	
	hold 64	OX	OX	
	portamento 65			
PROGRAM CHANGE		0 — 127	0 — 127	memorized (see note 3)
	True #			
SYSTEM EXCLUSIVE		OX	OX	
SYSTEM COMMON	Song Pos	X	X	
	Song Sel	X	X	
	Tune	X	X	
SYSTEM REAL TIME	Clock	X	X	
	Messages	X	X	
AUX	Local Control	X	O*	*default ON
	All Notes Off	O	O (123 — 127)	
	Active Sense	X	X	
	Reset	X	X	

NOTES: NOTE 1: Independent channel assignment for UP and LO
NOTE 2: Bender resolution is 8 bits. Range is 2, 3, 4, or 7 semitones.

NOTE 3: 0 — 99 as TONE #s (100 — 127 ignored if received.)
0 — 127 as PATCH #s
0 — 127 as optional program Prog # (transmitted only)

See each implementation notes for details.

Mode 1 : OMNI ON, POLY   Mode 2 : OMNI ON, MONO   O : Yes
Mode 3 : OMNI OFF, POLY   Mode 4: OMNI OFF, MONO   X : No

Manufacturer
Sequential
[6 Voice Synth/Sequencer]

Model
Max
Version 0.3   Date —

Function		Transmitted	Recognized	Remarks
CHANNEL	Default	3	1-16	
	Changed	1-16	1-16	
MODE	Default	Mode 1	Mode1	honors Modes 1, 3, 4
	Messages	X	OMNI ON/OFF, POLY, MONO	
	Altered		Mode 2 —> Mode 1	
NOTE NUMBER		36-84	0-127	
	True Voice		35-96	
VELOCITY	Note On	X	O	
	Note Off	X 9nH(v=0)	X	
TOUCH	Key's	X	X	
	Chan's	X	X	
PITCH BENDER		X	O	
CONTROL CHANGE	mod 1	X	O	
	parameters 2-36	X	O	
PROGRAM CHANGE		0-99	0-99	upper 20 programs must be loaded via MIDI
	True #			
SYSTEM EXCLUSIVE		O	O	data dumps
SYSTEM COMMON	Song Pos	X	X	
	Song Sel	X	X	
	Tune	O	O	
SYSTEM REAL TIME	Clock	O	O	
	Messages	Start, Stop	Start, Stop	
AUX	Local Control	O	O	
	All Notes Off	X	O (123-127)	
	Active Sense	X	X	
	Reset	X	X	
NOTES:				

Mode 1 : OMNI ON, POLY   Mode 2 : OMNI ON, MONO   O : Yes
Mode 3 : OMNI OFF, POLY   Mode 4: OMNI OFF, MONO   X : No

Manufacturer
Sequential
[6 Voice Synth/Sequencer]

Model
Multi Trak
Version —   Date —

Function		Transmitted	Recognized	Remarks
CHANNEL	Default	1	1	
	Changed	1-16	1-16	
MODE	Default	Mode 1	Mode 1	Honors Modes 1, 3, 4
	Messages	X	OMNI ON/OFF, POLY, MONO	
	Altered			
NOTE NUMBER		36-97	0-127	
	True Voice		36-91	
VELOCITY	Note On	X	O	
	Note Off	X	X	
TOUCH	Key's	X	X	Interpreted as mod
	Chan's	X	O	
PITCH BENDER		O	O	
CONTROL CHANGE	mod 1	O	O	
	Volume 7, 36	X	O	
PROGRAM CHANGE		0-99	0-99	
	True #			
SYSTEM EXCLUSIVE		O	O	data dumps
SYSTEM COMMON	Song Pos	X	X	
	Song Sel	O	O	
	Tune	X	X	
SYSTEM REAL TIME	Clock	O	O	
	Messages	Start, Stop	Start, Stop, Continue	
AUX	Local Control	X	O	
	All Notes Off	X	O (123-127)	
	Active Sense	X	X	
	Reset	X	X	

NOTES:

Mode 1 : OMNI ON, POLY   Mode 2 : OMNI ON, MONO   O : Yes
Mode 3 : OMNI OFF, POLY   Mode 4: OMNI OFF, MONO   X : No

Manufacturer	Model
Sequential	**Prophet 10**
[10 Voice Synth/Sequencer]	Version — Date 1/84

Function		Transmitted	Recognized	Remarks
CHANNEL	Default	1	1,6	1=lower keys/seq. 6 = upper keys
	Changed	1, 6	1-16	(Mode 3 only)
MODE	Default	Mode 1	Mode 1	honors Modes 1,3
	Messages	POLY	OMNI ON, POLY	
	Altered			
NOTE NUMBER		36-96	0-127	
	True Voice		36-96	
VELOCITY	Note On	X	X	
	Note Off	X	X	
TOUCH	Key's	X	X	
	Chan's	X	X	
PITCH BENDER		X	X	
CONTROL CHANGE		X	X	
PROGRAM CHANGE		0-31	0-31	
	True #			
SYSTEM EXCLUSIVE		O	O	data dumps
SYSTEM COMMON	Song Pos	X	X	
	Song Sel	X	X	
	Tune	O	O	
SYSTEM REAL TIME	Clock	X	X	
	Messages	X	X	
AUX	Local Control	X	X	
	All Notes Off	X	X	
	Active Sense	X	X	
	Reset	X	X	

NOTES:

Mode 1 : OMNI ON, POLY   Mode 2 : OMNI ON, MONO   O : Yes
Mode 3 : OMNI OFF, POLY   Mode 4: OMNI OFF, MONO   X : No

Manufacturer	Model
Sequential	**Six Trak**
[6 Voice Synth/Sequencer]	Version — Date 4/85

Function		Transmitted	Recognized	Remarks
CHANNEL	Default	1-16	1-16	memorized
	Changed	1-16	1-16	
MODE	Default	Mode 1	Mode 1	honors Modes 1, 3, 4
	Messages	X	OMNI ON/OFF, POLY, MONO	
	Altered		Mode 2 —>Mode 1	
NOTE		36-84	0-127	
NUMBER	True Voice		36-97	
VELOCITY	Note On	X	X	
	Note Off	X	X	
TOUCH	Key's	X	X	
	Chan's	X	X	
PITCH BENDER		O	O	
CONTROL	mod 1	O	O	
CHANGE	parameters 2-37	X	O	
PROGRAM		0-99	0-99	
CHANGE	True #			
SYSTEM EXCLUSIVE		O	O	data dumps
SYSTEM	Song Pos	X	X	
COMMON	Song Sel	X	X	
	Tune	X	X	
SYSTEM	Clock	O	O	
REAL TIME	Messages	Stop	Stop	
AUX	Local Control	X	O	
	All Notes Off	X	O (123-127)	
	Active Sense	X	X	
	Reset	X	X	
NOTES:				

Mode 1 : OMNI ON, POLY	Mode 2 : OMNI ON, MONO	O : Yes
Mode 3 : OMNI OFF, POLY	Mode 4: OMNI OFF, MONO	X : No

Manufacturer		Model	
Sequential		**T-8**	
[8 Voice Synth/Sequencer]		Version 3.7 Date 10/84	

Function		Transmitted	Recognized	Remarks
CHANNEL	Default	1	1-16	recognizes only 1-8 in Mode 4
	Changed	1-16	1-16	
MODE	Default	Mode 1	Mode 1	Honors Modes 1,3,4
	Messages	X	OMNI ON/OFF, POLY, MONO	
	Altered		Mode 2 —> Mode 4	
NOTE NUMBER		33-108	33-108	
	True Voice			
VELOCITY	Note On	O	O	
	Note Off	O	O	
TOUCH	Key's	X	X	
	Chan's	O	O	
PITCH BENDER		O	O	0-4 semitones
CONTROL CHANGE	mod 1	O	O	
	breath 2	X	O	interpereted as pressure
	2nd release 64	O	O	
PROGRAM CHANGE		0-127	0-127	
	True #			
SYSTEM EXCLUSIVE		O	O	data dumps
SYSTEM COMMON	Song Pos	X	X	
	Song Sel	X	X	
	Tune	O	O	
SYSTEM REAL TIME	Clock	O	O	
	Messages	Start, Stop	Start, Stop	
AUX	Local Control	X	O	
	All Notes Off	X	O (123-127)	
	Active Sense	X	X	
	Reset	X	X	
NOTES:				

Mode 1 : OMNI ON, POLY	Mode 2 : OMNI ON, MONO		O : Yes
Mode 3 : OMNI OFF, POLY	Mode 4: OMNI OFF, MONO		X : No

Hybrid Synthesizers

Manufacturer	Model
Siel	**DK-80**
[Dynamic Bi-timbral Synthesizer]	Version 0 Date —

Function		Transmitted	Recognized	Remarks
CHANNEL	Default	1 — 2	1	Selectable by Keyswitch
	Changed	*	1 — 16	*unavailable at printing
MODE	Default	Mode 3	Mode 1	honors Mode 1,3
	Messages	X	*	*unavailable at printing
	Altered		*	
NOTE NUMBER		36 — 96	36 — 96	
	True Voice			
VELOCITY	Note On	O	O	
	Note Off	X	X	
TOUCH	Key's	X		
	Chan's	X	X	
PITCH BENDER		X	X	
CONTROL CHANGE		O	O	see owner's manual for details
PROGRAM CHANGE		0-49	0-49	
	True #			
SYSTEM EXCLUSIVE		O	O	by "Request to send"
SYSTEM COMMON	Song Pos	X	X	
	Song Sel	X	X	
	Tune	X	X	
SYSTEM REAL TIME	Clock	O	O	used by on board sequencer
	Messages	O	O	
AUX	Local Control	O	O	
	All Notes Off	O	O	
	Active Sense	X	X	
	Reset	O	O	

NOTES: Instrument ID# — 02 H

Mode 1 : OMNI ON, POLY	Mode 2 : OMNI ON, MONO	O : Yes
Mode 3 : OMNI OFF, POLY	Mode 4: OMNI OFF, MONO	X : No

Manufacturer	Model	
Akai	AX-60	55
[Programmable Polyphonic Synthesizer]	Version 1.0 Date —	

Function		Transmitted	Recognized	Remarks
CHANNEL	Default	1 — 16	1 — 16 *	* memorized
	Changed	1 — 16	1 — 16 *	
MODE	Default	Mode 3, 4	Mode 3	memorized
	Messages	X	X	
	Altered			
NOTE NUMBER		36 — 96	0 — 127	
	True Voice		24 — 120	
VELOCITY	Note On	X	X	
	Note Off	X 9nH (v=0)	X	
TOUCH	Key's	X	X	
	Chan's	X	X	
PITCH BENDER		O	O	8 bit resolution
CONTROL CHANGE	mod 1	O	O	
	volume 7	X	O	
	sustain switch 64	O	O	
PROGRAM CHANGE		(0 — 63)	0 —127	
	True #		0 — 63	
SYSTEM EXCLUSIVE		X	X	
SYSTEM COMMON	Song Pos	X	X	
	Song Sel	X	X	
	Tune	X	O	
SYSTEM REAL TIME	Clock	X	X	
	Messages	X	X	
AUX	Local Control	X	X	* Set mode only
	All Notes Off	O*	O	
	Active Sense	X	X	
	Reset	X	X	

NOTES:

Mode 1 : OMNI ON, POLY   Mode 2 : OMNI ON, MONO   O : Yes
Mode 3 : OMNI OFF, POLY   Mode 4: OMNI OFF, MONO   X : No

Hybrid Synthesizers

Manufacturer

Akai
[Programmable Polyphonic Synthesizer]

Model

AX-73
Version 1.0   Date 3/28/86

Function		Transmitted	Recognized	Remarks
CHANNEL	Default	1 — 16	1 — 16 *	* memorized
	Changed	1 — 16	1 — 16 *	
MODE	Default	Mode 3, 4	Mode 3	memorized
	Messages	X	X	
	Altered			
NOTE NUMBER		24 — 96	0 — 127	
	True Voice		24 — 120	
VELOCITY	Note On	O	O	
	Note Off	X 9nH (v=0)	O	
TOUCH	Key's	X	X	
	Chan's	X	X	
PITCH BENDER		O	O	7 bit resolution
CONTROL CHANGE	mod 1	O	O	
	volume 7	X	O	
	sustain switch 64	O	O	
PROGRAM CHANGE		0 — 99	0 — 127	
	True #		0 — 99	
SYSTEM EXCLUSIVE		X	X	
SYSTEM COMMON	Song Pos	X	X	
	Song Sel	X	X	
	Tune	O	O	
SYSTEM REAL TIME	Clock	X	X	
	Messages	X	X	
AUX	Local Control	X	X	
	All Notes Off	O	O	
	Active Sense	X	X	
	Reset	X	X	

NOTES:

Mode 1 : OMNI ON, POLY   Mode 2 : OMNI ON, MONO   O : Yes
Mode 3 : OMNI OFF, POLY   Mode 4: OMNI OFF, MONO   X : No

FERRO TECHNOLOGIES

Manufacturer	Model
Korg	**DW-6000**
[6 Voice Polyphonic Synthesizer]	Version 1.0　　　Date 7/14/86

Function		Transmitted	Recognized	Remarks
CHANNEL	Default	1	1 — 16	memorized
	Changed	X	1 — 16	
MODE	Default	Mode 1	Mode 1	
	Messages	X	OMNI ON/OFF	
	Altered			
NOTE		36 — 96	0 — 127	
NUMBER	True Voice		24 — 108	
VELOCITY	Note On	X	X	
	Note Off	X	X	
TOUCH	Key's	X	X	
	Chan's	X	X	
PITCH BENDER		OX	OX	
CONTROL	DCO mod 1	OX	OX	
CHANGE	VCF mod 2	OX	OX	
	volume 7	X	OX	
	damper switch 64	OX	OX	
	portamento 65	OX	OX	
PROGRAM		0 — 63	0 — 127	enabled/disabled by setting of
CHANGE	True #		0 — 63 (see notes)	parameter 82
SYSTEM EXCLUSIVE		OX	OX	
SYSTEM	Song Pos	X	X	
COMMON	Song Sel	X	X	
	Tune	X	X	
SYSTEM	Clock	X	X	
REAL TIME	Messages	X	X	
AUX	Local Control	X	X	mode messages always received
	All Notes Off	X	O (123-127)	
	Active Sense	X	X	
	Reset	X	X	

NOTES: If parameter 82=1, only notes and mode messages will be transmitted and received.

OX means function can be enabled or disabled by value of parameter 82.

Program Change: 0=11, 7=18, 8=21, 56=81, 63=88

Mode 1 : OMNI ON, POLY	Mode 2 : OMNI ON, MONO	O : Yes
Mode 3 : OMNI OFF, POLY	Mode 4: OMNI OFF, MONO	X : No

Manufacturer

Korg

[8 Voice Polyphonic Synthesizer]

Model

DW-8000

Version 1.0   Date 7/16/86

Function		Transmitted	Recognized	Remarks
CHANNEL	Default	1 — 16	1 — 16	memorized
	Changed	1 — 16	1 — 16	
MODE	Default	Mode 1	Mode 1	
	Messages	X	OMNI ON/OFF	
	Altered			
NOTE NUMBER		36 — 96	0 — 127	
	True Voice		24 — 108	
VELOCITY	Note On	O	O	transmit: v=15 — 127
	Note Off	X	X	recognize: v=1 — 127
TOUCH	Key's	X	X	
	Chan's	OX	OX	
PITCH BENDER		OX	OX	
CONTROL CHANGE	OSC mod 1	OX	OX	
	VCF mod2	OX	OX	
	volume 7	X	OX	
	damper switch	OX	OX	
	64	OX	OX	
	portamento 65			
PROGRAM CHANGE		0 — 63	0 — 127	enabled/disabled by setting of parameter 85
	True #		0 — 63	
SYSTEM EXCLUSIVE		OX	OX	data dump/load
SYSTEM COMMON	Song Pos	X	X	
	Song Sel	X	X	
	Tune	X	X	
SYSTEM REAL TIME	Clock	OX	OX	
	Messages	OX	OX	
AUX	Local Control	X	X	
	All Notes Off	X	O (123 — 127)	
	Active Sense	X	OX	
	Reset	X	X	

NOTES: If parameter 85=1, only note data and mode messages will be transmitted and received.

OX means function can be enabled or disabled by value of parameter 85.

Progam Change: if # > 63, 64 is subtracted

Mode 1 : OMNI ON, POLY	Mode 2 : OMNI ON, MONO	O : Yes
Mode 3 : OMNI OFF, POLY	Mode 4: OMNI OFF, MONO	X : No

Manufacturer
Korg
[Programmable Polyphonic Synthesizer]

Model
POLY-61M
Version 1.0   Date 7/14/86

Function		Transmitted	Recognized	Remarks
CHANNEL	Default	1	1	
	Changed	X	X	
MODE	Default	Mode 1	Mode 1	
	Messages	X	OMNI ON/OFF	
	Altered			
NOTE NUMBER		36 — 96	0 — 127	
	True Voice		36 — 96	
VELOCITY	Note On	X	X	
	Note Off	X	X	
TOUCH	Key's	X	X	
	Chan's	X	X	
PITCH BENDER		X	X	
CONTROL CHANGE	damper pedal 64	O	O	
PROGRAM CHANGE	True #	O	0 — 63	
SYSTEM EXCLUSIVE		X	X	
SYSTEM COMMON	Song Pos	X	X	
	Song Sel	X	X	
	Tune	X	X	
SYSTEM REAL TIME	Clock	X	X	
	Messages	X	X	
AUX	Local Control	X	X	
	All Notes Off	X	O	
	Active Sense	X	X	
	Reset	X	O	

NOTES:

Mode 1 : OMNI ON, POLY   Mode 2 : OMNI ON, MONO   O : Yes
Mode 3 : OMNI OFF, POLY   Mode 4: OMNI OFF, MONO   X : No

Manufacturer
Oberheim
[8 Voice Synthesizer]

Model
OB-8
Version —   Date —

Function		Transmitted	Recognized	Remarks
CHANNEL	Default	1	1	upper keys=basic channel
	Changed	1 — 8	1 — 8	lower keys=basic + 1
MODE	Default	Mode 1	Mode 1	honors Modes 1, 3
	Messages	X	X	
	Altered			
NOTE NUMBER		36 — 96	36 — 96	
	True Voice			
VELOCITY	Note On	X	X	
	Note Off	X	X	
TOUCH	Key's	X	X	
	Chan's	X	X	
PITCH BENDER		O	O	
CONTROL CHANGE	mod 1	OX	OX	
PROGRAM CHANGE		0 — 119	0 — 119	enable/disable is selectable
	True #			
SYSTEM EXCLUSIVE		O	O	program dumps
SYSTEM COMMON	Song Pos	X	X	
	Song Sel	X	X	
	Tune	X	O	
SYSTEM REAL TIME	Clock	X	X	
	Messages	X	X	
AUX	Local Control	X	X	
	All Notes Off	X	X	
	Active Sense	X	X	
	Reset	X	X	

NOTES:

Mode 1 : OMNI ON, POLY   Mode 2 : OMNI ON, MONO   O : Yes
Mode 3 : OMNI OFF, POLY   Mode 4: OMNI OFF, MONO   X : No

Manufacturer	Model
Oberheim	**Matrix 6/6R**
[6 Voice Synthesizer]	Version 2 Date —

Function		Transmitted	Recognized	Remarks
CHANNEL	Default	1 — 16	1 — 16	memorized
	Changed	1 — 16	1 — 16	
MODE	Default	Mode 1,3,4	Mode 1,3,4	
	Messages	OMNI ON/OFF, POLY MONO	OMNI ON/OFF, POLY, MONO	
	Altered		Mode 2 -> Mode 4 (M≠6	
NOTE NUMBER		0 — 127	0 — 127	61 note keyboard, note range can be transposed
	True Voice			
VELOCITY	Note On	O	O	
	Note Off	O	O	
TOUCH	Key's	X	X	
	Chan's	X	X	
PITCH BENDER		O	O	lever 1
CONTROL CHANGE	pedal 1 7	O	O	any controller number from 0-121 can be assigned to numbers shown are system defaults
	pedal 2 64	O	O	
	lever 2 1	O	O	
	lever 3 2	O	O	
PROGRAM CHANGE		0 — 99	0 — 99	
	True #			
SYSTEM EXCLUSIVE		O	O	patches, parameters
SYSTEM COMMON	Song Pos	X	X	
	Song Sel	X	X	
	Tune	O	O	
SYSTEM REAL TIME	Clock	X	X	
	Messages	X	X	
AUX	Local Control	O	O	
	All Notes Off	O	O	
	Active Sense		O	
	Reset	X	X	

NOTES: The Matrix 6 is a stand alone instrument.
The Matrix 6R is a remote controllable slave unit. It only transmits System Exclusive messages.

Mode 1 : OMNI ON, POLY	Mode 2 : OMNI ON, MONO	O : Yes
Mode 3 : OMNI OFF, POLY	Mode 4 : OMNI OFF, MONO	X : No

Manufacturer		Model	
Oberheim		**Matrix 12/Xpander**	
[Polyphonic Synthesizer]		Version 1.4	Date —

Function		Transmitted	Recognized	Remarks
CHANNEL	Default	1 — 16	1 — 16	memorized
	Changed	1 — 16	1 — 16	
MODE	Default	Mode 1	Mode 1	Honors Modes 1 - 4
	Messages	X	X	
	Altered			
NOTE NUMBER		36 — 96	0 — 127	
	True Voice			
VELOCITY	Note On	O	O	
	Note Off	O	O	
TOUCH	Key's	X	X	
	Chan's	O	O	
PITCH BENDER		O	O	lever 1
CONTROL CHANGE	lever 2	O	O	can be assigned to any MIDI controller number (0-121)
	pedal 1	O	O	
	pedal 2	O	O	
PROGRAM CHANGE		0-99	0-99	
	True #			
SYSTEM EXCLUSIVE		O	O	
SYSTEM COMMON	Song Pos	X	X	
	Song Sel	X	X	
	Tune	X	O	
SYSTEM REAL TIME	Clock	X	X	
	Messages	X	X	
AUX	Local Control	X	X	see notes
	All Notes Off	X	O (123)	
	Active Sense	X	X	
	Reset	X	X	

NOTES: The Matrix 12 is a stand alone 12 voice instrument.

The Xpander is a remote controllable 6 voice slave unit. It only Transmits only System Exclusive messages.

For versions 1.4 and later, All Notes Off is channel dependent.
In earlier versions All Notes Off is effects all channels.

Mode 1 : OMNI ON, POLY	Mode 2 : OMNI ON, MONO	O : Yes
Mode 3 : OMNI OFF, POLY	Mode 4: OMNI OFF, MONO	X : No

Manufacturer Roland [6—Voice Synthesizer]		Model JP-6 Version 4	Date —	

Function		Transmitted	Recognized	Remarks
CHANNEL	Default	1,2	1,2	version1,2 (OLD MIDI)
	Changed	X	X	
MODE	Default	Mode 3	Mode 1	
	Messages	OMNI OFF, POLY	OMNI ON/OFF, POLY, MONO	
	Altered		MONO —>OMNI ON	
NOTE		36-96	0 — 127	
NUMBER	True Voice		36 — 96	
VELOCITY	Note On	X	X	
	Note Off	X 9nH (v=0)	X	
TOUCH	Key's	X	X	
	Chan's	X	X	
PITCH BENDER		X	X	
CONTROL CHANGE		X	X	
PROGRAM CHANGE	True #	0—31	0—31	
SYSTEM EXCLUSIVE		X	X	
SYSTEM COMMON	Song Pos	X	X	
	Song Sel	X	X	
	Tune	O	O	
SYSTEM REAL TIME	Clock	X	X	
	Messages	X	X	
AUX	Local Control	X	X	* versions 1, 2 :125—127
	All Notes Off	O (123)*	O (123—127)*	versions 3, 4 :123—127
	Active Sense	X	X	
	Reset	X	X	

NOTES: When power—up, the following mode messages are sent:
ver 1, 2 POLY ON
ver 3, 4 ALL Notes Off, OMNI OFF, POLY ON

Mode 1 : OMNI ON, POLY	Mode 2 : OMNI ON, MONO	O : Yes
Mode 3 : OMNI OFF, POLY	Mode 4: OMNI OFF, MONO	X : No

Manufacturer **Roland** [6—Voice Synthesizer]		Model **JP-6** Version 6	Date 12/10/84	

Function		Transmitted	Recognized	Remarks
CHANNEL	Default	1, 2	1, 2	versions 1, 2 (OLD MIDI)
	Changed	1—16	1—16	version 6 only
MODE	Default	Mode 3	Mode 3*	*versions 1-4 default to Mode 1
	Messages	OMNI OFF, POLY	OMNI ON/OFF, POLY, MONO	
	Altered		MONO —> OMNI ON	
NOTE NUMBER		36 — 96	0 — 127	
	True Voice		36 — 96	
VELOCITY	Note On	X	X	n = 0 or 1
	Note Off	X 9nH (v=0)	X	
TOUCH	Key's	X	X	
	Chan's	X	X	
PITCH BENDER		X	X	
CONTROL CHANGE		X	X	
PROGRAM CHANGE		0—31	0— 31	
	True #			
SYSTEM EXCLUSIVE		X	X	
SYSTEM COMMON	Song Pos	X	X	
	Song Sel	X	X	
	Tune	O	O	
SYSTEM REAL TIME	Clock	X	X	
	Messages	X	X	
AUX	Local Control	X	X	* versions 1,2 :125—127
	All Notes Off	O (123)*	O (123—127)*	versions 3,4, 6 :123—127
	Active Sense	X	X	
	Reset	X	X	

NOTES: When power—up, the following mode messages are sent:
    ver 1, 2   POLY ON
    ver 3, 4, 6, ALL Notes OFF, OMNI OFF, POLY ON

Mode 1 : OMNI ON, POLY   Mode 2 : OMNI ON, MONO   O : Yes
Mode 3 : OMNI OFF, POLY   Mode 4: OMNI OFF, MONO   X : No

Manufacturer	Model
Roland	**JU-1**
[6—Voice Polyphonic Synthesizer]	Version 1.0 Date 10/1/85

Function		Transmitted	Recognized	Remarks
CHANNEL	Default	1 — 16	1 — 16	memorized
	Changed	1 — 16	1 — 16	
MODE	Default	Mode 3	Mode 1, 3	memorized
	Messages	OMNI OFF, POLY	OMNI ON/OFF, POLY, MONO	
	Altered		MONO (m≠1) —> Mode 1, 3	
NOTE NUMBER		12 — 108	0 — 127	
	True Voice		12 — 108	
VELOCITY	Note On	OX*	O	*memorized
	Note Off	X 9n v=0	X	
TOUCH	Key's	X	X	*memorized
	Chan's	X	OX*	
PITCH BENDER		OX	OX	memorized (see note 1)
CONTROL CHANGE	mod 1	OX	OX	memorized
	foot control 4	OX*	OX	* see note 2
	portamento time	X	OX	
	5	OX	OX	
	volume 7	OX	OX	
	hold 64	OX	OX	
	portamento 65			
PROGRAM CHANGE		0 — 127	0 — 127	transmit/receive is memorized on power up
	True #			
SYSTEM EXCLUSIVE		OX	OX	memorized
SYSTEM COMMON	Song Pos	X	X	
	Song Sel	X	X	
	Tune	X	X	
SYSTEM REAL TIME	Clock	X	X	
	Messages	X	X	
AUX	Local Control	X	O	memorized
	All Notes Off	O (123)	O (123 — 127)	
	Active Sense	X	O	
	Reset	X	X	

NOTES: NOTE 1: Bender resolution is 9 bits. Range is 0-12 semitones

NOTE 2: The velocity value can be changed by FOOT CONTROL volume.

Mode 1 : OMNI ON, POLY	Mode 2 : OMNI ON, MONO	O : Yes
Mode 3 : OMNI OFF, POLY	Mode 4: OMNI OFF, MONO	X : No

Manufacturer	Model
Roland	**JU-1**
[6—Voice Polyphonic Synthesizer]	Version 1.1 Date 1/27/86

Function		Transmitted	Recognized	Remarks
CHANNEL	Default	1 — 16	1 — 16	memorized
	Changed	1 — 16	1 —16	
MODE	Default	Mode 3	Mode 1, 3	memorized
	Messages	OMNI OFF, POLY	OMNI ON/OFF, POLY, MONO	
	Altered		MONO (m≠1) —> Mode 1, 3	
NOTE NUMBER		12 — 108	0 — 127	
	True Voice		12 — 108	
VELOCITY	Note On	OX*	O	* memorized
	Note Off	X 9nH (v=0)	X	
TOUCH	Key's	X	X	*memorized
	Chan's	X	OX*	
PITCH BENDER		OX	OX	memorized
CONTROL CHANGE	mod 1	OX	OX	enable/disable memorized for all controllers
	foot control 4	OX	OX	
	portamento time	X	OX	controller 4 interpreted as AfterTouch
	5	OX	OX	
	volume 7	OX	OX	
	hold1 64	OX	OX	
	portamento 65			
PROGRAM CHANGE		0 — 127	0 — 127	set to OX and memorized
	True #			
SYSTEM EXCLUSIVE		OX	OX	memorized
SYSTEM COMMON	Song Pos	X	X	
	Song Sel	X	X	
	Tune	X	X	
SYSTEM REAL TIME	Clock	X	X	
	Messages	X	X	
AUX	Local Control	X	O	memorized
	All Notes Off	O (123)	O (123 — 127)	
	Active Sense	X	O	
	Reset	X	X	

NOTES: The velocity value can be changed by FOOT CONTROL volume.

Volume can adjust the volume of the sound within adjusted level by the panel volume knob.

Mode 1 : OMNI ON, POLY	Mode 2 : OMNI ON, MONO	O : Yes
Mode 3 : OMNI OFF, POLY	Mode 4: OMNI OFF, MONO	X : No

Manufacturer		Model	
Roland		**JU-2**	
[6—Voice Polyphonic Synthesizer]		Version 1.0	Date 11/5/85

Function		Transmitted	Recognized	Remarks
CHANNEL	Default	1 — 16	1 — 16	memorized
	Changed	1 — 16	1 — 16	
MODE	Default	Mode 3	Mode 1, 3	memorized
	Messages	OMNI OFF, POLY	OMNI ON/OFF, POLY, MONO	
	Altered		MONO (m≠1) —> Mode 1, 3	
NOTE NUMBER		12 —108	0 — 127	
	True Voice		12 — 108	
VELOCITY	Note On	O	O	
	Note Off	X 9nH (v=0)	X	
TOUCH	Key's	X	X	memorized
	Chan's	OX	OX	
PITCH BENDER		OX	OX	memorized (see notes)
CONTROL CHANGE	mod 1	OX	OX	memorized
	portatmento time	X	OX	
	5	OX	OX	
	volume 7	OX	OX	
	hold 64	OX	OX	
	portamento 65			
PROGRAM CHANGE		0 — 127	0 — 127	transmit receive set on power up
	True #			
SYSTEM EXCLUSIVE		OX	OX	memorized
SYSTEM COMMON	Song Pos	X	X	
	Song Sel	X	X	
	Tune	X	X	
SYSTEM REAL TIME	Clock	X	X	
	Messages	X	X	
AUX	Local Control	X	O*	*memorized
	All Notes Off	O (123)	O (123 — 127)	
	Active Sense	X	O	
	Reset	X	X	

NOTES: Bender resolution is 9 bits. Range is 0-12 semitones.

Mode 1 : OMNI ON, POLY	Mode 2 : OMNI ON, MONO	O : Yes
Mode 3 : OMNI OFF, POLY	Mode 4: OMNI OFF, MONO	X : No

Manufacturer	Model
Roland	**JU-2**
[6—Voice Polyphonic Synthesizer]	Version 1.1 Date 1/27/86

Function		Transmitted	Recognized	Remarks
CHANNEL	Default	1 —16	1 — 16	memorized
	Changed	1—16	1 — 16	
MODE	Default	Mode 3	Mode 1, 3	memorized
	Messages	OMNI OFF, POLY	OMNI ON/OFF, POLY, MONO	
	Altered	* * * * * * * * * * * * *	MONO (m≠1) —> Mode 1, 3	
NOTE NUMBER		12 — 108	0 — 127	
	True Voice		12 — 108	
VELOCITY	Note On	O	O	
	Note Off	X 9nH (v=0)	X	
TOUCH	Key's	X	X	memorized
	Chan's	OX	OX	
PITCH BENDER		OX	OX	memorized (see notes)
CONTROL CHANGE	mod 1	OX	OX	enable/disable memorized for all controllers
	portamento time5	X	OX	
	volume 7	OX	OX*	* volume can adjust the loudness of a sound within the level set by the volume knob on the panel
	hold1 64	OX	OX	
	portamento 65	OX	OX	
PROGRAM CHANGE		0 — 127	0 — 127	transmit /receive is set on power up
	True #			
SYSTEM EXCLUSIVE		OX	OX	
SYSTEM COMMON	Song Pos	X	X	
	Song Sel	X	X	
	Tune	X	X	
SYSTEM REAL TIME	Clock	X	X	
	Messages	X	X	
AUX	Local Control	X	O*	memorized
	All Notes Off	O (123)	O (123 — 127)	
	Active Sense	X	X	
	Reset	X	X	

NOTES: Bender resolution is 9 bits. Range is 0-12 semitones.

Mode 1 : OMNI ON, POLY	Mode 2 : OMNI ON, MONO	O : Yes
Mode 3 : OMNI OFF, POLY	Mode 4: OMNI OFF, MONO	X : No

Manufacturer	Model
Roland	**JX-8P**
[6—Voice Polyphonic Synthesizer]	Version 1.0　　Date 11/1/84

Function		Transmitted	Recognized	Remarks
CHANNEL	Default	1—16	1—16	memorized
	Changed	1—16	1—16	
MODE	Default	Mode 1, 3	Mode 1, 3	memorized
	Messages	OMNI ON/OFF, POLY	OMNI ON/OFF, POLY	
	Altered			
NOTE NUMBER		36—96	0 — 127	
	True Voice		21 — 108	
VELOCITY	Note On	O	OX	memorized
	Note Off	X	X	
TOUCH	Key's	X	X	memorized
	Chan's	OX	OX	
PITCH BENDER		OX	OX	memorized
CONTROL CHANGE	mod 1	OX	OX	memorized
	portamento time	OX	OX	
	5	OX	OX	
	volume 7	OX	OX	
	hold 64	OX	OX	
	portamento 65			
PROGRAM CHANGE		0 — 127	0 — 127	memorized
	True #			
SYSTEM EXCLUSIVE		OX	OX	memorized
SYSTEM COMMON	Song Pos	X	X	
	Song Sel	X	X	
	Tune	X	X	
SYSTEM REAL TIME	Clock	X	X	
	Messages	X	X	
AUX	Local Control	X	O	Local Control default: ON
	All Notes Off	O (123)	O (123—127)	* memorized
	Active Sense	OX*	OX*	
	Reset	X	X	
NOTES:				

Mode 1 : OMNI ON, POLY　　Mode 2 : OMNI ON, MONO　　O : Yes
Mode 3 : OMNI OFF, POLY　　Mode 4: OMNI OFF, MONO　　X : No

Manufacturer	Model
Roland	**JUNO-106**
[6—Voice Synthesizer]	Version 1.0 Date —

Function		Transmitted	Recognized	Remarks
CHANNEL	Default	1	1	tranmsit channel = receive channel
	Changed	1—16	1—16	
MODE	Default	Mode 3	Mode 1	
	Messages	OMNI OFF, POLY	OMNI ON/OFF, POLY	
	Altered		MONO (M≠1) —>1, (M=1)	
NOTE NUMBER		24 — 108	0 — 127	
	True Voice		24 — 108	
VELOCITY	Note On	X	X	
	Note Off	X 9nH (v=0)	X	
TOUCH	Key's	X	X	
	Chan's	X	X	
PITCH BENDER		O	O	F-2, F-3 only
CONTROL CHANGE	modulation 1	O*	O*	* F-2, F-3 only
	hold 64	O	O	
PROGRAM CHANGE		0-127	0-127	see notes
	True #			
SYSTEM EXCLUSIVE		O	O	F-3 only (Tone parameters)
SYSTEM COMMON	Song Pos	X	X	
	Song Sel	X	X	
	Tune	X	X	
SYSTEM REAL TIME	Clock	X	X	
	Messages	X	X	
AUX	Local Control	X	X	
	All Notes Off	O (123)	O (123 — 127)	
	Active Sense	X	X	
	Reset	X	X	

NOTES: Program changes messages are only transmitted when set to F-2. They are recognized only when set to F2 or F3.

When powered up, OMNI OFF, POLY ON are sent in channel 1.

Mode 1 : OMNI ON, POLY	Mode 2 : OMNI ON, MONO	O : Yes
Mode 3 : OMNI OFF, POLY	Mode 4: OMNI OFF, MONO	X : No

Manufacturer
Sequential
[5 Voice Synth]

Model
Prophet 5
Version 10.2   Date 1/84

Function		Transmitted	Recognized	Remarks
CHANNEL	Default	1	1-16	earlier versions only use channel 1
	Changed	1-16	1-16	
MODE	Default	Mode 1	Mode 1	honors Modes 1,3. (earlier versions only Mode 1)
	Messages			
	Altered			
NOTE NUMBER		36-96	0-127	
	True Voice		36-96	
VELOCITY	Note On	X	X	
	Note Off	X	X	
TOUCH	Key's	X	X	
	Chan's	X	X	
PITCH BENDER		X	O	
CONTROL CHANGE	release switch 64	O	O	only version 10.2
PROGRAM CHANGE		0-39, 64-103	0-39, 64-100	upper bank is for temperment
	True #			
SYSTEM EXCLUSIVE		O	O	program dumps
SYSTEM COMMON	Song Pos	X	X	
	Song Sel	X	X	
	Tune	O	O	
SYSTEM REAL TIME	Clock	X	X	
	Messages	X	X	
AUX	Local Control	X	X	
	All Notes Off	O	O 125,126,127	
	Active Sense	X	X	
	Reset	X	O	
NOTES:				

Mode 1 : OMNI ON, POLY   Mode 2 : OMNI ON, MONO   O : Yes
Mode 3 : OMNI OFF, POLY   Mode 4: OMNI OFF, MONO   X : No

Manufacturer	Model
Sequential	**Prophet 600**
[6 Voice Synth]	Version 6.07 Date 1/84

Function		Transmitted	Recognized	Remarks
CHANNEL	Default	1	1-16	
	Changed	1-16	1-16	
MODE	Default	Mode 1	Mode 1	honors Mode 1, 3
	Messages	X	X	see notes
	Altered			
NOTE NUMBER		36-96	0-127	
	True Voice		36-96	
VELOCITY	Note On	X	X	
	Note Off	X	X	
TOUCH	Key's	X	X	
	Chan's	X	X	
PITCH BENDER		O	O	0-4 semitones
CONTROL CHANGE	mod 1	O	O	
PROGRAM CHANGE		0-99	0-99	
	True #			
SYSTEM EXCLUSIVE		O	O	data dumps
SYSTEM COMMON	Song Pos	X	X	
	Song Sel	X	X	
	Tune	X	X	
SYSTEM REAL TIME	Clock	X	X	
	Messages	X	X	
AUX	Local Control	X	X	All Notes Off sent when onboard
	All Notes Off	O	O (123-127)	sequencer or arpeggiator are stopped
	Active Sense	X	X	
	Reset	X	X	

NOTES: Versions 6.04 and earlier always operate in Mode 1

Mode 1 : OMNI ON, POLY	Mode 2 : OMNI ON, MONO	O : Yes
Mode 3 : OMNI OFF, POLY	Mode 4: OMNI OFF, MONO	X : No

Manufacturer

Sequential

[6 Voice Vector Synthesizer]

Model

Prophet VS

Version —   Date —

Function		Transmitted	Recognized	Remarks
CHANNEL	Default	1	1	can transmit/receive on more than 1 channel
	Changed	1-16	1-16	
MODE	Default	*	*	*unavailable at printing. honors Modes 1,3,4
	Messages	X	X	
	Altered		*	
NOTE NUMBER		24-127	0-127	
	True Voice		24-127	
VELOCITY	Note On	O	O	
	Note Off	X (9n 0vH)	X	
TOUCH	Key's	X	O*	treated as Mod message (key # is ignored)
	Chan's	O	O	
PITCH BENDER		O	O	
CONTROL CHANGE	mod 1	O	O	VS can Transmit/Receive all panel parameters via Control Change messages 62,63,06,26. (see owner's manual for details)
	2	X	O treated as chan pressure	
	foot control 4	X	O treated as Mod change	
	volume 7	O	O	
	pan 10	O	O	
	X 16, Y 17	O	O	
	hold 64,rlse2 69	O, X	O	
	Parameters	O	O	
PROGRAM CHANGE		0-63	0-63	
	True #			
SYSTEM EXCLUSIVE		O	O	see note
SYSTEM COMMON	Song Pos	X	X	
	Song Sel	X	X	
	Tune	X	X	
SYSTEM REAL TIME	Clock	O	O	MIDI arpeggiator
	Messages	Start, Stop, Continue	Start, Stop, Conitnue	
AUX	Local Control	X	X	
	All Notes Off	X	O (123)	
	Active Sense	X	X	
	Reset	X	X	

NOTES: data dumps, sample dump standard (waveforms)

Mode 1 : OMNI ON, POLY   Mode 2 : OMNI ON, MONO   O : Yes
Mode 3 : OMNI OFF, POLY   Mode 4: OMNI OFF, MONO   X : No

Hybrid Synthesizers

Manufacturer		Model	
Siel		DK 600	
[Dynamic Programmable Synthesizer]		Version 8	Date 3/9/84

Function		Transmitted	Recognized	Remarks
CHANNEL	Default	1	1	*unavailable at printing
	Changed	*	Channel 1 — 16	
MODE	Default	Mode 1	Mode 1	*unavailable at printing
	Messages	*	*	
	Altered			
NOTE NUMBER		36 — 96	36 — 96	
	True Voice			
VELOCITY	Note On	O	O	
	Note Off	X	X	
TOUCH	Key's	X	X	
	Chan's	X	X	
PITCH BENDER		X	X	
CONTROL CHANGE		X	X	
PROGRAM CHANGE		0-94	0-94	
	True #			
SYSTEM EXCLUSIVE		O	O	
SYSTEM COMMON	Song Pos	X	X	
	Song Sel	X	X	
	Tune	X	X	
SYSTEM REAL TIME	Clock	X	X	
	Messages	X	X	
AUX	Local Control	X	X	
	All Notes Off	O	O	
	Active Sense	X	X	
	Reset	O	O	

NOTES: Instrument ID# — 00 H

Mode 1 : OMNI ON, POLY   Mode 2 : OMNI ON, MONO   O : Yes
Mode 3 : OMNI OFF, POLY   Mode 4: OMNI OFF, MONO   X : No

Manufacturer	Model
Siel	DK 700
[6Voice Synth/Controller]	Version — Date —

Function		Transmitted	Recognized	Remarks
CHANNEL	Default	1	1	see note 1
	Changed	1-16	X	
MODE	Default	Mode 1	Mode 1	honors modes 1,3
	Messages	OMNI OFF, POLY	OMNI OFF	
	Altered			
NOTE NUMBER		36-96 *	36-96	*can be shifted up/down 2 octaves
	True Voice			
VELOCITY	Note On	O	O	
	Note Off	O	O	
TOUCH	Key's	X	X	
	Chan's	X	X	
PITCH BENDER		O	O	
CONTROL CHANGE	mod 1	O	O	
	sustain 64	O	X	
	latch 65	O	X	
PROGRAM CHANGE		0-127 note 1	0-72*	*0-54 controller mode
	True #			0-72 DK 700 mode
SYSTEM EXCLUSIVE		O	O	data dumps
SYSTEM COMMON	Song Pos	X	X	
	Song Sel	X	X	
	Tune	X	X	
SYSTEM REAL TIME	Clock	O	O	
	Messages	Start, Stop	X	
AUX	Local Control	X	X	
	All Notes Off	X	X	
	Active Sense	X	X	
	Reset	X	X	

NOTES: Note 1: The DK 700 can operate as either a stand alone synthesizer or a master controller. In the controller mode, the DK 700 transmits on up to four independent channels. Each channel has selectable program program change and transpose, mod and velocity ranges are also programmable per channel. See owner's manual for more details.

Mode 1 : OMNI ON, POLY	Mode 2 : OMNI ON, MONO	O : Yes
Mode 3 : OMNI OFF, POLY	Mode 4: OMNI OFF, MONO	X : No

Hybrid Synthesizers

Manufacturer	Model
Hohner	**MR 250**
[Multi Timbral Expander]	Version 1.0 Date 8/8/86

Function		Transmitted	Recognized	Remarks
CHANNEL	Default	X	1 2 3 4 5 16	
	Changed	X	1 — 16	
MODE	Default	X	Mode 1	
	Messages	X	OMNI ON/OFF	
	Altered			
NOTE NUMBER		X	35 — 96	
	True Voice			
VELOCITY	Note On	X	O	
	Note Off	X	X	
TOUCH	Key's	X	X	
	Chan's	X	X	
PITCH BENDER		X	X	
CONTROL CHANGE		X	O	see owner's manual
PROGRAM CHANGE	True #	X	O	see owner's manual
SYSTEM EXCLUSIVE		X	X	
SYSTEM COMMON	Song Pos	X	X	
	Song Sel	X	X	
	Tune	X	X	
SYSTEM REAL TIME	Clock	X	O	
	Messages	X	O	
AUX	Local Control	X	X	
	All Notes Off	X	O	
	Active Sense	X	O	
	Reset	X	O	

NOTES:

Mode 1 : OMNI ON, POLY   Mode 2 : OMNI ON, MONO   O : Yes
Mode 3 : OMNI OFF, POLY   Mode 4: OMNI OFF, MONO   X : No

Function		Transmitted	Recognized	Remarks
CHANNEL	Default	1	1	*unavailable at printing
	Changed	*	1-16	
MODE	Default	Mode 1	Mode 1	honors Modes 1,3
	Messages		*	*unavailable at printing
	Altered			
NOTE NUMBER		36 — 96	36 — 96	
	True Voice			
VELOCITY	Note On	O	O	
	Note Off	X	X	
TOUCH	Key's			
	Chan's	X	X	
PITCH BENDER		X	X	
CONTROL CHANGE		X	X	
PROGRAM CHANGE		0-99	0-99	
	True #			
SYSTEM EXCLUSIVE		O	O	
SYSTEM COMMON	Song Pos	X	X	
	Song Sel	X	X	
	Tune	X	X	
SYSTEM REAL TIME	Clock	X	X	
	Messages	X	X	
AUX	Local Control	X	X	
	All Notes Off	O	O	
	Active Sense	X	X	
	Reset	O	O	

NOTES: Instrument ID# — 01 H

Mode 1 : OMNI ON, POLY   Mode 2 : OMNI ON, MONO   O : Yes
Mode 3 : OMNI OFF, POLY   Mode 4: OMNI OFF, MONO   X : No

Manufacturer Siel — Model EX-600 [Dynamic Programmable Expander] Version 0 Date 3/9/84

Hybrid Synthesizers

Manufacturer
Akai
[MIDI Sound Module]

Model
VX-90
Version 1.0   Date 4/1/86

Function		Transmitted	Recognized	Remarks
CHANNEL	Default	1 — 16	1 — 16 *	* memorized
	Changed	1 — 16	1 — 16 *	
MODE	Default	Mode 3, 4	Mode 3	memorized
	Messages	X	X	
	Altered			
NOTE NUMBER		24 — 96	0 — 127	
	True Voice		24 — 120	
VELOCITY	Note On	X	O	
	Note Off	X 9nH (v=0)	O	
TOUCH	Key's	X	X	
	Chan's	x	X	
PITCH BENDER		X	O	7 bit resolution
CONTROL CHANGE	mod 1	X	O	
	volume 7	X	O	
	sustain 64	X	O	
PROGRAM CHANGE		0 — 99	0 — 127	
	True #		0 — 99	
SYSTEM EXCLUSIVE		X	X	
SYSTEM COMMON	Song Pos	X	X	
	Song Sel	X	X	
	Tune	O	O	
SYSTEM REAL TIME	Clock	X	X	
	Messages	X	X	
AUX	Local Control	X	X	
	All Notes Off	O	O	
	Active Sense	X	X	
	Reset	X	X	

NOTES:

Mode 1 : OMNI ON, POLY   Mode 2 : OMNI ON, MONO   O : Yes
Mode 3 : OMNI OFF, POLY   Mode 4: OMNI OFF, MONO   X : No

FERRO TECHNOLOGIES

Manufacturer	Model
Korg	**EX-800**
[Polyphonic Synthesizer Module]	Version 1.0 Date 7/14/86

Function		Transmitted	Recognized	Remarks
CHANNEL	Default	X	1 — 16	memorized
	Changed	X	1 — 16	
MODE	Default	X	Mode 1	
	Messages	X	OMNI ON/OFF	
	Altered			
NOTE NUMBER		X	0 — 127	
	True Voice		36 — 96	
VELOCITY	Note On	X	X	
	Note Off	X	X	
TOUCH	Key's	X	X	
	Chan's	X	X	
PITCH BENDER		X	O	
CONTROL CHANGE	OSC mod 1	X	O	
	VCF mod 2	X	O	
	volume 7	X	O	
PROGRAM CHANGE		X	0 — 127	enable/disable is set by parameter 86
	True #		0 — 63	
SYSTEM EXCLUSIVE		O	O	
SYSTEM COMMON	Song Pos	X	X	
	Song Sel	X	X	
	Tune	X	X	
SYSTEM REAL TIME	Clock	X	O	
	Messages	X	O	
AUX	Local Control	X	X	
	All Notes Off	X	X	
	Active Sense	X	O	
	Reset	X	X	
NOTES:				

Mode 1 : OMNI ON, POLY	Mode 2 : OMNI ON, MONO	O : Yes
Mode 3 : OMNI OFF, POLY	Mode 4: OMNI OFF, MONO	X : No

Manufacturer

Korg
[8 Voice Synthesizer Module]

Model

EX-8000
Version 1.0   Date 7/14/86

Function		Transmitted	Recognized	Remarks
CHANNEL	Default	1 — 16	1 — 16	memorized
	Changed	1 — 16	1 — 16	
MODE	Default	Mode 1, 3	Mode 1, 3	memorized
	Messages	X	OMNI ON/OFF	
	Altered			
NOTE NUMBER		X	0 — 127	set by Key Window function
	True Voice		24 — 108	
VELOCITY	Note On	X	O	
	Note Off	X	X	
TOUCH	Key's	X	X	
	Chan's	X	OX	
PITCH BENDER		X	OX	
CONTROL CHANGE	OSC mod 1	X	OX	
	VCF mod 2	X	OX	
	volume 7	X	OX	
	damper 64	X	OX	
	portamento 65	X	OX	
PROGRAM CHANGE		0 — 63	0 — 127	enabled/disabled by setting of parameter 85
	True #		0 — 63	
SYSTEM EXCLUSIVE		OX	OX	
SYSTEM COMMON	Song Pos	X	X	
	Song Sel	X	X	
	Tune	X	X	
SYSTEM REAL TIME	Clock	X	X	
	Messages	X	X	
AUX	Local Control	X	X	
	All Notes Off	X	O (123-127)	
	Active Sense	X	OX	
	Reset	X	X	

NOTES: Only program change + sys exclusive transmitted.
If parameter 85=1, only note data + mode messages are transmitted and received.
OX means function can be enabled or disabled by value of parameter 85.
Program Change: if n>63, 64 is subtracted

Mode 1 : OMNI ON, POLY   Mode 2 : OMNI ON, MONO   O : Yes
Mode 3 : OMNI OFF, POLY   Mode 4: OMNI OFF, MONO   X : No

Manufacturer	Model	
Roland	**MKS-7**	
[Sound Module (BASS Part—1 Voice)]	Version 1.0	Date 1/21/85

Function		Transmitted	Recognized	Remarks
CHANNEL	Default	X	2	
	Changed	X	1 — 16	
MODE	Default	X	Mode 4	
	Messages	X	X	
	Altered			
NOTE NUMBER		X	0 — 127	1 octave down
	True Voice		31 — 96	
VELOCITY	Note On	X	O	
	Note Off	X	X	
TOUCH	Key's	X	X	
	Chan's	X	X	
PITCH BENDER		X	X	
CONTROL CHANGE		X	X	
PROGRAM CHANGE		X	0 — 127	
	True #		0 — 19	
SYSTEM EXCLUSIVE		X	O	Tone parameters
SYSTEM COMMON	Song Pos	X	X	
	Song Sel	X	X	
	Tune	X	X	
SYSTEM REAL TIME	Clock	X	X	
	Messages	X	X	
AUX	Local Control	X	X	
	All Notes Off	X	O (123 — 127)	
	Active Sense	X	O	
	Reset	X	X	

NOTES:

Mode 1 : OMNI ON, POLY   Mode 2 : OMNI ON, MONO   O : Yes
Mode 3 : OMNI OFF, POLY   Mode 4: OMNI OFF, MONO   X : No

| Manufacturer **Roland** [Sound Module (Melody part-2 voices)] | | Model **MKS-7** Version 1.0 Date 1/21/85 | | |

Function		Transmitted	Recognized	Remarks
CHANNEL	Default	X	1	
	Changed	X	1 — 16	
MODE	Default	X	Mode 3	
	Messages	X	X	
	Altered			
NOTE NUMBER		X	0 — 127	
	True Voice		24 — 108	
VELOCITY	Note On	X	O	
	Note Off	X	X	
TOUCH	Key's	X	X	
	Chan's	X	X	
PITCH BENDER		X	O	
CONTROL CHANGE	mod 1	X	O	
	hold 64	X	O	
PROGRAM CHANGE		X	0 — 127	
	True #		0 — 99	
SYSTEM EXCLUSIVE		X	O	Tone parameters
SYSTEM COMMON	Song Pos	X	X	
	Song Sel	X	X	
	Tune	X	X	
SYSTEM REAL TIME	Clock	X	X	
	Messages	X	X	
AUX	Local Control	X	X	
	All Notes Off	X	O (123 — 127)	
	Active Sense	X	O	
	Reset	X	X	

NOTES: When the CHORD part is in 6 voice mode, the MELODY part cannot sound.

Mode 1 : OMNI ON, POLY   Mode 2 : OMNI ON, MONO   O : Yes
Mode 3 : OMNI OFF, POLY   Mode 4: OMNI OFF, MONO   X : No

Manufacturer	Model	
Roland	**MKS-7**	
[Sound Module (CHORD Part-4 Voices)]	Version 1.0	Date 1/21/85

Function		Transmitted	Recognized	Remarks
CHANNEL	Default	X	3	
	Changed	X	1—16	
MODE	Default	X	Mode 3	
	Messages	X	X	
	Altered			
NOTE NUMBER		X	0 — 127	
	True Voice		24 — 108	
VELOCITY	Note On	X	O	
	Note Off	X	X	
TOUCH	Key's	X	X	
	Chan's	X	X	
PITCH BENDER		X	O	
CONTROL CHANGE	mod 1	X	O	voice select = 6/4 voices
	sustain 64	X	O	
	voice select 121	X	O	
PROGRAM CHANGE		X	0 — 127	
	True #		0 — 99	
SYSTEM EXCLUSIVE		X	X	Tone parameters
SYSTEM COMMON	Song Pos	x	x	
	Song Sel	X	X	
	Tune	X	X	
SYSTEM REAL TIME	Clock	X	X	
	Messages	X	X	
AUX	Local Control	X	X	
	All Notes Off	X	O (123 — 127)	
	Active Sense		O	
	Reset	X	X	
NOTES:				

Mode 1 : OMNI ON, POLY   Mode 2 : OMNI ON, MONO   O : Yes
Mode 3 : OMNI OFF, POLY   Mode 4: OMNI OFF, MONO   X : No

Hybrid Synthesizers

Manufacturer	Model
Roland	**MKS-7**
[Sound Module (Rhythm Part—11 Voices)]	Version 1.0 Date 1/21/85

Function		Transmitted	Recognized	Remarks
CHANNEL	Default	X	10	
	Changed	X	1—16	
MODE	Default	X	Mode 3	
	Messages	X	X	
	Altered		X	
NOTE NUMBER		X	35 — 51	
	True Voice			
VELOCITY	Note On	X	O	
	Note Off	X	X	
TOUCH	Key's	X	X	
	Chan's	X	X	
PITCH BENDER		X	X	
CONTROL CHANGE		X	X	
PROGRAM CHANGE		X	X	
	True #			
SYSTEM EXCLUSIVE		X	X	
SYSTEM COMMON	Song Pos	X	X	
	Song Sel	X	X	
	Tune	X	X	
SYSTEM REAL TIME	Clock	X	X	
	Messages	X	X	
AUX	Local Control	X	X	
	All Notes Off	X	X	
	Active Sense		X	
	Reset	X	X	

NOTES: Note # to instruments assignment
  35, 36 — Bass Dr   48, 50 — Hi Tom   46 — Opn HH
  38, 40 — Snr Dr   37   — Rim Sht   49 — Crsh Cym
  41, 43 — Low Tom   39   — Hnd Clp   51 — Ride Cym
  45, 47 — Mid Tom   42, 44 — Cls HH

Mode 1 : OMNI ON, POLY   Mode 2 : OMNI ON, MONO   O : Yes
Mode 3 : OMNI OFF, POLY   Mode 4: OMNI OFF, MONO   X : No

Manufacturer	Model
Roland	**MKS-80**
[8—Voice Sound Module]	Version 1.0 Date 9/11/84

Function		Transmitted	Recognized	Remarks
CHANNEL	Default	1 — 16	1 — 16	memorized
	Changed	1 — 16	1 — 16	
MODE	Default	Mode 3	Mode 3	MONO (M≠1) ignored
	Messages	X	OMNI ON/OFF, POLY, MONO	
	Altered			
NOTE NUMBER		X	0 — 127	
	True Voice		21 — 108	
VELOCITY	Note On	X	O	
	Note Off	X	X	
TOUCH	Key's	X	X	
	Chan's	X	O*	
PITCH BENDER		X	O*	*see note
CONTROL CHANGE	mod 1	X	O*	*not recognized when MIDI FUNCTION is set to I
	volume 7	X	O*	
	bender sense 31	X	O*	
	hold 64	X	OX	Hold O or X is memorized with patch
PROGRAM CHANGE		0—63	0—127	see notes
	True #			
SYSTEM EXCLUSIVE		O	O	FUNCTION III only
SYSTEM COMMON	Song Pos	X	X	*not recognized when MIDI FUNCTION is set to I
	Song Sel	X	X	
	Tune	O*	O*	
SYSTEM REAL TIME	Clock	X	X	
	Messages	X	X	
AUX	Local Control	X	X	
	All Notes Off	X	O (123-127)	
	Active Sense	X	O	
	Reset	X	X	

NOTES: Received messages are usually transmitted.

Program Change:

MIDI FUNCTION	Tx	Rx
I		
II	Tone #	Tone #
III	———	Patch #

Mode 1 : OMNI ON, POLY   Mode 2 : OMNI ON, MONO   O : Yes
Mode 3 : OMNI OFF, POLY   Mode 4: OMNI OFF, MONO   X : No

Manufacturer
Emu
[8 Voice Sampler]

Model
Emulator II
Version —   Date —

Function		Transmitted	Recognized	Remarks
CHANNEL	Default	1	1	
	Changed	1 — 16	1 — 16	
MODE	Default	Mode 1	Mode 1	Honors Modes 1,3
	Messages	X	OMNI ON/OFF	
	Altered			
NOTE NUMBER		36-96	36-96	
	True Voice			
VELOCITY	Note On	O	O	
	Note Off	X	X	
TOUCH	Key's	X	X	
	Chan's	OX	OX	
PITCH BENDER		OX	OX	
CONTROL CHANGE	Left Wheel	OX	OX	assignable to controllers 0—31
	Right Wheel	OX	OX	
	Pedal	OX	OX	
	Sustain Pedal	OX	OX	
PROGRAM CHANGE		0 — 98	0 — 98	
	True #		1 — 99	
SYSTEM EXCLUSIVE		X	X	
SYSTEM COMMON	Song Pos	X	X	
	Song Sel	X	X	
	Tune	X	X	
SYSTEM REAL TIME	Clock	O	OX	recognition of commands is selectable
	Messages	Start, Stop	Start, Stop	
AUX	Local Control	X	O	
	All Notes Off	O	O (123-127)	
	Active Sense	X	X	
	Reset	O	X	
NOTES:				

Mode 1 : OMNI ON, POLY   Mode 2 : OMNI ON, MONO   O : Yes
Mode 3 : OMNI OFF, POLY   Mode 4: OMNI OFF, MONO   X : No

Manufacturer	Model
Ensoniq	Mirage
[Standard Operating System]	Version 3.2 Date 6/3/86

Function		Transmitted	Recognized	Remarks
CHANNEL	Default	1	1	
	Changed	1 — 16	1 — 16	
MODE	Default	Mode 1	Mode1	
	Messages	OMNI ON/OFF	OMNI ON/OFF	
	Altered		OMNI OFF > Mode 3	
NOTE NUMBER		36 — 96	36 — 96	
	True Voice			
VELOCITY	Note On	O	O	
	Note Off	O	O	
TOUCH	Key's	X	O	
	Chan's	X	O	
PITCH BENDER		O	O	
CONTROL CHANGE	mod 1	O	O	2—7 are programmable
	2	X	O	
	3	X	O	
	4	X	O	
	5	X	O	
	6	X	O	
	7	X	O	
	sustain 64	O	O	
PROGRAM CHANGE		0 — 47	0 — 47	
	True #			
SYSTEM EXCLUSIVE		X	X	
SYSTEM COMMON	Song Pos	X	X	
	Song Sel	X	X	
	Tune	X	X	
SYSTEM REAL TIME	Clock	O	*	on-board sequencer
	Messages	X	Start, Stop, Cont	*unavailable at printing
AUX	Local Control	X	X	
	All Notes Off	O	O	
	Active Sense	X	X	
	Reset	X	X	
NOTES:				

Mode 1 : OMNI ON, POLY	Mode 2 : OMNI ON, MONO	O : Yes
Mode 3 : OMNI OFF, POLY	Mode 4: OMNI OFF, MONO	X : No

Manufacturer		Model		
Ensoniq		**Mirage**		
[MASOS Operating System]		Version 2.0	Date 6/3/86	

Function		Transmitted	Recognized	Remarks
CHANNEL	Default	1	1	
	Changed	1 — 16	1 — 16	
MODE	Default	Mode 1	Mode 1	
	Messages	OMNI ON/OFF	OMNI ON/OFF	
	Altered		OMNI OFF > Mode 3	
NOTE NUMBER		36 — 96	36 — 96	
	True Voice			
VELOCITY	Note On	O	O	
	Note Off	O	O	
TOUCH	Key's	X	X	
	Chan's	X	X	
PITCH BENDER		O	O	
CONTROL CHANGE	mod 1	O	O	
	sustain 64	O	O	
PROGRAM CHANGE		X	X	
	True #			
SYSTEM EXCLUSIVE		O	O	
SYSTEM COMMON	Song Pos	X	X	
	Song Sel	X	X	
	Tune	X	X	
SYSTEM REAL TIME	Clock	X	X	
	Messages	X	X	
AUX	Local Control	X	X	
	All Notes Off	X	O	
	Active Sense	X	X	
	Reset	X	X	

NOTES:

Mode 1 : OMNI ON, POLY	Mode 2 : OMNI ON, MONO	O : Yes
Mode 3 : OMNI OFF, POLY	Mode 4: OMNI OFF, MONO	X : No

Manufacturer	Model
Emu	E-Max
[Sampler]	Version 0.12 A Date —

Function		Transmitted	Recognized	Remarks
CHANNEL	Default	1	1	
	Changed	1 — 16	1 — 16	
MODE	Default	Mode 1	Mode 1	honors Mode 1, 3
	Messages	X	X	
	Altered			
NOTE NUMBER		21-108	21-108	
	True Voice			
VELOCITY	Note On	O	O	
	Note Off	X	X	
TOUCH	Key's	X	X	
	Chan's	O	O	
PITCH BENDER		O	O	7 bit resolution
CONTROL CHANGE	0—31	O	O	
PROGRAM CHANGE		0 — 99	0 — 99	
	True #			
SYSTEM EXCLUSIVE		O	O	data dumps, sample dumps, parameters
SYSTEM COMMON	Song Pos	X	X	
	Song Sel	O	O	
	Tune	X	X	
SYSTEM REAL TIME	Clock	O	O	
	Messages	Start, Stop	Start, Stop	
AUX	Local Control	X	O	
	All Notes Off	O	123, 127	
	Active Sense	X	X	
	Reset	X	X	

NOTES: The E-Max can do high-speed sample dumps. Sample data format follows the MIDI sample dump format.

Mode 1 : OMNI ON, POLY	Mode 2 : OMNI ON, MONO	O : Yes
Mode 3 : OMNI OFF, POLY	Mode 4: OMNI OFF, MONO	X : No

Manufacturer **Sequential**			Model **Prophet 2000**	
[6 Voice Sampler]			Version —	Date —

Function		Transmitted	Recognized	Remarks
CHANNEL	Default	1	1	
	Changed	1-16	1-16	
MODE	Default	Mode 1	Mode 1	Honors Modes 1,3,4
	Messages	X	X	
	Altered			
NOTE NUMBER		36-96	0-127	
	True Voice		36-96	
VELOCITY	Note On	O	O	
	Note Off	X	X	
TOUCH	Key's	X	X	
	Chan's	O	O	
PITCH BENDER		O	O	
CONTROL CHANGE	mod 1	O	O	
	2,3,4,	X	O (interpreted as mod)	
	volume 7	X	O	
	hold 64	X	O	
	2nd release 68	O	O	
PROGRAM CHANGE		0-127	0-127	
	True #			
SYSTEM EXCLUSIVE		O	O	see note 2
SYSTEM COMMON	Song Pos	X	X	
	Song Sel	X	X	
	Tune	X	X	
SYSTEM REAL TIME	Clock	O	O	MIDI Arpgeggiator
	Messages	Start, Stop	Start, Stop	
AUX	Local Control	X	O	
	All Notes Off	X	O (123)	
	Active Sense	X	X	
	Reset	X	X	

NOTES: Note 1: The Prophet 2000 offers several variations of the standard MIDI modes. See owner's manuals for details

Note 2: data dumps, sample dump standard

Mode 1 : OMNI ON, POLY	Mode 2 : OMNI ON, MONO	O : Yes
Mode 3 : OMNI OFF, POLY	Mode 4: OMNI OFF, MONO	X : No

Manufacturer Akai [6 Voice Sampler]		Model S-612 Version — Date 8/86		
Function		Transmitted	Recognized	Remarks
CHANNEL	Default	N/A	1	
	Changed		1 — 9	
MODE	Default	N/A	1	Honors Modes 1 — 4
	Messages		OMNI ON/OFF, POLY, MONO	
	Altered			
NOTE NUMBER		N/A	36 — 72	
	True Voice			
VELOCITY	Note On	N/A	O	
	Note Off		X	
TOUCH	Key's	N/A	X	
	Chan's		X	
PITCH BENDER		N/A	O	
CONTROL CHANGE	mod 1	N/A	O	
	sustain 64		O	
PROGRAM CHANGE	True #	N/A	X	
SYSTEM EXCLUSIVE		N/A	O	
SYSTEM COMMON	Song Pos	N/A	X	
	Song Sel		X	
	Tune		X	
SYSTEM REAL TIME	Clock	N/A	X	
	Messages		X	
AUX	Local Control	N/A	X	
	All Notes Off		X	
	Active Sense		X	
	Reset		X	

NOTES: N/A : Not Applicable

Mode 1 : OMNI ON, POLY	Mode 2 : OMNI ON, MONO	O : Yes
Mode 3 : OMNI OFF, POLY	Mode 4: OMNI OFF, MONO	X : No

Manufacturer	Model
Akai	S900
[MIDI Digital Sampler]	Version 1.2 Date —

Function		Transmitted	Recognized	Remarks
CHANNEL	Default	X	1	without Disk
	Changed	X	1 — 16	Memorized (Disk)
MODE	Default	X	Mode1*	* without disk, 1-4 memorized with
	Messages	X	OMNI ON/OFF, POLY, MONO	disk
	Altered			
NOTE NUMBER		X	0 — 127	
	True Voice		24 — 96	
VELOCITY	Note On	X	O	see note 1
	Note Off	X	O	
TOUCH	Key's	X	X	treated as modulation
	Chan's	X	O	see note 1
PITCH BENDER		X	O	see note 2
CONTROL CHANGE	mod 1	X	O*	*see note 1
	volume7	X	O*	
	sustain 64	X	O	
PROGRAM CHANGE		X	0 — 31	see note 1
	True #			
SYSTEM EXCLUSIVE		O	O	ID:47
SYSTEM COMMON	Song Pos	X	X	
	Song Sel	X	X	
	Tune	X	X	
SYSTEM REAL TIME	Clock	X	X	
	Messages	X	X	
AUX	Local Control	X	X	
	All Notes Off	X	O (123)	
	Active Sense	X	X	
	Reset	X	X	

NOTES: NOTE 1: Can be set O or X manually, and memorized.

NOTE 2: 7 bit resolution. 0-12 semitone step.

Mode 1 : OMNI ON, POLY	Mode 2 : OMNI ON, MONO	O : Yes
Mode 3 : OMNI OFF, POLY	Mode 4: OMNI OFF, MONO	X : No

Manufacturer	Model
Kurzweil	**Ensemble Grande**
—	Version — Date 7/86

Function		Transmitted	Recognized	Remarks
CHANNEL	Default	1 — 6	1 (Drums) 6 (Keybd)	sequencer transmits on CH 2 — 5
	Changed	X	1 — 16 (Keyboard)	
MODE	Default	Mode 3	Mode 3	
	Messages	X	X	
	Altered	X	X	
NOTE NUMBER		9 — 120	9 — 120	depends on transposition
	True Voice			
VELOCITY	Note On	O	O	
	Note Off	X	X	
TOUCH	Key's	X	X	
	Chan's	X	X	
PITCH BENDER		X	X	
CONTROL CHANGE	tuning slider 0	O	O	brightness data = 0-4
	brightness 10	O	O	
	sustain pedal 64	O	O	
	soft pedal 65	O	O	
PROGRAM CHANGE		(0 — 23)	(0 — 23)	Voice Select Buttons
	True #			
SYSTEM EXCLUSIVE		O	O	see note 1
SYSTEM COMMON	Song Pos	X	X	
	Song Sel			
	Tune			
SYSTEM REAL TIME	Clock	O	O	
	Messages	Start, Stop	Start, Stop	
AUX	Local Control	X	X	*at end of sequence
	All Notes Off	O*	O*	
	Active Sense	X	X	
	Reset	X	X	
NOTES: NOTE 1: Keyboard split & bulk sequence				

Mode 1 : OMNI ON, POLY	Mode 2 : OMNI ON, MONO	O : Yes
Mode 3 : OMNI OFF, POLY	Mode 4: OMNI OFF, MONO	X : No

Manufacturer	Model
Technics	**SX-PX1M**
[16-Voice Digital Piano]	Version — Date —

Function		Transmitted	Recognized	Remarks
CHANNEL	Default	1—16	1—16	memorized
	Changed	1—16	1-16	
MODE	Default	3	1, 3	memorized
	Messages	X	X	
	Altered			
NOTE NUMBER		1—126	15—124	see note
	True Voice		21—119	
VELOCITY	Note On	O	N/A	
	Note Off	X 9nH (V=0)		
TOUCH	Key's	X	N/A	
	Chan's	X		
PITCH BENDER		X	N/A	
CONTROL CHANGE	volume 7	O	X	
	sustain 64	OX	OX	
	sustenuto 66	OX	OX	
	soft pedal 67	OX	OX	
	ext 91	OX	OX	
	tremolo 92	OX	OX	
	chorus 93	OX	OX	
PROGRAM CHANGE		0-127	0-5	transmit/receive is user selectable
	True #			
SYSTEM EXCLUSIVE		X	X	
SYSTEM COMMON	Song Pos	X	X	
	Song Sel	O	O	
	Tune	X	X	
SYSTEM REAL TIME	Clock	O	X	
	Messages	Start, Stop	X	
AUX	Local Control	X	X	
	All Notes Off	O	O	
	Active Sense	O	O	
	Reset	X	X	

NOTES: Note Number ranges can be altered by settings of TRANSPOSE slide control.

Mode 1 : OMNI ON, POLY	Mode 2 : OMNI ON, MONO	O : Yes
Mode 3 : OMNI OFF, POLY	Mode 4: OMNI OFF, MONO	X : No

Manufacturer	Model
Ensoniq	**SDP-1**
[Digital Piano/Bass]	Version 1.0 Date 6/3/86

Function		Transmitted	Recognized	Remarks
CHANNEL	Default	1	1	Bass can be on different Channel
	Changed	1 — 16	1 — 16	
MODE	Default	Mode 3	Mode 3	
	Messages	X	X	
	Altered	X	X	
NOTE NUMBER	True Voice	22 — 108	22 — 108	
VELOCITY	Note On	O	O	
	Note Off	O	O	
TOUCH	Key's	X	X	
	Chan's	X	X	
PITCH BENDER		X	X	
CONTROL CHANGE	sustain 64	O	O	
	sostenudo 66	O	O	
	chorus on/off 93	O	O	
PROGRAM CHANGE	True #	0 — 22	0 — 22	
SYSTEM EXCLUSIVE		X	X	
SYSTEM COMMON	Song Pos	X	X	
	Song Sel	X	X	
	Tune	X	X	
SYSTEM REAL TIME	Clock	X	X	
	Messages	X	X	
AUX	Local Control	X	X	
	All Notes Off	O	O	
	Active Sense	X	X	
	Reset	X	X	

NOTES:

Mode 1 : OMNI ON, POLY   Mode 2 : OMNI ON, MONO   O : Yes
Mode 3 : OMNI OFF, POLY   Mode 4: OMNI OFF, MONO   X : No

Pianos

Manufacturer

Manufacturer	Model
Roland	**EP-50**
[Electronic Piano]	Version 1.0 Date 1/30/85

Function		Transmitted	Recognized	Remarks
CHANNEL	Default	1	1	
	Changed	1—16	1—16	
MODE	Default	Mode 3	Mode 1	
	Messages	OMNI OFF, POLY	OMNI ON, POLY	
	Altered		MONO (M≠1) —>1, (M=1)	
NOTE NUMBER		22 — 108	0 — 127	
	True Voice		21 — 108	
VELOCITY	Note On	O	O	
	Note Off	X 9n (v=0)	X	
TOUCH	Key's	X	X	
	Chan's	X	X	
PITCH BENDER		X	X	
CONTROL CHANGE	damper pedal 64	O	O	
PROGRAM CHANGE		0 — 127	0 — 7	can be ignored by power—up setting
	True #			
SYSTEM EXCLUSIVE		X	X	
SYSTEM COMMON	Song Pos	X	X	
	Song Sel	X	X	
	Tune	X	X	
SYSTEM REAL TIME	Clock	X	X	
	Messages	X	X	
AUX	Local Control	X	X	
	All Notes Off	O (123)	O (123—127)	
	Active Sense	O	O	
	Reset	X	X	

NOTES: When powered up, ch—1 OMNI OFF and POLY are sent.
When MIDI channel is changed, MODE is set to 3.

Mode 1 : OMNI ON, POLY	Mode 2 : OMNI ON, MONO	O : Yes
Mode 3 : OMNI OFF, POLY	Mode 4: OMNI OFF, MONO	X : No

FERRO TECHNOLOGIES

Manufacturer	Model
Roland	**HP-100**
[Piano Plus]	Version 1.0 Date 1/30/85

Function		Transmitted	Recognized	Remarks
CHANNEL	Default	1	1	see note 1
	Changed	1—16	1—16	
MODE	Default	Mode 3	Mode 1	see note 1
	Messages	OMNI OFF, POLY	OMNI ON, POLY	
	Altered		MONO (M≠1) —>1, (M=1)	
NOTE NUMBER		22 — 108	0 — 127	
	True Voice		21 — 108	
VELOCITY	Note On	O	O	
	Note Off	X 9nH (v=0)	X	
TOUCH	Key's	X	X	
	Chan's	X	X	
PITCH BENDER		X	X	
CONTROL CHANGE	damper pedal 64	O	O	
PROGRAM CHANGE	True #	0 — 127	0 — 7	can be ignored by power—up setting
SYSTEM EXCLUSIVE		X	X	
SYSTEM COMMON	Song Pos	X	X	
	Song Sel	X	X	
	Tune	X	X	
SYSTEM REAL TIME	Clock	X	X	
	Messages	X	X	
AUX	Local Control	X	X	
	All Notes Off	O (123)	O (123—127)	
	Active Sense	O	O	
	Reset	X	X	
NOTES: NOTE 1: When MIDI channel is changed, MODE is set to 3.				
NOTE 2: When powered up, OMNI OFF, POLY are sent on channel 1.				

Mode 1 : OMNI ON, POLY	Mode 2 : OMNI ON, MONO	O : Yes	
Mode 3 : OMNI OFF, POLY	Mode 4: OMNI OFF, MONO	X : No	

Manufacturer	Model
Roland	**HP-300**
[Piano Plus]	Version 1.0 Date —

Function		Transmitted	Recognized	Remarks
CHANNEL	Default	1	1	OLD MIDI
	Changed	X	X	
MODE	Default	Mode 3	Mode 1	
	Messages	POLY	OMNI ON, POLY	
	Altered		MONO —> OMNI	
NOTE NUMBER		29 — 103	0 — 127	
	True Voice		21 — 108	
VELOCITY	Note On	O	O	
	Note Off	X 90H (v=0)	X	
TOUCH	Key's	X	X	
	Chan's	X	X	
PITCH BENDER		X	X	
CONTROL CHANGE	damper 64	O	O	right pedal
	soft pedal65	O	O	left pedal
PROGRAM CHANGE	True #	X	X	
SYSTEM EXCLUSIVE		X	X	
SYSTEM COMMON	Song Pos	X	X	
	Song Sel	X	X	
	Tune	X	X	
SYSTEM REAL TIME	Clock	X	X	
	Messages	X	X	
AUX	Local Control	X	X	
	All Notes Off	O (127)	O (127)	
	Active Sense	X	X	
	Reset	X	X	

NOTES: When powered up, POLY ON is sent in channel 1.

Mode 1 : OMNI ON, POLY	Mode 2 : OMNI ON, MONO	O : Yes
Mode 3 : OMNI OFF, POLY	Mode 4: OMNI OFF, MONO	X : No

Manufacturer **Roland** [Piano Plus]		Model **HP-35.0** Version 1.0 Date 9/20/84		
Function		**Transmitted**	**Recognized**	**Remarks**
CHANNEL	Default	1	1	*set by power—up setting
	Changed	1—16	1—16*	
MODE	Default	Mode 3	Mode 1, 3*	* set by power-up setting
	Messages	OMNI OFF, POLY	OMNI ON, POLY, MONO	
	Altered		MONO (M≠1) —> 1, (M=1)	
NOTE NUMBER		28 — 103	0 — 127	
	True Voice		21 — 108	
VELOCITY	Note On	O	O	
	Note Off	X	X	
TOUCH	Key's	X	X	
	Chan's	X	X	
PITCH BENDER		X	X	
CONTROL CHANGE	damper 64	O	O	right pedal
	soft pedal 65	X*	X*	left pedal
	soft pedal67	O	O	left pedal * soft pedal can be changed to 65 by circuitry change
PROGRAM CHANGE		0 — 7	0 — 127	can be ignored by power—up setting
	True #		0 — 31	
SYSTEM EXCLUSIVE		X	X	
SYSTEM COMMON	Song Pos	X	X	
	Song Sel	X	X	
	Tune	X	X	
SYSTEM REAL TIME	Clock	X	X	
	Messages	X	X	
AUX	Local Control	X	X	
	All Notes Off	O (123)	O (123—127)	
	Active Sense	O	O	
	Reset	X	X	

NOTES: When powered up, OMNI OFF and POLY are sent on channel 1.

Mode 1 : OMNI ON, POLY   Mode 2 : OMNI ON, MONO   O : Yes
Mode 3 : OMNI OFF, POLY   Mode 4: OMNI OFF, MONO   X : No

Pianos

Manufacturer	Model
Roland	**HP-400**
[Piano Plus]	Version 1.0 Date —

Function		Transmitted	Recognized	Remarks
CHANNEL	Default	1	1	OLD MIDI
	Changed	X	X	
MODE	Default	Mode 3	Mode 1	
	Messages	POLY	OMNI ON, POLY, MONO	
	Altered		MONO —> OMNI	
NOTE NUMBER		21 — 108	0 — 127	
	True Voice		21 — 108	
VELOCITY	Note On	O	O	
	Note Off	X 90H (v=0)	X	
TOUCH	Key's	X	X	
	Chan's	X	X	
PITCH BENDER		X	X	
CONTROL CHANGE	damper 64	O	O	right pedal
	soft pedal 65	O	O	left pedal
PROGRAM CHANGE	True #	X	X	
SYSTEM EXCLUSIVE		X	X	
SYSTEM COMMON	Song Pos	X	X	
	Song Sel	X	X	
	Tune	X	X	
SYSTEM REAL TIME	Clock	X	X	
	Messages	X	X	
AUX	Local Control	X	X	
	All Notes Off	O (127)	O (125—127)	
	Active Sense	X	X	
	Reset	X	X	

NOTES: When powered up, POLY ON is sent on channel 1.

Mode 1 : OMNI ON, POLY   Mode 2 : OMNI ON, MONO   O : Yes
Mode 3 : OMNI OFF, POLY   Mode 4: OMNI OFF, MONO   X : No

Manufacturer	Model
Roland	**HP-450**
[Piano Plus]	Version 1.0 Date 9/20/84

Function		Transmitted	Recognized	Remarks
CHANNEL	Default	1	1	*by power up setting
	Changed	1—16	1—16*	
MODE	Default	Mode 3	Mode 1,3*	* by power up setting
	Messages	OMNI OFF, POLY	OMNI ON, POLY	
	Altered		MONO (M≠1)—> 1,	
NOTE NUMBER		21 — 108	0 — 127	
	True Voice		21 — 108	
VELOCITY	Note On	O	O	
	Note Off	X	X	
TOUCH	Key's	X	X	
	Chan's	X	X	
PITCH BENDER		X	X	
CONTROL CHANGE	damper 64	O	O	right pedal
	(soft pedal) 65	X *	X	left pedal
	soft pedal 67	O	O	left pedal
				* can be set by circuitry change
PROGRAM CHANGE		0—7	0 — 127	can be ignored by power-up setting
	True #		0 — 31	
SYSTEM EXCLUSIVE		X	X	
SYSTEM COMMON	Song Pos	X	X	
	Song Sel	X	X	
	Tune	X	X	
SYSTEM REAL TIME	Clock	X	X	
	Messages	X	X	
AUX	Local Control	X	X	
	All Notes Off	O (123)	O (123—127)	
	Active Sense	O	O	
	Reset	X	X	
NOTES: When powered up, OMNI OFF, POLY ON are sent on channel 1.				

Mode 1 : OMNI ON, POLY   Mode 2 : OMNI ON, MONO   O : Yes
Mode 3 : OMNI OFF, POLY   Mode 4 : OMNI OFF, MONO   X : No

Manufacturer	Model
Roland	HP-5500,5600
[Piano Plus]	Version 1.0 Date 12/20/85

Function		Transmitted	Recognized	Remarks
CHANNEL	Default	1	1	
	Changed	1 — 16	1 — 16	
MODE	Default	Mode 3	Mode 1	
	Messages	OMNI OFF, POLY	OMNI ON/OFF, POLY	
	Altered		MONO (M≠1) —>1, (M=1)	
NOTE NUMBER		15 — 113	0 — 127	
	True Voice		15 — 113	
VELOCITY	Note On	O	O	
	Note Off	X 9nH (v=0)	X	
TOUCH	Key's	X	X	
	Chan's	X	X	
PITCH BENDER		X	X	
CONTROL CHANGE	damper pedal 64	O	O	
	soft pedal 67	O	O	
	tremolo 92	O	O	
	chorus 93	O	O	
PROGRAM CHANGE		0 — 127	0 — 31	can be ignored by power—up setting
	True #			
SYSTEM EXCLUSIVE		X	X	
SYSTEM COMMON	Song Pos	X	X	
	Song Sel	X	X	
	Tune	X	X	
SYSTEM REAL TIME	Clock	X	X	
	Messages	X	X	
AUX	Local Control	X	X	
	All Notes Off	O	O (123—127)	
	Active Sense	O	O	
	Reset	X	X	

NOTES: When powered up, OMNI OFF and POLY are sent on channel 1.
When Basic channel is changed, Mode is set to 3.

Mode 1 : OMNI ON, POLY	Mode 2 : OMNI ON, MONO	O : Yes
Mode 3 : OMNI OFF, POLY	Mode 4: OMNI OFF, MONO	X : No

Manufacturer	Model
Roland	**RD-1000**
[Electronic Piano]	Version 1.0 Date 12/20/85

Function		Transmitted	Recognized	Remarks
CHANNEL	Default	1 — 16	1 — 16	
	Changed	1 — 16	1 — 16	memorized
MODE	Default	Mode 3	Mode 1, 3	memorized
	Messages	OMNI OFF, POLY	OMNI ON/OFF, POLY, MONO	
	Altered		MONO (M≠1) —>1, (M=1) —>	
NOTE NUMBER		115-113	0 — 127	
	True Voice		15 — 113	
VELOCITY	Note On	O	O	
	Note Off	X 9nH (v=0)	X	
TOUCH	Key's	X	X	
	Chan's	X	X	
PITCH BENDER		X	X	
CONTROL CHANGE	foot control 4	O	O	
	volume 7	O	O	
	expression 11	O	O	
	damper pedal 64	O	O	
	soft pedal 67	O	O	
	tremolo 92	O	O	
	chorus 93	O		
PROGRAM CHANGE		0 — 127	0 — 63	can be ignored by
	True #			power—up setting
SYSTEM EXCLUSIVE		X	X	
SYSTEM COMMON	Song Pos	X	X	
	Song Sel	X	X	
	Tune	X	X	
SYSTEM REAL TIME	Clock	X	X	
	Messages	X	X	
AUX	Local Control	X	O	
	All Notes Off	O	O (123 — 127)	
	Active Sense	O	O	
	Reset	X	X	

NOTES: When powered up, OMNI OFF, POLY ON are sent on memorized transmitter's channel.

Mode 1 : OMNI ON, POLY	Mode 2 : OMNI ON, MONO	O : Yes
Mode 3 : OMNI OFF, POLY	Mode 4: OMNI OFF, MONO	X : No

Pianos

Manufacturer	Model
Yamaha [Electronic Piano]	**PF70** Version 1.0 Date 8/23/85

Function		Transmitted	Recognized	Remarks
CHANNEL	Default	1 — 16	1 — 16	memorized
	Changed	1 — 16	1 — 16	
MODE	Default	Mode 3	Mode 1	honors modes 1 and 3
	Messages	X	OMNI ON/OFF	
	Altered			
NOTE NUMBER		16 — 115	0 — 127	
	True Voice		1 — 127	
VELOCITY	Note On	O	O	note 1
	Note Off	X 9nH (v=0)	X	
TOUCH	Key's	X	X	
	Chan's	X	X	
PITCH BENDER		X	O	see note 3
CONTROL CHANGE	Tremolo depth 1	O	O*	note 1
	Tremolo speed 4	O	O*	* recognized when F1 or F2 switch is on.
	Master volume 7	X	O	
	Sustain 64	O	O	
	Key hold 66	O	O	
	Soft pedal 67	O	O	
	Tremolo on/off 92	O	O	
	Chorus on/off 93	O	O	
PROGRAM CHANGE		0 — 98	0 — 9	
	True #			
SYSTEM EXCLUSIVE		O	O	Tuning, etc. note 1
SYSTEM COMMON	Song Pos	X	X	
	Song Sel	X	X	
	Tune	X	X	
SYSTEM REAL TIME	Clock	X	X	
	Messages	X	X	
AUX	Local Control	X	X	
	All Notes Off	X	O (123—127)	
	Active Sense	O	O	
	Reset	X	X	

NOTES: NOTE 1: These messages are transmitted when note event switch is on.

NOTE 2: Received messages are merged to MIDI OUT when MIDI merge switch is on.

NOTE 3: 7 bit resolution 0-12 semitones.

Mode 1 : OMNI ON, POLY	Mode 2 : OMNI ON, MONO	O : Yes
Mode 3 : OMNI OFF, POLY	Mode 4: OMNI OFF, MONO	X : No

FERRO TECHNOLOGIES

Manufacturer		Model	
Yamaha		**PF80**	
[Electronic Piano]		Version 1.0	Date 8/23/85

Function		Transmitted	Recognized	Remarks
CHANNEL	Default	1 — 16	1 - 16	memorized
	Changed	1 — 16	1 — 16	
MODE	Default	Mode 3	Mode 1	
	Messages	X	OMNI ON/OFF	
	Altered			
NOTE		9 — 120	0 — 127	
NUMBER	True Voice		1 – 127	
VELOCITY	Note On	O	O	note 1
	Note Off	X 9nH (v=0)	X	
TOUCH	Key's	X	X	
	Chan's	X	X	
PITCH BENDER		X	O	see note 3
CONTROL	Tremolo depth 1	O	O*	note 1
CHANGE	Tremolo speed 4	O	O*	
	Master volume 7	X	O	* recognized when F1 or F2 switch is on
	Sustain 64	O	O	
	Key hold 66	O	O	
	Soft pedal 67	O	O	
	Tremolo on/off	O	O	
	92	O	O	
	Chorus on/off 93			
PROGRAM		0 — 98	0 — 9	
CHANGE	True #			
SYSTEM EXCLUSIVE		O	O	note 1
SYSTEM	Song Pos	X	X	
COMMON	Song Sel	X	X	
	Tune	X	X	
SYSTEM	Clock	X	X	
REAL TIME	Messages	X	X	
AUX	Local Control	X	X	
	All Notes Off	X	O (123—127)	
	Active Sense	O	O	
	Reset	X	X	

NOTES: NOTE 1: These messages are transmitted when note event switch is on.

NOTE 2: Received messages are merged to MIDI OUT when MIDI merge switch is on.

NOTE 3: 7 bit resolution 0-12 semitones.

Mode 1 : OMNI ON, POLY	Mode 2 : OMNI ON, MONO	O : Yes
Mode 3 : OMNI OFF, POLY	Mode 4: OMNI OFF, MONO	X : No

Pianos

		Manufacturer **Roland** [12—Voice Piano Module]		

Model
MKS-10
Version 1.0   Date 8/11/84

Function		Transmitted	Recognized	Remarks
CHANNEL	Default	N/A	1—16	memorized
	Changed		1—16	
MODE	Default	N/A	Mode 3	
	Messages		OMNI ON/OFF, POLY	
	Altered		MONO (M≠1) —>1, (M=1)	
NOTE NUMBER		N/A	0 —127	
	True Voice		21 —108	
VELOCITY	Note On	N/A	O	
	Note Off		X	
TOUCH	Key's	N/A	X	
	Chan's		X	
PITCH BENDER		N/A	X	
CONTROL CHANGE	damper pedal 64		O	recognition can be set from panel
	soft pedal 65		X*	
	soft pedal 67		O	
PROGRAM CHANGE		N/A	0 —127	see notes
	True #			
SYSTEM EXCLUSIVE		N/A	X	
SYSTEM COMMON	Song Pos	N/A	X	
	Song Sel		X	
	Tune		X	
SYSTEM REAL TIME	Clock	N/A	X	
	Messages		X	
AUX	Local Control	N/A	X	
	All Notes Off		O (123—127)	
	Active Sense		O	
	Reset		X	

NOTES: While pressing any tone selector, except #1, the program changes are disabled.

Receiver only.

Mode 1 : OMNI ON, POLY	Mode 2 : OMNI ON, MONO	O : Yes
Mode 3 : OMNI OFF, POLY	Mode 4: OMNI OFF, MONO	X : No

Manufacturer	Model
Roland	MKS-20
[Electronic Piano Module]	Version 1.0 Date 12/20/85

Function		Transmitted	Recognized	Remarks
CHANNEL	Default	N/A	1 — 16	memorized
	Changed		1 — 16	
MODE	Default	N/A	Mode 1, 3	memorized
	Messages		OMNI ON/OFF, POLY, MONO	
	Altered	* * * * * * * * * * * * *	MONO (M≠1) —>1, (M=1)	
NOTE		N/A	0 — 127	
NUMBER	True Voice		15 — 113	
VELOCITY	Note On	N/A	O	
	Note Off		X	
TOUCH	Key's	N/A	X	
	Chan's		X	
PITCH BENDER		N/A	X	
CONTROL	foot control 4	N/A	O	
CHANGE	volume 7		O	
	expression 11		O	
	damper pedal 64		O	
	soft pedal 67		O	
	tremolo 92		O	
	chorus 93		O	
PROGRAM		N/A	0 — 63	can be ignored by
CHANGE	True #			power—up setting
SYSTEM EXCLUSIVE		N/A	X	
SYSTEM	Song Pos	N/A	X	
COMMON	Song Sel		X	
	Tune		X	
SYSTEM	Clock	N/A	X	
REAL TIME	Messages		X	
AUX	Local Control	N/A	X	
	All Notes Off		O (123 — 127)	
	Active Sense		O	
	Reset		X	
NOTES:				

Mode 1 : OMNI ON, POLY	Mode 2 : OMNI ON, MONO	O : Yes
Mode 3 : OMNI OFF, POLY	Mode 4: OMNI OFF, MONO	X : No

Preset Instruments

Manufacturer

Casio

[Casiotone Keyboard Instrument]

Model

CT-6000

Version —   Date —

Function		Transmitted	Recognized	Remarks
CHANNEL	Default	1	1 — 16	see note 1
	Changed	X	X	
MODE	Default	Mode 1	Mode 1	see note 1
	Messages	X	X	
	Altered			
NOTE NUMBER		36 — 96	36 — 96	see note 1
	True Voice			
VELOCITY	Note On	O	O	6 bit resolution
	Note Off	X 9nH (v=0)	O	
TOUCH	Key's	X	X	4 bit resoluton
	Chan's	O	O	
PITCH BENDER		O	O	see note 3
CONTROL CHANGE	sustain 64	O	O	
PROGRAM CHANGE	True #	X	X	
SYSTEM EXCLUSIVE		X	X	
SYSTEM COMMON	Song Pos	X	X	
	Song Sel	X	X	
	Tune	X	X	
SYSTEM REAL TIME	Clock	O	O	
	Messages	Start, Stop	Start, Stop	
AUX	Local Control	X	O	
	All Notes Off	X	X	
	Active Sense	X	X	
	Reset	X	X	

NOTES: NOTE 1: A retrofit is available the allows Mode 3 operation (with channel assignment) and a MIDI ON/OFF function for the lowest 18 keys.

NOTE 2: The CT-6000 transmits the MIDI clock when it is started from its on-board controls. It recognizes incoming MIDI clock messages only when they follow an incoming Start message. No incoming clock messages will be recognized while the internal clock is running.

NOTE 3: 8 bit resolution. 0-12 semitones.

Mode 1 : OMNI ON, POLY   Mode 2 : OMNI ON, MONO   O : Yes
Mode 3 : OMNI OFF, POLY   Mode 4: OMNI OFF, MONO   X : No

Manufacturer	Model
Casio	**CT-6500**
[Instrument/Rhythmn & Chords]	Version — Date —

Function		Transmitted	Recognized	Remarks
CHANNEL	Default	1	1	see note 1
	Changed	X	X	
MODE	Default	Mode 3	Mode 3	
	Messages	X	X	
	Altered			
NOTE NUMBER		36 — 96	0 — 127	
	True Voice		36 — 96	
VELOCITY	Note On	X	X	
	Note Off	X	X	
TOUCH	Key's	X	X	
	Chan's	X	X	
PITCH BENDER		O	O	see note 3
CONTROL CHANGE	mod 1	O	O	
	portamento time	X	O	
	5	X	O	
	master tune 6	O	O	
	sustain 64	O	O	
	portamento 65			
PROGRAM CHANGE		0—47,100—119,125—127	0—47,100—119,125—127	see note 2
	True #			
SYSTEM EXCLUSIVE		O	O	TONE data, etc.
SYSTEM COMMON	Song Pos	X	X	
	Song Sel	X	X	
	Tune	X	X	
SYSTEM REAL TIME	Clock	O	O (MIDI mode)	
	Messages	Start, Stop	Start, Stop	
AUX	Local Control	X	O	
	All Notes Off	X	X	
	Active Sense		X	
	Reset	X	X	

NOTES: NOTE 1: The data above is for the NORMAL mode, which is in effect when power is first switched ON. MULTI CHANNEL mode settings are also possible for 5 basic channels (CH 1= MELODY, CH 2 = BASS, CH 3 = CHORD, CH 4 = OBLIGATO, CH 5 = RHYTHM)

NOTE 2: TONE memories: 0-47, RHYTHM memories: 100-119, OPERATION memories: 125-127.

NOTE 3: 8 bit resolution. 0-12 semitones.

Mode 1 : OMNI ON, POLY	Mode 2 : OMNI ON, MONO	O : Yes
Mode 3 : OMNI OFF, POLY	Mode 4: OMNI OFF, MONO	X : No

Preset Instruments

Manufacturer	Model
Siel	**MK 1000**
[Stereo MIDI Keyboard]	Version 1.0 Date 2/25/85

Function		Transmitted	Recognized	Remarks
CHANNEL	Default	1	1	*Split ON
	Changed	Left 2/Right 1*	Left 2/Right 1*	
MODE	Default	Mode 3	Mode 1	Mode 3 = Split ON
	Messages	X	*	*unavailable at printing
	Altered			
NOTE NUMBER		36—96	36—96	
	True Voice			
VELOCITY	Note On	X	X	
	Note Off	X	X	
TOUCH	Key's	X	X	
	Chan's	X	X	
PITCH BENDER		X	X	
CONTROL CHANGE		X	X	
PROGRAM CHANGE		X	X	
	True #			
SYSTEM EXCLUSIVE		X	X	
SYSTEM COMMON	Song Pos	X	X	
	Song Sel	X	X	
	Tune	X	X	
SYSTEM REAL TIME	Clock	O	X	on board sequencer
	Messages	O	X	
AUX	Local Control	X	X	
	All Notes Off	X	O	
	Active Sense	X	X	
	Reset	X	X	
NOTES:				

Mode 1 : OMNI ON, POLY   Mode 2 : OMNI ON, MONO   O : Yes
Mode 3 : OMNI OFF, POLY   Mode 4: OMNI OFF, MONO   X : No

FERRO TECHNOLOGIES

Manufacturer	Model
Casio	CZ-230S
[PD Synthesis Instrument]	Version — Date —

Function		Transmitted	Recognized	Remarks
CHANNEL	Default	1 — 16	1 — 16	memorized
	Changed	1 — 16	1 — 16	
MODE	Default	Mode 3, 4	Mode 3,4	see note 1
	Messages	X	X	
	Altered			
NOTE NUMBER		36 — 84	0 — 127	
	True Voice		36 — 96	
VELOCITY	Note On	X	X	
	Note Off	X 9nH (v=0)	X	
TOUCH	Key's	X	X	X
	Chan's	X	X	X
PITCH BENDER		O	O	see note 2
CONTROL CHANGE	portamento time 5	X	O	
	portamento 65	O	O	
PROGRAM CHANGE		0 — 99	0 — 99	0 — 99 preset
	True #			96 — 99 rewrite
SYSTEM EXCLUSIVE		O	O	see note 3
SYSTEM COMMON	Song Pos	X	X	
	Song Sel	X	X	
	Tune	X	X	
SYSTEM REAL TIME	Clock	O	O	
	Messages	O	O	
AUX	Local Control	X	O	
	All Notes Off	X	X	
	Active Sense	X	X	
	Reset	X	X	

NOTES: NOTE 1: When power is turned on the 230S normally defaults to Mode 3. If the SOLO switch is held down when the power is turned on, the 230S will default to Mode 4.

NOTE 2: 8 bit resolution. 0-12 semitones.

NOTE 3: TONE DATA, TRANSPOSE, BEND RANGE

Mode 1 : OMNI ON, POLY	Mode 2 : OMNI ON, MONO	O : Yes
Mode 3 : OMNI OFF, POLY	Mode 4: OMNI OFF, MONO	X : No

Preset Instruments

Manufacturer		Model	
Siel		**MK-610/MK-890**	
[Stereo MIDI Keyboard]		Version 1.0	Date 10/4/84

Function		Transmitted	Recognized	Remarks
CHANNEL	Default	1	1	*Split on
	Changed	Left 2/Right 1*	Left 2/Right 1*	honors Mode 1,3
MODE	Default	Mode 3	Mode 1	Mode 3 = Split on
	Messages	X	X	
	Altered			
NOTE NUMBER		36 — 96	36 — 96	
	True Voice			
VELOCITY	Note On	X	X	
	Note Off	X	X	
TOUCH	Key's	X	X	
	Chan's	X	X	
PITCH BENDER		X	X	
CONTROL CHANGE		X	X	
PROGRAM CHANGE	True #	X	X	
SYSTEM EXCLUSIVE		X	X	
SYSTEM COMMON	Song Pos	X	X	
	Song Sel	X	X	
	Tune	X	X	
SYSTEM REAL TIME	Clock	X	X	
	Messages	X	X	
AUX	Local Control	X	X	
	All Notes Off	X	O (123-127)	
	Active Sense	X	X	
	Reset	X	X	

NOTES:

Mode 1 : OMNI ON, POLY   Mode 2 : OMNI ON, MONO   O : Yes
Mode 3 : OMNI OFF, POLY   Mode 4: OMNI OFF, MONO   X : No

FERRO TECHNOLOGIES

Manufacturer **Hohner** [Personal Keyboard]		Model **PK 150** Version — Date 1/86		

Function		Transmitted	Recognized	Remarks
CHANNEL	Default	1	1 — 16	see note 1
	Changed	1 2	1 — 6 16	
MODE	Default	Mode 1	Mode 1	
	Messages	X	OMNI ON, POLY	
	Altered			
NOTE NUMBER		36 — 96	36 — 96	
	True Voice			
VELOCITY	Note On	X	X	
	Note Off	X	X	
TOUCH	Key's	X	X	
	Chan's	X	X	
PITCH BENDER		X	X	
CONTROL CHANGE		X	X	
PROGRAM CHANGE		X	X	
	True #		X	
SYSTEM EXCLUSIVE		O	O	for switch dump
SYSTEM COMMON	Song Pos	X	X	
	Song Sel	X	X	
	Tune	X	X	
SYSTEM REAL TIME	Clock	O	O	
	Messages	Start, Stop	Start, Stop	
AUX	Local Control	X	X	
	All Notes Off	X	O	channel ignored
	Active Sense	X	X	
	Reset	X	O	

NOTES: NOTE 1:
mode 3 select: push (break) & (memory)
notes below keyboard split are sent on CH 2
notes on CH 1...6 control keyboard voice
notes on CH 16 control percussion

Mode 1 : OMNI ON, POLY　　Mode 2 : OMNI ON, MONO　　O : Yes
Mode 3 : OMNI OFF, POLY　　Mode 4: OMNI OFF, MONO　　X : No

Preset Instruments

Manufacturer	Model
360 Systems	**MIDI Bass**
[Sampled Bass Expander]	Version — Date 7/27/86

Function		Transmitted	Recognized	Remarks
CHANNEL	Default	X	unavailable at printing	
	Changed		1—14	
MODE	Default	X	unavailable at printing	Honors Modes 1, 3
	Messages			
	Altered			
NOTE NUMBER		X	36 — *	*see note 1
	True Voice			
VELOCITY	Note On	X	O	Selectable by user
	Note Off	X	X	
TOUCH	Key's	X	X	
	Chan's	X	X	
PITCH BENDER		X	O	+/- minor third
CONTROL CHANGE		X	X	
PROGRAM CHANGE		X	0 — 1	2 chip version
	True #		0 — 3	4 chip version
SYSTEM EXCLUSIVE		X	X	
SYSTEM COMMON	Song Pos	X	X	
	Song Sel	X	X	
	Tune	X	X	
SYSTEM REAL TIME	Clock	X	X	
	Messages	X	X	
AUX	Local Control	X	X	
	All Notes Off	X	X	
	Active Sense	X	X	
	Reset	X	X	

NOTES: As each sound chip contains its operating system — each chip has its own Note # range — typical range is 2 to 4 octaves (24—28 notes).

Mode 1 : OMNI ON, POLY	Mode 2 : OMNI ON, MONO	O : Yes
Mode 3 : OMNI OFF, POLY	Mode 4: OMNI OFF, MONO	X : No

Manufacturer	Model
Hohner	**PK 250**
[Personal Keyboard]	Version 7.0 Date 8/8/86

Function		Transmitted	Recognized	Remarks
CHANNEL	Default	1 2	1 2 16	
	Changed	1 — 16	1 — 16	
MODE	Default	Mode 3	Mode 3	
	Messages	X	X	
	Altered			
NOTE NUMBER		36 — 96	35 — 96	drums from 35
	True Voice			keyboard from 36
VELOCITY	Note On	X	X	
	Note Off	X	X	
TOUCH	Key's	X	X	
	Chan's	X	X	
PITCH BENDER		X	X	
CONTROL CHANGE		X	X	
PROGRAM CHANGE		X	X	
	True #		X	
SYSTEM EXCLUSIVE		O	O	
SYSTEM COMMON	Song Pos	X	X	
	Song Sel	X	X	
	Tune	X	X	
SYSTEM REAL TIME	Clock	O	O	* if enabled
	Messages	START, STOP*	START, STOP*	
AUX	Local Control	X	X	
	All Notes Off	X	O	
	Active Sense	O	O	
	Reset	X	O	
NOTES:				

Mode 1 : OMNI ON, POLY   Mode 2 : OMNI ON, MONO   O : Yes
Mode 3 : OMNI OFF, POLY   Mode 4: OMNI OFF, MONO   X : No

Preset Instruments

<table>
<tr><td colspan="2">Manufacturer
Roland
[8—Voice Sound Module]</td><td colspan="3">Model
EM-101
Version 1.0   Date 7/24/85</td></tr>
</table>

Function		Transmitted	Recognized	Remarks
CHANNEL	Default	X	1	
	Changed	X	1 — 8	
MODE	Default	X	Mode 1	
	Messages	X	OMNI ON/OFF	
	Altered			
NOTE NUMBER		X	0 — 127	
	True Voice		24 — 108	
VELOCITY	Note On	X	O	
	Note Off	X	X	
TOUCH	Key's	X	X	
	Chan's	X	X	
PITCH BENDER		X	X	
CONTROL CHANGE	hold 64	X	OX	O or X selected when power—up
PROGRAM CHANGE		X	0 —127	
	True #		0 — 15	
SYSTEM EXCLUSIVE		X	X	
SYSTEM COMMON	Song Pos	X	X	
	Song Sel	X	X	
	Tune	X	X	
SYSTEM REAL TIME	Clock	X	X	
	Messages	X	X	
AUX	Local Control	X	X	
	All Notes Off	X	O (123-127)	
	Active Sense		O	
	Reset	X	X	

NOTES: Receiver only

Mode 1 : OMNI ON, POLY	Mode 2 : OMNI ON, MONO	O : Yes
Mode 3 : OMNI OFF, POLY	Mode 4: OMNI OFF, MONO	X : No

Manufacturer
Roland
[6—Voice Module]

Model
MKS-30
Version 1.0   Date 5/25/84

Function		Transmitted	Recognized	Remarks
CHANNEL	Default	N/A	1 — 16	memorized
	Changed		1 — 16	
MODE	Default	N/A	Mode 3	
	Messages		OMNI ON/OFF, POLY	
	Altered			
NOTE NUMBER		N/A	0 —127	
	True Voice		21 —108	
VELOCITY	Note On	N/A	O	
	Note Off		X	
TOUCH	Key's	N/A	X	
	Chan's		X	
PITCH BENDER		N/A	O	see note 2
CONTROL CHANGE	mod 1	N/A	O	see notes
	hold 64		O	
PROGRAM CHANGE	True #	N/A	0—127	see notes
SYSTEM EXCLUSIVE		N/A	X	
SYSTEM COMMON	Song Pos	N/A	X	
	Song Sel		X	
	Tune		X	
SYSTEM REAL TIME	Clock	N/A	X	
	Messages		X	
AUX	Local Control		X	
	All Notes Off		O (123—127)	
	Active Sense		X	
	Reset		X	

NOTES: N/A: Not Applicable

Note1: Recognition of these MIDI functions are selectable by panel operations. Selections are memorized.

Note 2: 9—bit resolution 0-7 semitones.

Mode 1 : OMNI ON, POLY   Mode 2 : OMNI ON, MONO   O : Yes
Mode 3 : OMNI OFF, POLY   Mode 4 : OMNI OFF, MONO   X : No

Organs

Manufacturer
Hohner
[2 Manual Digital Organ]

Model
D 160
Version — Date 1/86

Function		Transmitted	Recognized	Remarks
CHANNEL	Default	1	1 — 16	
	Changed	1 2 3	1 2 3 16	
MODE	Default	Mode 1	Mode 1	set mode 3: push (+) & (memory)
	Messages	X	OMNI ON, POLY	buttons
	Altered			
NOTE NUMBER		36 — 84	36 — 84*	both Keyboards
	True Voice			bass pedal: 36 — 48
VELOCITY	Note On	X	X	
	Note Off	X	X	
TOUCH	Key's	X	X	
	Chan's	X	X	
PITCH BENDER		X	X	
CONTROL CHANGE		X	X	
PROGRAM CHANGE		X	X	
	True #		X	
SYSTEM EXCLUSIVE		O	O	for switch dump
SYSTEM COMMON	Song Pos	X	X	
	Song Sel	X	X	
	Tune	X	X	
SYSTEM REAL TIME	Clock	O	O	note 1
	Messages	START, STOP	START, STOP	
AUX	Local Control	X	X	
	All Notes Off	X	O	channel ignored
	Active Sense	X	X	
	Reset	X	O	

NOTES: NOTE 1) enable external clock: push (+) & (Arrangeur) buttons

Mode 1 : OMNI ON, POLY   Mode 2 : OMNI ON, MONO   O : Yes
Mode 3 : OMNI OFF, POLY   Mode 4: OMNI OFF, MONO   X : No

Manufacturer	Model
Hohner	**D 180**
[2 Manual Digital Organ]	Version — Date 1/86

Function		Transmitted	Recognized	Remarks
CHANNEL	Default	1	1 — 16	
	Changed	1 2 3	1 2 3 16	
MODE	Default	Mode1	Mode1	set mode 3: push (+) &
	Messages	X	OMNI ON, POLY	(memory) buttons
	Altered			
NOTE NUMBER		36 — 84	36 — 84	both keyboards
	True Voice			bass pedal: 36 — 48
VELOCITY	Note On	X	X	
	Note Off	X	X	
TOUCH	Key's	X	X	
	Chan's	X	X	
PITCH BENDER		X	X	
CONTROL CHANGE		X	X	
PROGRAM CHANGE		X	X	
	True #		X	
SYSTEM EXCLUSIVE		O	O	for switch dump
SYSTEM COMMON	Song Pos	X	X	
	Song Sel	X	X	
	Tune	X	X	
SYSTEM REAL TIME	Clock	O	O	
	Messages	O	O	
AUX	Local Control	X	X	
	All Notes Off	X	O	channel ignored
	Active Sense	X	X	
	Reset	X	O	

NOTES: 1) enable external clock: push (+) & (Arrangeur) buttons

Mode 1 : OMNI ON, POLY	Mode 2 : OMNI ON, MONO	O : Yes
Mode 3 : OMNI OFF, POLY	Mode 4: OMNI OFF, MONO	X : No

Manufacturer	Model
Hohner	**GP 180/D 180**
[2 Manual Electronic Organ]	Version 7.2 Date 7/10/86

Function		Transmitted	Recognized	Remarks
CHANNEL	Default	1 2 3	1 2 3 16	see notes
	Changed	1 — 16	1 — 16	
MODE	Default	Mode 3	Mode 3	
	Messages	X	X	
	Altered			
NOTE NUMBER		36 — 96	35 — 96	see notes
	True Voice			
VELOCITY	Note On	X	X	
	Note Off	X	X	
TOUCH	Key's	X	X	
	Chan's	X	X	
PITCH BENDER		X	X	
CONTROL CHANGE		O	O	see owner's manuals for details
PROGRAM CHANGE	True #	O	O	see owner's manuals for details
SYSTEM EXCLUSIVE		X	X	
SYSTEM COMMON	Song Pos	X	X	
	Song Sel	X	X	
	Tune	X	X	
SYSTEM REAL TIME	Clock	O	O	receive must be enabled
	Messages	Start, Stop	Start, Stop	
AUX	Local Control	X	O	
	All Notes Off	X	O	
	Active Sense	O	O	
	Reset	O	O	

NOTES: upper manual: default channel 1,   note range 48—96
            lower manual: default channel 2,   note range 36—84
            pedal   : default channel 3,   note range 36—48
            drums   : default channel 16, note range 35—66

Mode 1 : OMNI ON, POLY	Mode 2 : OMNI ON, MONO	O : Yes
Mode 3 : OMNI OFF, POLY	Mode 4: OMNI OFF, MONO	X : No

Manufacturer	Model
Technics	**SX-EX50(L)**
[Organ]	Version — Date 8/86

Function		Transmitted	Recognized	Remarks
CHANNEL	Default	1-16	1-16	memorized
	Changed	1-16	1-16	note 1
MODE	Default	Mode 3	Mode 3	honors Mode 3
	Messages	X	X	
	Altered			
NOTE		36-127 (36-84 Solo)	35-119*	*upper/lower
NUMBER	True Voice		36-119	note 2, 3, 4
VELOCITY	Note On	X	X	
	Note Off	X 9nH (v=0)	X	
TOUCH	Key's	X	X	
	Chan's	X	X	
PITCH BENDER		X	X	
CONTROL	sustain 64	OX	OX	control change messages are not
CHANGE	tremolo 92	OX	OX	transmitted or recognized on bass or
	chorus 93	OX	OX	solo channels (see note 1)
	celeste 94	OX	OX	
			OX	
PROGRAM		OX	OX	note 1
CHANGE	True #			
SYSTEM EXCLUSIVE		X	X	
SYSTEM	Song Pos	X	X	
COMMON	Song Sel	O	O	
	Tune	X	X	
SYSTEM	Clock	O	O	
REAL TIME	Messages	OX	OX	
AUX	Local Control	X	X	
	All Notes Off	O	O (123-127)	
	Active Sense	O	O	
	Reset	X	X	

NOTES: NOTE 1: upper, lower, bass, and solo can each transmit/recognize Note Numbers, Program Changes, and All Notes Off independently on seperate MIDI channels.
NOTE 2: bass transmits 36-84, recognizes 24-95 True Voice 36-95 (changes depending on the selected voice).
NOTE 3: solo recognizes 48-107.
NOTE 4: note numbers recognized are effected by TRANSPOSE and OCTAVE controls.

Mode 1 : OMNI ON, POLY	Mode 2 : OMNI ON, MONO	O : Yes
Mode 3 : OMNI OFF, POLY	Mode 4 : OMNI OFF, MONO	X : No

Manufacturer	Model
Technics	**SX-EX60**
[Organ]	Version — Date —

Function		Transmitted	Recognized	Remarks
CHANNEL	Default	1 — 16	1 — 16	memorized
	Changed	1 — 16	1 — 16	note 1
MODE	Default	Mode 3	Mode 3	honors Mode 3
	Messages	X	X	
	Altered			
NOTE NUMBER		36-127 (36-108 bass)	35-119	upper/lower
	True Voice			note 2, 3, 4
VELOCITY	Note On	X	X	
	Note Off	X 9nH (v=0)	X	
TOUCH	Key's	X	X	
	Chan's	X	X	
PITCH BENDER		X	X	
CONTROL CHANGE	sustain 64	OX	OX	note 1
	multi-tremolo			
	fast 92	OX	OX	
	slow 93	OX	OX	
	celeste 94	OX	OX	
PROGRAM CHANGE		OX	OX	note 1
	True #			
SYSTEM EXCLUSIVE		X	X	
SYSTEM COMMON	Song Pos	X	X	
	Song Sel	O	O	
	Tune	X	X	
SYSTEM REAL TIME	Clock	O	O	
	Messages	OX	OX	
AUX	Local Control	X	X	
	All Notes Off	O	O (123-127)	
	Active Sense	O	O	
	Reset	X	X	

NOTES: NOTE 1:   upper, lower, bass and solo can each function independently on seperate MIDI   channels
             NOTE 2:   bass transmits 36-108,   recognizes 24-95 True Voice 36-95 (changes depending on the selected voice)
             NOTE 3:   solo recognizes 48-107
             NOTE 4:   note numbers recognized are effected by TRANSPOSE and OCTAVE controls

Mode 1 : OMNI ON, POLY	Mode 2 : OMNI ON, MONO	O : Yes
Mode 3 : OMNI OFF, POLY	Mode 4: OMNI OFF, MONO	X : No

Manufacturer	Model
Hohner	**Atlantic**
[Accordian]	Version — Date 7/18/86

Function		Transmitted	Recognized	Remarks
CHANNEL	Default	1 2 3	X	descant 1
	Changed	X	X	chords 2, bass 3
MODE	Default	Mode 3	X	
	Messages	X	X	
	Altered		X	
NOTE NUMBER		24-104	X	default Ch1/53—93,
	True Voice		X	Ch2/60—71, Ch3/36—47
VELOCITY	Note On	X	X	
	Note Off	X	X	
TOUCH	Key's	X	X	
	Chan's	X	X	
PITCH BENDER		X	X	
CONTROL CHANGE		X	X	
PROGRAM CHANGE		X	X	
	True #		X	
SYSTEM EXCLUSIVE		X	X	
SYSTEM COMMON	Song Pos	X	X	
	Song Sel	X	X	
	Tune	X	X	
SYSTEM REAL TIME	Clock	X	X	
	Messages	X	X	
AUX	Local Control	X	X	
	All Notes Off	X	X	
	Active Sense	O	X	
	Reset	X	X	

NOTES: Octave transpose: Press lowest C or following keys at power up

	Up 1 Oct — Down 1 Oct
CH 1	C C#
CH 2	D D#
CH 3	E F#

Mode 1 : OMNI ON, POLY   Mode 2 : OMNI ON, MONO   O : Yes
Mode 3 : OMNI OFF, POLY   Mode 4: OMNI OFF, MONO   X : No

Manufacturer	Model
Hohner	**Fortuna**
[Accordian]	Version — Date 7/18/86

Function		Transmitted	Recognized	Remarks
CHANNEL	Default	1 2 3	X	descant 1
	Changed	X	X	chords 2, bass 3
MODE	Default	Mode 3	X	
	Messages	X	X	
	Altered		X	
NOTE NUMBER		24 — 108	X	default CH1/52—97;
	True Voice		X	CH2/60—71; CH3/36—47
VELOCITY	Note On	X	X	
	Note Off	X	X	
TOUCH	Key's	X	X	
	Chan's	X	X	
PITCH BENDER		X	X	
CONTROL CHANGE		X	X	
PROGRAM CHANGE		X	X	
	True #		X	
SYSTEM EXCLUSIVE		X	X	
SYSTEM COMMON	Song Pos	X	X	
	Song Sel	X	X	
	Tune	X	X	
SYSTEM REAL TIME	Clock	X	X	
	Messages	X	X	
AUX	Local Control	X	X	
	All Notes Off	X	X	
	Active Sense	O	X	
	Reset	X	X	

NOTES: Octave transpose: Press lowest C or following keys at power up

Up 1 Oct — Down 1 Oct

	Up 1 Oct	Down 1 Oct
CH 1}	C	C#
CH 2}	D	D#
CH 3}	E	F#

Mode 1 : OMNI ON, POLY	Mode 2 : OMNI ON, MONO	O : Yes
Mode 3 : OMNI OFF, POLY	Mode 4: OMNI OFF, MONO	X : No

		Manufacturer	Model		

Manufacturer
Hohner
[Accordian]

Model
Morino
Version —   Date 7/18/86

Function		Transmitted	Recognized	Remarks
CHANNEL	Default	1 2 3	X	descant 1
	Changed	X	X	chords 2, bass 3
MODE	Default	Mode 3	X	
	Messages	X	X	
	Altered		X	
NOTE NUMBER		24 — 104	X	default Ch1/53—93;
	True Voice		X	Ch2/60—71;Ch3/36—47
VELOCITY	Note On	X	X	
	Note Off	X	X	
TOUCH	Key's	X	X	
	Chan's	X	X	
PITCH BENDER		X	X	
CONTROL CHANGE		X	X	
PROGRAM CHANGE		X	X	
	True #		X	
SYSTEM EXCLUSIVE		X	X	
SYSTEM COMMON	Song Pos	X	X	
	Song Sel	X	X	
	Tune	X	X	
SYSTEM REAL TIME	Clock	X	X	
	Messages	X	X	
AUX	Local Control	X	X	
	All Notes Off	X	X	
	Active Sense	O	X	
	Reset	X	X	

NOTES: Octave transpose: Press lowest C or following keys at power up

Up 1 Oct — Down 1 Oct

	Up 1 Oct	Down 1 Oct
CH 1	C	C#
CH 2	D	D#
CH 3	E	F#

Mode 1 : OMNI ON, POLY   Mode 2 : OMNI ON, MONO   O : Yes
Mode 3 : OMNI OFF, POLY   Mode 4: OMNI OFF, MONO   X : No

Manufacturer	Model
Hohner	**Tango**
[Accordian]	Version — Date 7/18/86

Function		Transmitted	Recognized	Remarks
CHANNEL	Default	1 2 3	X	descant 1
	Changed	X	X	chords 2, bass 3
MODE	Default	Mode 3	X	
	Messages	X	X	
	Altered			
NOTE NUMBER		24 — 100	X	default Ch1/53—89;
	True Voice			Ch2/60—72;Ch3/36—47
VELOCITY	Note On	X	X	
	Note Off	X	X	
TOUCH	Key's	X	X	
	Chan's	X	X	
PITCH BENDER		X	X	
CONTROL CHANGE		X	X	
PROGRAM CHANGE		X	X	
	True #		X	
SYSTEM EXCLUSIVE		X	X	
SYSTEM COMMON	Song Pos	X	X	
	Song Sel	X	X	
	Tune	X	X	
SYSTEM REAL TIME	Clock	X	X	
	Messages	X	X	
AUX	Local Control	X	x	
	All Notes Off	X	X	
	Active Sense	O	X	
	Reset	X	X	

NOTES: Octave transpose: Press lowest C or following keys at power up

Up 1 Oct — Down 1 Oct

	Up 1 Oct	Down 1 Oct
CH 1	C	C#
CH 2	D	D#
CH 3	E	F#

Mode 1 : OMNI ON, POLY   Mode 2 : OMNI ON, MONO   O : Yes
Mode 3 : OMNI OFF, POLY   Mode 4: OMNI OFF, MONO   X : No

Manufacturer		Model
Hohner		**VOX 5**
[Accordian]		Version — Date 7/18/86

Function		Transmitted	Recognized	Remarks
CHANNEL	Default	1 2 3	X	descan 1
	Changed	X	X	chords 2, bass 3
MODE	Default	Mode 3	X	
	Messages	X	X	
	Altered			
NOTE NUMBER		24 — 104	X	default: Ch1/53—93;
	True Voice			Ch2/60—71; Ch3/36—47
VELOCITY	Note On	X	X	
	Note Off	X	X	
TOUCH	Key's	X	X	
	Chan's	X	X	
PITCH BENDER		X	X	
CONTROL CHANGE	tremolo 92	O	X	
	chorus 93	O		
PROGRAM CHANGE		0 - 16	X	
	True #		X	
SYSTEM EXCLUSIVE		X	X	
SYSTEM COMMON	Song Pos	X	X	
	Song Sel	X	X	
	Tune	X	X	
SYSTEM REAL TIME	Clock	X	X	
	Messages	X	X	
AUX	Local Control	X	X	
	All Notes Off	X	X	
	Active Sense	O	X	
	Reset	X	X	

NOTES: Octave transpose: Press lowest C or following keys at power up

	Up 1 Oct —	Down 1 Oct
CH 1	C	C#
CH 2	D	D#
CH 3	E	F#

Mode 1 : OMNI ON, POLY   Mode 2 : OMNI ON, MONO   O : Yes
Mode 3 : OMNI OFF, POLY   Mode 4: OMNI OFF, MONO   X : No

MIDI Performance Controllers

Manufacturer	Model
Roland	**PAD-8**
[Pad Controlor]	Version 1.0 Date 12/24/84

Function		Transmitted	Recognized	Remarks
CHANNEL	Default	1 — 16	X	Memorized
	Changed	1 — 16	X	
MODE	Default	Mode 3	X	*unavailable at printing
	Messages	*	X	
	Altered			
NOTE NUMBER		0 — 99	X	
	True Voice		X	
VELOCITY	Note On	O 9nH (v=10—127)	X	
	Note Off	X 9nH (v=0)	X	
TOUCH	Key's	X	X	
	Chan's	X	X	
PITCH BENDER		X	X	
CONTROL CHANGE		X	X	
PROGRAM CHANGE		0 — 127	X	
	True #			
SYSTEM EXCLUSIVE		X	X	
SYSTEM COMMON	Song Pos	*	X	*unavailable at printing
	Song Sel	*	X	
	Tune	*	X	
SYSTEM REAL TIME	Clock	*	X	*unavailable at printing
	Messages	*	X	
AUX	Local Control	X	X	*unavailable at printing
	All Notes Off	X	X	
	Active Sense	*	X	
	Reset	*	X	
NOTES:				

Mode 1 : OMNI ON, POLY   Mode 2 : OMNI ON, MONO   O : Yes
Mode 3 : OMNI OFF, POLY   Mode 4: OMNI OFF, MONO   X : No

| Manufacturer
Korg
[MIDI Pedal Keyboard] | | Model
MPK-130
Version 1.0 | Date 7/14/86 |

Function		Transmitted	Recognized	Remarks
CHANNEL	Default	1 — 16	N/A	set by DIP switches
	Changed	1 — 16		
MODE	Default	Mode 1	N/A	set by rear panel switch
	Messages	POLY, MONO		
	Altered			
NOTE NUMBER	True Voice	24 — 60	N/A	24—36=Low, 36—48=Mid, 48—60=High
VELOCITY	Note On	X	N/A	
	Note Off	X		
TOUCH	Key's	X	N/A	
	Chan's	X		
PITCH BENDER		X	N/A	
CONTROL CHANGE		X	N/A	
PROGRAM CHANGE	True #	X	N/A	
SYSTEM EXCLUSIVE		X	N/A	
SYSTEM COMMON	Song Pos	X	N/A	
	Song Sel	X		
	Tune	X		
SYSTEM REAL TIME	Clock	X	N/A	
	Messages	X		
AUX	Local Control	X	N/A	
	All Notes Off	X		
	Active Sense	O		
	Reset	X		
NOTES: N/A: Not Applicable				

Mode 1 : OMNI ON, POLY	Mode 2 : OMNI ON, MONO	O : Yes
Mode 3 : OMNI OFF, POLY	Mode 4: OMNI OFF, MONO	X : No

MIDI Performance Controllers

Manufacturer		Model	
Ibanez		**MC1**	
[MIDI Guitar]		Version 1.1	Date 3/5/86

Function		Transmitted	Recognized	Remarks
CHANNEL	Default	1 — 16	N/A	channel assignment progammable per string
	Changed	1 — 16	N/A	
MODE	Default	Mode 3	N/A	
	Messages	x	N/A	
	Altered		N/A	
NOTE NUMBER		16 — 103	N/A	
	True Voice		N/A	
VELOCITY	Note On	O	N/A	
	Note Off	X 9nH (v=0)	N/A	
TOUCH	Key's	X	N/A	
	Chan's	X	N/A	
PITCH BENDER		O	N/A	
CONTROL CHANGE	control change 0-31	O O	N/A	assignment is memorized
	bender arm 0-31	O		
	hold pedal 64			
PROGRAM CHANGE		0 — 127	N/A	
	True #		N/A	
SYSTEM EXCLUSIVE		X	N/A	
SYSTEM COMMON	Song Pos	X	N/A	
	Song Sel	X	N/A	
	Tune	X	N/A	
SYSTEM REAL TIME	Clock	X	N/A	
	Messages	X	N/A	
AUX	Local Control	X	N/A	
	All Notes Off	O (123)	N/A	
	Active Sense	O	N/A	
	Reset	X	N/A	

NOTES: N/A: Not Applicable

Mode 1 : OMNI ON, POLY	Mode 2 : OMNI ON, MONO	O : Yes
Mode 3 : OMNI OFF, POLY	Mode 4: OMNI OFF, MONO	X : No

Manufacturer **K-Muse** [Guitar to MIDI Converter]		Model **Photon** Version 1.0	Date 8/14/86	
Function		Transmitted	Recognized	Remarks
CHANNEL	Default	1	N/A	see notes
	Changed	1 — 16		
MODE	Default	Mode 3	N/A	
	Messages	X		
	Altered			
NOTE NUMBER	True Voice	1 — 127	N/A	Extreme notes reached by transpose/harmonize
VELOCITY	Note On	O	N/A	
	Note Off	X 9nH (v=0)		
TOUCH	Key's	X	N/A	
	Chan's	X		
PITCH BENDER		X	N/A	
CONTROL CHANGE		X	N/A	
PROGRAM CHANGE	True #	X	N/A	
SYSTEM EXCLUSIVE		X	N/A	
SYSTEM COMMON	Song Pos	X	N/A	
	Song Sel	X		
	Tune	X		
SYSTEM REAL TIME	Clock	X	N/A	
	Messages	X		
AUX	Local Control	X	N/A	
	All Notes Off	X		
	Active Sense	X		
	Reset	X		

NOTES: N/A: Not Applicable

Each string is individually assignable and saved as programs

Mode 1 : OMNI ON, POLY Mode 2 : OMNI ON, MONO O : Yes
Mode 3 : OMNI OFF, POLY Mode 4: OMNI OFF, MONO X : No

Manufacturer		Model	
K-Muse		**Photon**	
[Guitar to MIDI Converter]		Version 2.0	Date 8/14/86

Function		Transmitted	Recognized	Remarks
CHANNEL	Default	1	N/A	see notes
	Changed	1 — 16		
MODE	Default	Mode 3	N/A	
	Messages	X		
	Altered			
NOTE NUMBER		1 — 127	N/A	
	True Voice			
VELOCITY	Note On	O	N/A	
	Note Off	X 9nH (v=0)		
TOUCH	Key's	X	N/A	
	Chan's	X		
PITCH BENDER		O	N/A	
CONTROL CHANGE	pedal 1 (mod)	O	N/A	
	0-31	O		
	pedal 2 (pitch)	O		
	0-31			
	sustain 64			
PROGRAM CHANGE		1 — 99	1 — 99	
	True #			
SYSTEM EXCLUSIVE		X	X	
SYSTEM COMMON	Song Pos	X	X	
	Song Sel	X	X	
	Tune	X	O	
SYSTEM REAL TIME	Clock	O	O	sequencer/arpeggiator clock
	Messages	X	X	
AUX	Local Control	X	N/A	
	All Notes Off	X		
	Active Sense	X		
	Reset	X		

NOTES: N/A: Not Applicable

Each string is individually assignable and saved as programs

Mode 1 : OMNI ON, POLY	Mode 2 : OMNI ON, MONO	O : Yes
Mode 3 : OMNI OFF, POLY	Mode 4: OMNI OFF, MONO	X : No

Manufacturer		Model	
Synthaxe		**Controller**	
[Guitar Controller]		Version 1 Date 7/27/86	

Function		Transmitted	Recognized	Remarks
CHANNEL	Default	1	N/A	:Axe Only
	Changed	1 — 16		:With Console
MODE	Default	Mode 3	N/A	Mono/Poly Switch on Console
	Messages	X		
	Altered			
NOTE NUMBER	True Voice	40—88	N/A	0—127 with Console
VELOCITY	Note On	O	N/A	
	Note Off	X		
TOUCH	Key's	O	N/A	
	Chan's	unavailable at printing		
PITCH BENDER		O	N/A	String Bend or Wang Bar
CONTROL CHANGE	string pitch bend 1	O	N/A	These Controllers only used in Mono Mode.
	wang bar bend 2	O		
	string damping 31	O		
PROGRAM CHANGE	True #	0-99	N/A	only possible with System Console
SYSTEM EXCLUSIVE		O	N/A	Pedal status sent to console
SYSTEM COMMON	Song Pos	X	N/A	
	Song Sel	X		
	Tune	X		
SYSTEM REAL TIME	Clock	X	N/A	
	Messages	X		
AUX	Local Control	X	N/A	Transmitted by console on synth or port change.
	All Notes Off	O		
	Active Sense	O		
	Reset	X		

NOTES: N/A : Not Applicable

The MIDI Transmission channels, controller numbers and MONO/POLY Modes may be altered using the Synthaxe System Console.

Mode 1 : OMNI ON, POLY   Mode 2 : OMNI ON, MONO   O : Yes
Mode 3 : OMNI OFF, POLY   Mode 4: OMNI OFF, MONO   X : No

MIDI Performance Controllers

Manufacturer	Model
Casio	AZ-1
[Remote Strap-on Master Keyboard]	Version — Date —

Function		Transmitted	Recognized	Remarks
CHANNEL	Default	1 — 16	X	transmits on 2 channels (A & B) at once
	Changed	1 — 16(A) 1 — 16(B)	X	
MODE	Default	Mode 3	X	
	Messages	POLY, MONO (M=1)	X	
	Altered		X	
NOTE NUMBER		45 — 88 (Normal)	X	36 — 76 (Down)
	True Voice		X	60 — 100 (Up)
VELOCITY	Note On	O	X	
	Note Off	X 9nH (v=0)	X	
TOUCH	Key's	X	X	
	Chan's	O	X	
PITCH BENDER		O	X	8 bit resolution
CONTROL CHANGE	mod 1	O	N/A	The AZ-1 has 10 controllers, five of which are user definable.
	2 — 4	O		
	portamento time 5	O		
	master tune 6	O		
	volume 7	O		
	8 — 31	O		
	sustain 64	O		
	portamento 65	O		
	66-121			
PROGRAM CHANGE		0 — 127	X	
	True #			
SYSTEM EXCLUSIVE		O	X	see note 1
SYSTEM COMMON	Song Pos	X	X	
	Song Sel	X	X	
	Tune	X	X	
SYSTEM REAL TIME	Clock	X	X	
	Messages	X	X	
AUX	Local Control	X	X	
	All Notes Off	X	X	
	Active Sense	X	X	
	Reset	X	X	

NOTES: NOTE 1: GLIDE ON/OFF, etc. definable on an operation knob.

NOTE 2: Following messages will be transmitted at Default: Omni Off, Poly On, Sustain Off, Pitch Wheel Change (Center Value), Portamento Off, Definable Wheel*, Definable Slider*, Definable Switch Off, Program Change* (* Value or number currently backed up).

Mode 1 : OMNI ON, POLY	Mode 2 : OMNI ON, MONO	O : Yes
Mode 3 : OMNI OFF, POLY	Mode 4: OMNI OFF, MONO	X : No

Manufacturer	Model
Korg	RK-100
[Remote Keyboard]	Version 1.0 Date 7/14/86

Function		Transmitted	Recognized	Remarks
CHANNEL	Default	1	N/A	
	Changed	X		
MODE	Default	Mode 1	N/A	
	Messages	X		
	Altered			
NOTE NUMBER		36 — 100	N/A	range set by octave selector
	True Voice			
VELOCITY	Note On	X	N/A	
	Note Off	X		
TOUCH	Key's	X	N/A	
	Chan's	X		
PITCH BENDER		O		
CONTROL CHANGE	OSC mod 1	O	N/A	
	VCF mod 2	O		
	volume 7	O		
PROGRAM CHANGE		0 — 63	N/A	
	True #			
SYSTEM EXCLUSIVE		X	N/A	
SYSTEM COMMON	Song Pos	X	N/A	
	Song Sel	X		
	Tune	X		
SYSTEM REAL TIME	Clock	X	N/A	
	Messages	X		
AUX	Local Control	X	N/A	
	All Notes Off	X		
	Active Sense	O		
	Reset	X		

NOTES: N/A: Not Applicable

Mode 1 : OMNI ON, POLY	Mode 2 : OMNI ON, MONO	O : Yes
Mode 3 : OMNI OFF, POLY	Mode 4: OMNI OFF, MONO	X : No

MIDI Performance Controllers

Manufacturer	Model
Lync Systems	**LN-1**
[Remote Keyboard]	Version 1.02A Date 11/85

Function		Transmitted	Recognized	Remarks
CHANNEL	Default	1 — 4	N/A	Global
	Changed	1 — 4		
MODE	Default	Mode 3	N/A	
	Messages	OMNI OFF, POLY		
	Altered			
NOTE NUMBER		24 — 72 or 36 — 84	N/A	Programmable
	True Voice			
VELOCITY	Note On	O	N/A	Programmable
	Note Off	X		
TOUCH	Key's	X	N/A	*option available 1/86
	Chan's	*		
PITCH BENDER		O	N/A	direction changes
CONTROL CHANGE	mod 1	O	N/A	Programmable
	volume 7	O		
	sustain 64	O		
PROGRAM CHANGE		0 — 127	N/A	Programmable
	True #			
SYSTEM EXCLUSIVE		X	N/A	
SYSTEM COMMON	Song Pos	X	N/A	
	Song Sel	X		
	Tune	X		
SYSTEM REAL TIME	Clock	X	N/A	
	Messages	Start, Stop		
AUX	Local Control	X	N/A	
	All Notes Off	O		
	Active Sense	X	X	
	Reset	X		

NOTES: N/A: Not applicable

Mode 1 : OMNI ON, POLY	Mode 2 : OMNI ON, MONO	O : Yes
Mode 3 : OMNI OFF, POLY	Mode 4: OMNI OFF, MONO	X : No

FERRO TECHNOLOGIES

Manufacturer			Model	
Roland			**AXIS-1**	
[Remote Keyboard]			Version 1.0	Date 9/4/84

Function		Transmitted	Recognized	Remarks
CHANNEL	Default	1 — 16	X	Memorized
	Changed	1 — 16	X	
MODE	Default	Mode 1 — 4	X	
	Messages	OMNI ON/OFF, POLY, MONO	X	
	Altered			
NOTE NUMBER		0 — 127	X	
	True Voice		X	
VELOCITY	Note On	o	X	
	Note Off	X 9nH (v=0)	X	
TOUCH	Key's	X	X	* After Touch Function = 2
	Chan's	O*	X	
PITCH BENDER		O	X	
CONTROL CHANGE	1 —31	O	X	
	32—63	X	X	
	64—95	O	X	
	96—121	X	X	
PROGRAM CHANGE		O	X	0 — 119
	True #		X	
SYSTEM EXCLUSIVE		O	X	see note 2
SYSTEM COMMON	Song Pos	X	X	
	Song Sel	X	X	
	Tune	O	X	
SYSTEM REAL TIME	Clock	X	X	
	Messages	X	X	
AUX	Local Control	X	X	Active Sense not sent or recognized when After Touch Function is 3
	All Notes Off	O	X	
	Active Sense	O	X	
	Reset	X	X	

NOTES: Note 1: When powered up, memorized mode is transmitted on memorized channel.

Note 2: After Touch Function = 3 ($FO 43 F7 for old MIDI)

Mode 1 : OMNI ON, POLY   Mode 2 : OMNI ON, MONO   O : Yes
Mode 3 : OMNI OFF, POLY   Mode 4: OMNI OFF, MONO   X : No

Manufacturer			Model	
Yamaha			**KX5**	
[Remote Keyboard]			Version —	Date —

Function		Transmitted	Recognized	Remarks
CHANNEL	Default	1	N/A	
	Changed	1, 2		
MODE	Default	Mode 3	N/A	
	Messages	X		
	Altered			
NOTE NUMBER	True Voice	48-84	N/A	can be transposed up/down 1 octave
VELOCITY	Note On	O	N/A	
	Note Off	X		
TOUCH	Key's	X	N/A	
	Chan's	O		
PITCH BENDER		O	N/A	
CONTROL CHANGE	mod 1	O	N/A	
	breath 2	O		
	after touch 3	O		
	P. time 5	O		
	volume 7	O		
	sustain 64	O		
	portamento 65	O		
PROGRAM CHANGE	True #	0-63	N/A	
SYSTEM EXCLUSIVE		X	N/A	
SYSTEM COMMON	Song Pos	X	N/A	
	Song Sel	X		
	Tune	X		
SYSTEM REAL TIME	Clock	X	N/A	
	Messages	X		
AUX	Local Control	X	N/A	
	All Notes Off	X		
	Active Sense	O	O	
	Reset	X		

NOTES: N/A: Not Applicable

Mode 1 : OMNI ON, POLY   Mode 2 : OMNI ON, MONO   O : Yes
Mode 3 : OMNI OFF, POLY   Mode 4: OMNI OFF, MONO   X : No

| Manufacturer
Akai
[MIDI Master Keyboard] | | Model
MX-73
Version 1.0   Date 4/1/86 | | |

Function		Transmitted	Recognized	Remarks
CHANNEL	Default	1 — 16	X	memorized
	Changed	1 — 16	X	
MODE	Default	Mode 1, 2, 3, 4	X	memorized
	Messages	OMNI ON/OFF MONO, POLY	X	
	Altered		X	
NOTE NUMBER		0-120	X	
	True Voice		X	
VELOCITY	Note On	O	X	
	Note Off	X 9nH (v=0)	X	
TOUCH	Key's	X	X	
	Chan's	X	X	
PITCH BENDER		O	X	7 bit resolution
CONTROL CHANGE	mod 1	O	X	
	foot controller 4	O	X	
	volume 7	O	X	
	continous 8—31	O	X	
	sustain 64	O	X	
	portamento 65	O	X	
	switches 66—95	O	X	
PROGRAM CHANGE		0 —127	X	
	True #		X	
SYSTEM EXCLUSIVE		X	X	
SYSTEM COMMON	Song Pos	X	X	
	Song Sel	X	X	
	Tune	O	X	
SYSTEM REAL TIME	Clock	X	X	
	Messages	X	X	
AUX	Local Control	X	X	
	All Notes Off	O	X	
	Active Sense	X	X	
	Reset	X	X	

NOTES:
The MIDI EXT output jack transmits only Progam Change messages (0—99) when the EXT CONTROL switch is "ON", otherwise it works as other MIDI OUT jacks.

Mode 1 : OMNI ON, POLY   Mode 2 : OMNI ON, MONO   O : Yes
Mode 3 : OMNI OFF, POLY   Mode 4: OMNI OFF, MONO   X : No

MIDI Performance Controllers

Manufacturer	Model
Kurzweil	**MIDIBOARD**
[MIDI Keyboard Controller]	Version 1.1 Date 7/7/86

Function		Transmitted	Recognized	Remarks
CHANNEL	Default	1	N/A	
	Changed	1 — 16		
MODE	Default	Mode 2	N/A	
	Messages	OMNI ON/OFF, MONO, POLY		
	Altered			
NOTE NUMBER		0 — 127	N/A	kbd range: AO—C8
	True Voice			default 21-108
VELOCITY	Note On	O	N/A	
	Note Off	O		
TOUCH	Key's	O	N/A	
	Chan's	O		
PITCH BENDER		O	N/A	
CONTROL CHANGE	0-31	O	N/A	control destinations are programmable
	64-95	O		
PROGRAM CHANGE		0 — 127	N/A	
	True #			
SYSTEM EXCLUSIVE		O	N/A	see note
SYSTEM COMMON	Song Pos	X	N/A	
	Song Sel	X		
	Tune	X		
SYSTEM REAL TIME	Clock	X	N/A	
	Messages	X		
AUX	Local Control	X	N/A	
	All Notes Off	O		
	Active Sense	X		
	Reset	X		

NOTES: N/A: Not Applicable

NOTE: Programmable list allows arbitrary MIDI information to be sent with setup change.

Mode 1 : OMNI ON, POLY	Mode 2 : OMNI ON, MONO	O : Yes
Mode 3 : OMNI OFF, POLY	Mode 4: OMNI OFF, MONO	X : No

Manufacturer **Mimetics** [Console Keyboard]		Model **Soundscape** Version 1	Date —	

Function		Transmitted	Recognized	Remarks
CHANNEL	Default	1	X	
	Changed	1 — 16	X	
MODE	Default	Mode 3	X	
	Messages	X	X	
	Altered	X	X	
NOTE NUMBER		0 — 127	X	
	True Voice		X	
VELOCITY	Note On	X	X	
	Note Off	X	X	
TOUCH	Key's	X	X	
	Chan's	X	X	
PITCH BENDER		X	X	
CONTROL CHANGE		*	X	*unavailable at printing
PROGRAM CHANGE		X	X	
	True #		X	
SYSTEM EXCLUSIVE		X	X	
SYSTEM COMMON	Song Pos	X	X	
	Song Sel	X	X	
	Tune	X	X	
SYSTEM REAL TIME	Clock	O	X	
	Messages	O	X	
AUX	Local Control	X	X	
	All Notes Off	X	X	
	Active Sense	X	X	
	Reset	X	X	

NOTES:

Mode 1 : OMNI ON, POLY   Mode 2 : OMNI ON, MONO   O : Yes
Mode 3 : OMNI OFF, POLY   Mode 4: OMNI OFF, MONO   X : No

Manufacturer	Model
Oberheim	**XK**
[Remote MIDI Keyboard Controller]	Version 1.0 Date —

Function		Transmitted	Recognized	Remarks
CHANNEL	Default	1	N/A	
	Changed	1 — 16		
MODE	Default	Mode 1	N/A	honors Modes 1, 4
	Messages	*		*unavailable at printing
	Altered			
NOTE NUMBER		0 — 120	N/A	
	True Voice			
VELOCITY	Note On	O	N/A	
	Note Off	O		
TOUCH	Key's	X	N/A	
	Chan's	O		
PITCH BENDER		O	N/A	
CONTROL CHANGE	continuous 0-63	O	N/A	
	mod lever 0-63	O		
	footswitch 64-95	O		
PROGRAM CHANGE		0 — 99	N/A	
	True #			
SYSTEM EXCLUSIVE		O	N/A	Xpander functions
SYSTEM COMMON	Song Pos	X	N/A	
	Song Sel	O		
	Tune	O		
SYSTEM REAL TIME	Clock	X	N/A	
	Messages	Start, Stop, Continue		
AUX	Local Control	X	N/A	
	All Notes Off	X		
	Active Sense	X		
	Reset	X		

NOTES: N/A : Not Applicable

Mode 1 : OMNI ON, POLY	Mode 2 : OMNI ON, MONO	O : Yes
Mode 3 : OMNI OFF, POLY	Mode 4: OMNI OFF, MONO	X : No

Manufacturer **Roland** [MIDI Keyboard]		Model **MKB-200** Version 1.0 Date 11/15/85		
Function		**Transmitted**	**Recognized**	**Remarks**
CHANNEL	Default	1 — 16	X	memorized
	Changed	1 — 16	X	
MODE	Default	Mode 3	X	
	Messages	OMNI, POLY, MONO	X	
	Altered			
NOTE NUMBER		24 — 108	X	
	True Voice		X	
VELOCITY	Note On	O	X	
	Note Off	X 9nH (v=0)	X	
TOUCH	Key's	X	X	
	Chan's	O	X	
PITCH BENDER		O	X	9 blt resolution
CONTROL CHANGE	mod 1	O	X	
	volume 7	O		continuous controllers (0-127)
	damper pedal 64	O	X	switch controllers (0,127)
	continuous 0—63	O	X	
	switches 64—121	O	X	
PROGRAM CHANGE		0 — 127	X	
	True #		X	
SYSTEM EXCLUSIVE		O	X	MKS 7 parameter changes
SYSTEM COMMON	Song Pos	X	X	
	Song Sel	X	X	
	Tune	O	X	
SYSTEM REAL TIME	Clock	X	X	
	Messages	X	X	
AUX	Local Control	X	X	
	All Notes Off	O	X	
	Active Sense	O	X	
	Reset	X	X	
NOTES:				

Mode 1 : OMNI ON, POLY   Mode 2 : OMNI ON, MONO   O : Yes
Mode 3 : OMNI OFF, POLY   Mode 4: OMNI OFF, MONO   X : No

MIDI Performance Controllers

Manufacturer			Model	
Roland			**MKB-300, 1000**	
[MIDI Keyboard]			Version —	Date —

Function		Transmitted	Recognized	Remarks
CHANNEL	Default	1 — 16	1-16	memorized
	Changed	1 — 16	X	
MODE	Default	Mode 3 , 4	X	memorized
	Messages	OMNI OFF, POLY, MONO	OMNI OFF, POLY, MONO	
	Altered			
NOTE NUMBER		22-108 , 15-113　*	0 — 127	22-108 = MKB 300
	True Voice			15-113 = MKB 1000
VELOCITY	Note On	O	O	
	Note Off	X 90H (v=0)	O	
TOUCH	Key's	X	O	
	Chan's	X	O	
PITCH BENDER		O	O	
CONTROL CHANGE	1	O	O*	* 1-121 are recognized
	64	O		
	67	O (can be changed to 65)		
PROGRAM CHANGE		0 — 127	0 — 127	
	True #			
SYSTEM EXCLUSIVE		X	O	
SYSTEM COMMON	Song Pos	X	O	
	Song Sel	X	O	
	Tune	X	O	
SYSTEM REAL TIME	Clock	O	O	
	Messages	O	O	
AUX	Local Control	X	O	*not merged with MIDI OUT
	All Notes Off	O (123)	O (123—127)	
	Active Sense	O	O*	
	Reset	X	O*	

NOTES: When powered up (or CHANNEL or MODE is changed), OMNI OFF for all channels and MONO or POLY for the basic channel are sent.

Recognized messages are only merged into MIDI OUT.

Mode 1 : OMNI ON, POLY	Mode 2 : OMNI ON, MONO	O : Yes
Mode 3 : OMNI OFF, POLY	Mode 4: OMNI OFF, MONO	X : No

FERRO TECHNOLOGIES

Manufacturer	Model
Yamaha	**KX88**
[MIDI Master Keyboard	Version 1.0 Date 12/4/84

Function		Transmitted	Recognized	Remarks
CHANNEL	Default	1 — 16 *	1-16	* memorized
	Changed	1 — 16	X	
MODE	Default	Mode 3	X	
	Messages	OMNI ON/OFF, POLY, MONO	OMNI ON/OFF, POLY, MONO	
	Altered			
NOTE NUMBER		1 — 127	0 — 127	
	True Voice			
VELOCITY	Note On	O	O	
	Note Off	X 9nH (v=0)	O	
TOUCH	Key's	X	O	
	Chan's	O	O	
PITCH BENDER		O	O	7 bit resolution
CONTROL CHANGE	0—121	O	O	
PROGRAM CHANGE		0 — 127	0 —127	
	True #			
SYSTEM EXCLUSIVE		O (program change)	O (all)	
SYSTEM COMMON	Song Pos	X	O	
	Song Sel	0 — 9	O	
	Tune	O	O	
SYSTEM REAL TIME	Clock	O	O	
	Messages	O	O	
AUX	Local Control	O	O	
	All Notes Off	O	O	
	Active Sense	O	O	
	Reset	O	O	

NOTES: Received messages are only bypassed to MIDI OUT.

Mode 1 : OMNI ON, POLY   Mode 2 : OMNI ON, MONO   O : Yes
Mode 3 : OMNI OFF, POLY   Mode 4: OMNI OFF, MONO   X : No

Manufacturer	Model
Casio	**SZ-1**
[Multi-Track Sequencer]	Version 1 Date —

Function		Transmitted	Recognized	Remarks
CHANNEL	Default	1 — 16	1 — 16	No basic channels
	Changed	1 — 16	X	
MODE	Default	Mode 3		
	Messages	X	X	
	Altered			
NOTE NUMBER		0 — 127	0 — 127	
	True Voice			
VELOCITY	Note On	O	O*	*Touch data switch enabled, real-time only
	Note Off	O 9nH (v=0)	X	
TOUCH	Key's	X	X	
	Chan's	X	X	
PITCH BENDER		X	X	
CONTROL CHANGE	0 — 63	O	O	continuous data
	64 — 121	O	O	switch data
PROGRAM CHANGE		1 — 127	1 — 127	
	True #			
SYSTEM EXCLUSIVE		O	O	GLIDE ON/OFF
SYSTEM COMMON	Song Pos	X	X	
	Song Sel	X	X	
	Tune	X	X	
SYSTEM REAL TIME	Clock	O	O	
	Messages	O	O	
AUX	Local Control	X	X	
	All Notes Off	X	X	
	Active Sense	X	X	
	Reset	X	X	
NOTES:				

Mode 1 : OMNI ON, POLY   Mode 2 : OMNI ON, MONO   O : Yes
Mode 3 : OMNI OFF, POLY   Mode 4: OMNI OFF, MONO   X : No

| Manufacturer **Korg** [1 Voice Sequencer] | Model **MP-100** Version 1.0 Date 7/14/86 |

Function		Transmitted	Recognized	Remarks
CHANNEL	Default	1	N/A	
	Changed	X		
MODE	Default	Mode 4	N/A	
	Messages	X		
	Altered			
NOTE NUMBER		44 — 92	N/A	
	True Voice			
VELOCITY	Note On	X	N/A	
	Note Off	X		
TOUCH	Key's	X	N/A	
	Chan's	X		
PITCH BENDER		X	N/A	
CONTROL CHANGE		X	N/A	
PROGRAM CHANGE		X	N/A	
	True #			
SYSTEM EXCLUSIVE		X	N/A	
SYSTEM COMMON	Song Pos	X	N/A	
	Song Sel	X		
	Tune	X		
SYSTEM REAL TIME	Clock	O	N/A	see notes
	Messages	O		
AUX	Local Control	X	N/A	
	All Notes Off	X		
	Active Sense	X		
	Reset	X		

NOTES: N/A: Not Applicable

These messages can only be sent when MIDI OUT/SYNC OUT switch is set to MIDI OUT.

Mode 1 : OMNI ON, POLY Mode 2 : OMNI ON, MONO O : Yes
Mode 3 : OMNI OFF, POLY Mode 4: OMNI OFF, MONO X : No

Manufacturer	Model
Korg	**SQD-1**
[MIDI Recorder]	Version 1.0 Date 7/14/86

Function		Transmitted	Recognized	Remarks
CHANNEL	Default	1 — 16	1 — 16	has no basic channel
	Changed	X	X	
MODE	Default	Mode 3	X	
	Messages	X	X	
	Altered			
NOTE NUMBER		0 — 127	0 — 127	
	True Voice			
VELOCITY	Note On	O	OX	set by function switch
	Note Off	O	OX	
TOUCH	Key's	O	OX	set by function switch
	Chan's	O	OX	
PITCH BENDER		O	OX	set by switch
CONTROL CHANGE	0 — 63	O	OX*	*set by function switch
	64—121	O	O	
PROGRAM CHANGE		0 — 127	0 — 127	
	True #			
SYSTEM EXCLUSIVE		O	O	sequence data
SYSTEM COMMON	Song Pos	O	O	play only mode
	Song Sel	X	X	
	Tune	X	X	
SYSTEM REAL TIME	Clock	O	O	set by clock switch
	Messages	O	O	
AUX	Local Control	X	X	
	All Notes Off	X	X	
	Active Sense	X	X	
	Reset	X	X	

NOTES:

Mode 1 : OMNI ON, POLY	Mode 2 : OMNI ON, MONO	O : Yes
Mode 3 : OMNI OFF, POLY	Mode 4: OMNI OFF, MONO	X : No

Manufacturer
Linn
[Sequencer/Sampling Drum Machine]

Model
Linn 9000 & Linn Sequencer
Version —   Date —

Function		Transmitted	Recognized	Remarks
CHANNEL	Default	1	1 — 16	
	Changed	1 to 16	1 — 16	
MODE	Default	X	Mode 1	
	Messages	OMNI OFF	X	
	Altered			
NOTE NUMBER		0 to 127	0 to 127	
	True Voice			
VELOCITY	Note On	O	O	
	Note Off	O	O	
TOUCH	Key's	O	O	Modulation ON
	Chan's	O	O	
PITCH BENDER		O	O	Pitch Bend ON
CONTROL CHANGE	1	O	O	Mod Wheel ON
	64, 65	O	O	Sustain ON
PROGRAM CHANGE		O	O	Preset Changes ON
	True #			
SYSTEM EXCLUSIVE		X	X	
SYSTEM COMMON	Song Pos	O	O	
	Song Sel	O	O	
	Tune	O	X	
SYSTEM REAL TIME	Clock	O	O	
	Messages	start,stop, continue	start,stop, continue	
AUX	Local Control	O	X	
	All Notes Off	O	X	
	Active Sense	X	X	
	Reset	X	X	

NOTES: User can transmit OMNI OFF message from the front panel. Received messages can be "echoed" on channels 1 to 16 when MIDI Echo is on.

Mode 1 : OMNI ON, POLY   Mode 2 : OMNI ON, MONO   O : Yes
Mode 3 : OMNI OFF, POLY   Mode 4: OMNI OFF, MONO   X : No

Manufacturer	Model
Roland	**MCP-PC8**
[MIDI Compu—Music]	Version 1.00 Date 4/15/85

Function		Transmitted	Recognized	Remarks
CHANNEL	Default	1, 10	X	
	Changed	1—16	X	
MODE	Default	Mode 3	X	
	Messages	OMNI ON/OFF POLY, MONO	X *	
	Altered			
NOTE NUMBER		0—127	X *	
	True Voice			
VELOCITY	Note On	O	X *	
	Note Off	X 9nH (v=0)	X *	
TOUCH	Key's	O	X *	
	Chan's	O	X *	
PITCH BENDER		O	X *	
CONTROL CHANGE	0—121	O	X *	
PROGRAM CHANGE		(0—127)	X *	
	True #			
SYSTEM EXCLUSIVE		X	X	
SYSTEM COMMON	Song Pos	O	X *	
	Song Sel	X	X *	
	Tune	O	X *	
SYSTEM REAL TIME	Clock	O	O*	*SYNC mode = 2, 3
	Messages	O	O**	**SYNC mode = 3
AUX	Local Control	O	X	
	All Notes Off	O (123)	X *	
	Active Sense	X	X	
	Reset	X	X	

NOTES:
   * These received messages are transmitted.

Mode 1 : OMNI ON, POLY	Mode 2 : OMNI ON, MONO	O : Yes
Mode 3 : OMNI OFF, POLY	Mode 4: OMNI OFF, MONO	X : No

Manufacturer **Roland** [Real Time Recorder]		Model **MRC-PC98** Version 1.00 Date 9/19/85	

Function		Transmitted	Recognized	Remarks
CHANNEL	Default	1-16	1-16	No basic channel
	Changed			
MODE	Default	Mode 3	X	
	Messages	OMNI ON/OFF, MONO, POLY	X	
	Altered			
NOTE NUMBER		0 — 127	0 — 127	
	True Voice			
VELOCITY	Note On	O	O	
	Note Off	O	O	
TOUCH	Key's	O	O*	* see note 1
	Chan's	O	O*	
PITCH BENDER		O	O*	* see note 1
CONTROL CHANGE	0— 63	O	O*	* see note 1
	64— 95	O	O	
	96—121	O	O*	
PROGRAM CHANGE		0 — 127	0 — 127	
	True #			
SYSTEM EXCLUSIVE		O	O	
SYSTEM COMMON	Song Pos	O	O*	* see note 2
	Song Sel	X	X	
	Tune	O	X	
SYSTEM REAL TIME	Clock	O	O*	* see note 3
	Messages	O	O*	
AUX	Local Control	X	X	
	All Notes Off	O	O (123 — 127)	
	Active Sense	X	X	
	Reset	X	X	

NOTES: NOTE 1: When the 'bender' switch is set to 'on'.
NOTE 2: When the 'sync' switch is set to 'midi', and in 'STOP' mode.
NOTE 3: When the 'sync' switch is set to 'midi'. (Clock)
When the 'midi-ctl' switch is set to 'on'. (Commands)

Mode 1 : OMNI ON, POLY	Mode 2 : OMNI ON, MONO	O : Yes
Mode 3 : OMNI OFF, POLY	Mode 4: OMNI OFF, MONO	X : No

Manufacturer
Roland
[MIDI Music Recorder]

Model
MRC-PC8,FM7,X1
Version 1.00   Date 9/19/85

Function		Transmitted	Recognized	Remarks
CHANNEL	Default	X	X	
	Changed	X	X	
MODE	Default	Mode 3	X	
	Messages	OMNI, MONO, POLY	X	
	Altered			
NOTE NUMBER		0 — 127	0 — 127	
	True Voice			
VELOCITY	Note On	O	O	
	Note Off	O	O	
TOUCH	Key's	O	O*	* see note 1
	Chan's	O	O*	
PITCH BENDER		O	O*	*see note 1
CONTROL CHANGE	0— 63	O	O*	*see note 1
	64— 95	O	O	
	96—121	O	O*	
PROGRAM CHANGE		0 — 127	0 — 127	
	True #			
SYSTEM EXCLUSIVE		X	X	
SYSTEM COMMON	Song Pos	O	O*	*see note 2
	Song Sel	X	X	
	Tune	X	X	
SYSTEM REAL TIME	Clock	O	O*	*see note 3
	Messages	O	O*	
AUX	Local Control	X	X	
	All Notes Off	O	O (123 — 127)	
	Active Sense		X	
	Reset	X	X	

NOTES: NOTE 1: When the 'bender' switch is set to 'on'.
     NOTE 2: When the 'sync' switch is set to 'midi', and in ' STOP' mode.
     NOTE 3: When the 'sync' switch is set to 'midi'. (Clock)
          When the 'midi-ctl' switch is set to 'on'. (Commands)

Mode 1 : OMNI ON, POLY   Mode 2 : OMNI ON, MONO   O : Yes
Mode 3 : OMNI OFF, POLY   Mode 4: OMNI OFF, MONO   X : No

Manufacturer		Model	
Roland		**MSQ-100**	
[MIDI Digital Keyboard Recorder]		Version 1.0	Date _

Function		Transmitted	Recognized	Remarks
CHANNEL	Default	1-16	1-16	no basic channel
	Changed	X	X	
MODE	Default	Mode 3	X	mode not changed
	Messages	X	X	
	Altered			
NOTE		0 — 120	0 — 127	
NUMBER	True Voice		0 — 120	
VELOCITY	Note On	O	XO*	* recognized when VELOCITY is ON
	Note Off	O 9nH (v=0), 8nH	XO*	
TOUCH	Key's	O	XO*	* recognized when AFTER TOUCH is ON
	Chan's	O	XO*	
PITCH BENDER		O	XO*	recognized when BENDER/CONTROL is
CONTROL	0—63	O	XO*	* recognized when Bender/Control is
CHANGE	64—95	O	O	set ON
	96—121	O	XO*	
		O		
PROGRAM		O	0 — 127	
CHANGE	True #			
SYSTEM EXCLUSIVE		O	O	For sequence data
SYSTEM	Song Pos	O	O	in STOP mode
COMMON	Song Sel	X	X	
	Tune	X	X	
SYSTEM	Clock	O	O*	*MIDI clock mode
REAL TIME	Messages	O	O*	
AUX	Local Control	X	X	
	All Notes Off	O (123)	O (123—127)	
	Active Sense	X	X	
	Reset	X	X	

NOTES: When power–up, OMNI OFF, POLY ON are sent in ALL channels. (1 — 16)

Mode 1 : OMNI ON, POLY	Mode 2 : OMNI ON, MONO	O : Yes
Mode 3 : OMNI OFF, POLY	Mode 4: OMNI OFF, MONO	X : No

Manufacturer	Model
Roland	**MSQ-700**
[Digital Keyboard Recorder]	Version 1.41 Date 12/13/83

Function		Transmitted	Recognized	Remarks
CHANNEL	Default	1-16	1-16	no basic channel
	Changed	X	1-16	
MODE	Default	Mode 3	X	
	Messages	OMNI OFF, POLY	X	mode not changed
	Altered			
NOTE NUMBER		9 — 120	0 — 127	
	True Voice		9 — 120	
VELOCITY	Note On	O	O	see note 1
	Note Off	X 9nH (v=0)	X	
TOUCH	Key's	O	O*	*recognized when After touch = ON
	Chan's	O	O*	
PITCH BENDER		O	O	see note 1
CONTROL CHANGE	0 — 121	O	O	see note 1
PROGRAM CHANGE		0-127	0-127	see note 1
	True #			
SYSTEM EXCLUSIVE		X	X	
SYSTEM COMMON	Song Pos	X	X	
	Song Sel	X	X	
	Tune	X	X	
SYSTEM REAL TIME	Clock	O	O	MIDI Sync on
	Messages	O	O	
AUX	Local Control	X	X	
	All Notes Off	O (123)	O (123—127)	
	Active Sense	X	X	
	Reset	X	X	

NOTES: NOTE 1: When received, these messages can be enabled or disabled from being transmitted to MIDI OUT.

NOTE 2: When powered up, OMNI OFF, POLY ON are sent in ALL channels. (1—16).

Mode 1 : OMNI ON, POLY	Mode 2 : OMNI ON, MONO	O : Yes
Mode 3 : OMNI OFF, POLY	Mode 4: OMNI OFF, MONO	X : No

Manufacturer **Roland** [Piano Recorder]		Model **PR-800** Version 1.0	Date —	

Function		Transmitted	Recognized	Remarks
CHANNEL	Default	1	1	OLD MIDI
	Changed	X	X	
MODE	Default	Mode 3	Mode 1	
	Messages	POLY	OMNI ON, POLY, MONO	
	Altered		MONO —>OMNI	
NOTE NUMBER		0 — 127	0 — 127	
	True Voice			
VELOCITY	Note On	O	O	
	Note Off	X 90H (v=0)	X	
TOUCH	Key's	X	X	
	Chan's	X	X	
PITCH BENDER		X	X	
CONTROL CHANGE	damper pedal 64	O	O	
	soft pedal 65	O	O	
	66	O	O	
	67	O	O	
PROGRAM CHANGE		0-127	0 — 127	
	True #			
SYSTEM EXCLUSIVE		X	X	
SYSTEM COMMON	Song Pos	X	X	
	Song Sel	X	X	
	Tune	X	X	
SYSTEM REAL TIME	Clock	O	O*	*MIDI Sync on
	Messages	O	O*	
AUX	Local Control	X	X	
	All Notes Off	O (127)	O (125—127)	
	Active Sense	X	X	
	Reset	X	X	

NOTES: When powered up, ch—1 POLY ON is sent.

Received voice and mode mess are sent.

Mode 1 : OMNI ON, POLY   Mode 2 : OMNI ON, MONO   O : Yes
Mode 3 : OMNI OFF, POLY   Mode 4: OMNI OFF, MONO   X : No

Sequencers

Manufacturer

Yamaha

[Digital Sequence Recorder]

Model

QX1

Version 1.0   Date 10/1/84

Function		Transmitted	Recognized	Remarks
CHANNEL	Default	1	1	no basic channel
	Changed	1 — 16	1 — 16	
MODE	Default			see note
	Messages	OMNI ON/OFF, POLY, MONO	OMNI ON/OFF, POLY, MONO	
	Altered			
NOTE NUMBER		0 — 127	0 — 127	see note
	True Voice			
VELOCITY	Note On	O	O	see note
	Note Off	X	X	
TOUCH	Key's	X	X	
	Chan's	X	X	
PITCH BENDER		O	OX	see note
CONTROL CHANGE	0—63	O	OX	see note
	64—121	O	O	
PROGRAM CHANGE		O	0—127	see note
	True #			
SYSTEM EXCLUSIVE		O	O	see note
SYSTEM COMMON	Song Pos	X	X	
	Song Sel	X	X	
	Tune	X	X	
SYSTEM REAL TIME	Clock	O*	O	*only from track 8
	Messages	O*	O	
AUX	Local Control	O	O *	* see note
	All Notes Off	O	X	
	Active Sense	O	X	
	Reset	X	X	

NOTES: NOTE: These messages are recognized and transmitted as record data.

Mode 1 : OMNI ON, POLY   Mode 2 : OMNI ON, MONO   O : Yes
Mode 3 : OMNI OFF, POLY   Mode 4: OMNI OFF, MONO   X : No

Function		Transmitted	Recognized	Remarks
Manufacturer Yamaha [Digital Sequence Recorder]			**Model** QX7 Version 1.0 Date 11/16/84	

Function		Transmitted	Recognized	Remarks
CHANNEL	Default	1-16	1-16	no basic channel
	Changed	X	X	
MODE	Default			
	Messages	OMNI ON/OFF, POLY, MONO	OMNI ON/OFF, POLY, MONO	
	Altered			
NOTE NUMBER		1 — 111	1 — 127	
	True Voice		1 — 111	
VELOCITY	Note On	O	OX	
	Note Off	X 9nH (v=0)	X	
TOUCH	Key's	O	OX	
	Chan's	O	OX	
PITCH BENDER		O	OX	
CONTROL CHANGE	0—63	O	OX	
	64—122	O	O	
	124—127	O	O	
PROGRAM CHANGE		0 — 127	0 — 127	
	True #			
SYSTEM EXCLUSIVE		O	O	sequence data
SYSTEM COMMON	Song Pos	O	O	* see note
	Song Sel	O *	O *	
	Tune	O	O	
SYSTEM REAL TIME	Clock	O	OX	
	Messages	O	O	
AUX	Local Control	O	O	* see note
	All Notes Off	X	X	
	Active Sense	O	X	
	Reset	X*	O*	

NOTES: These messages are not recognized by QX7, only bypassed to MIDI OUT in ECHO BACK ON mode. All other messages, except System Exclusive and Real Time, are bypassed in ECHO BACK ON mode.

Mode 1 : OMNI ON, POLY   Mode 2 : OMNI ON, MONO   O : Yes
Mode 3 : OMNI OFF, POLY   Mode 4: OMNI OFF, MONO   X : No

Manufacturer	Model
Yamaha	**QX21**
[Digital Sequence Recorder]	Version 1.0 Date 10/23/85

Function		Transmitted	Recognized	Remarks
CHANNEL	Default	1-16	1-16	no basic channel
	Changed	X	X	
MODE	Default			
	Messages	OMNI ON/OFF POLY, MONO	OMNI ON/OFF POLY, MONO	
	Altered			
NOTE		1 — 111	1 — 127	
NUMBER	True Voice		1 — 111	
VELOCITY	Note On	O	OX	
	Note Off	X 9nH (v=0)	X	
TOUCH	Key's	O	OX	
	Chan's	O	OX	
PITCH BENDER		O	OX	
CONTROL	0— 63	O	OX	
CHANGE	64—122	O	O	
	124—127	O	O	
PROGRAM		0 — 127	0 — 127	
CHANGE	True #			
SYSTEM EXCLUSIVE		O	O	sequence data
SYSTEM	Song Pos	O	O	* see note
COMMON	Song Sel	O *	O*	
	Tune	O	O	
SYSTEM	Clock	O	OX	
REAL TIME	Messages	O	O	
AUX	Local Control	O	O	* see note
	All Notes Off	X	X	
	Active Sense	O	X	
	Reset	O*	O*	

NOTES: These messages are not recognized by QX21, only bypassed to MIDI OUT in ECHO BACK
ON mode. All other messages except System Exclusive and Real Time are bypassed in ECHO BACK ON mode.

Mode 1 : OMNI ON, POLY	Mode 2 : OMNI ON, MONO	O : Yes
Mode 3 : OMNI OFF, POLY	Mode 4: OMNI OFF, MONO	X : No

Manufacturer	Model
Casio	RZ-1
[Digital Sampling Rhythm Composer]	Version 1 Date —

Function		Transmitted	Recognized	Remarks
CHANNEL	Default	1 — 16*	1 — 16*	*memorized
	Changed	1 — 16	1 — 16	Rx chan=Tx chan
MODE	Default	Mode 3	Mode 3	Fixed
	Messages	X	X	
	Altered			
NOTE NUMBER		36 — 62	35 — 64*	when enabled
	True Voice			
VELOCITY	Note On	O	O	see note 1
	Note Off			
TOUCH	Key's	X	X	
	Chan's	X	X	
PITCH BENDER		X	X	
CONTROL CHANGE		X	X	
PROGRAM CHANGE		X	X	
	True #			
SYSTEM EXCLUSIVE		O	O	GLIDE ON/OFF
SYSTEM COMMON	Song Pos	X	X	
	Song Sel	O	O	
	Tune			
SYSTEM REAL TIME	Clock	O	O*	*When CLOCK=EXT.
	Messages	O	O	
AUX	Local Control	X	X	
	All Notes Off	X	X	
	Active Sense	X	X	
	Reset	X	X	

NOTES: NOTE 1: 3 dynamic levels, 1—48: MUTE, 49—96: NORMAL, 97—127: ACCENT

Mode 1 : OMNI ON, POLY	Mode 2 : OMNI ON, MONO	O : Yes
Mode 3 : OMNI OFF, POLY	Mode 4: OMNI OFF, MONO	X : No

Manufacturer	Model
J L Cooper	**Sound Chest II**
[Sound Module]	Version — Date —

Function		Transmitted	Recognized	Remarks
CHANNEL	Default	1 — 16	1 — 16	
	Changed			
MODE	Default	mode 3	mode 3	
	Messages			
	Altered			
NOTE NUMBER		24 — 96	24 — 96	
	True Voice			
VELOCITY	Note On	O	O	
	Note Off	X	X	
TOUCH	Key's	X	X	
	Chan's			
PITCH BENDER		X	X	
CONTROL CHANGE		X	X	
PROGRAM CHANGE		1 — 99	1 — 99	
	True #			
SYSTEM EXCLUSIVE		O	O	Data Dump
SYSTEM COMMON	Song Pos	X	X	
	Song Sel			
	Tune			
SYSTEM REAL TIME	Clock	X	X	
	Messages			
AUX	Local Control			
	All Notes Off	X	X	
	Active Sense			
	Reset			
NOTES:				

Mode 1 : OMNI ON, POLY   Mode 2 : OMNI ON, MONO   O : Yes
Mode 3 : OMNI OFF, POLY   Mode 4: OMNI OFF, MONO   X : No

Manufacturer	Model
Korg	**MR-16**
[MIDI Rhythm Sound Unit]	Version 1.0 Date 7/14/86

Function		Transmitted	Recognized	Remarks
CHANNEL	Default	N/A	1 — 16	set by DIP switches
	Changed		1 — 16	
MODE	Default	N/A	Mode 3	
	Messages		X	
	Altered			
NOTE NUMBER		N/A	35 — 65	
	True Voice			
VELOCITY	Note On	N/A	O	accents = v of 96 or greater
	Note Off		X	
TOUCH	Key's	N/A	X	
	Chan's		X	
PITCH BENDER		N/A	X	
CONTROL CHANGE	volume 7	N/A	O	
PROGRAM CHANGE		N/A	X	
	True #		X	
SYSTEM EXCLUSIVE		N/A	X	
SYSTEM COMMON	Song Pos	N/A	X	
	Song Sel		X	
	Tune		X	
SYSTEM REAL TIME	Clock	N/A	O	*for metronome sound only
	Messages		Start, Stop, Continue*	
AUX	Local Control	N/A	X	
	All Notes Off		X	
	Active Sense		X	
	Reset		X	
NOTES: N/A: Not Applicable				

Mode 1 : OMNI ON, POLY   Mode 2 : OMNI ON, MONO   O : Yes
Mode 3 : OMNI OFF, POLY   Mode 4: OMNI OFF, MONO   X : No

Drum Machines

Manufacturer	Model
Oberheim	**DX**
[Drum Machine]	Version — Date —

Function		Transmitted	Recognized	Remarks
CHANNEL	Default	1 — 16	1 — 16	memorized
	Changed	1 — 16	1 — 16	
MODE	Default	Mode 1,3	Mode 1,3	memorized
	Messages	OMNI ON/OFF	OMNI ON/OFF	
	Altered			
NOTE NUMBER		0 — 127	0 — 127	any 32 notes, default is 36-68
	True Voice			
VELOCITY	Note On	X	X	
	Note Off	X	X	
TOUCH	Key's	X	X	
	Chan's	X	X	
PITCH BENDER		X	X	
CONTROL CHANGE		X	X	
PROGRAM CHANGE	True #	X	X	
SYSTEM EXCLUSIVE		O	O	
SYSTEM COMMON	Song Pos	X	X	
	Song Sel	0 — 49	0 — 49	
	Tune	X	X	
SYSTEM REAL TIME	Clock	O	O	
	Messages	Start, Stop	Start, Stop	
AUX	Local Control	X	X	
	All Notes Off	X	X	
	Active Sense	X	X	
	Reset	X	X	
NOTES:				

Mode 1 : OMNI ON, POLY   Mode 2 : OMNI ON, MONO   O : Yes
Mode 3 : OMNI OFF, POLY   Mode 4: OMNI OFF, MONO   X : No

Manufacturer
Roland
[Rhythm Machine]

Model
TR-505
Version 1.1   Date 2/5/86

Function		Transmitted	Recognized	Remarks
CHANNEL	Default	1 — 16	1 — 16	Memorized
	Changed	1 — 16	1 — 16	
MODE	Default	Mode 3	Mode 1	
	Messages		OMNI ON/OFF	
	Altered			
NOTE NUMBER		25 — 99	25 — 99	see note 1
	True Voice			
VELOCITY	Note On	O 9nH (v=48—127)	O 9bH (v=1—127)	n = Inst CH, b = Basic CH
	Note Off	X 9nH (v=0)	X	see note 2
TOUCH	Key's	X	X	
	Chan's	X	X	
PITCH BENDER		X	X	
CONTROL CHANGE		X	X	
PROGRAM CHANGE		X	X	
	True #			
SYSTEM EXCLUSIVE		X	X	
SYSTEM COMMON	Song Pos	O	O*	*SYNC mode=MIDI
	Song Sel	0-5	0-5*	
	Tune	X	X	
SYSTEM REAL TIME	Clock	O	O *	*SYNC mode=MIDI
	Messages	O	O *	
AUX	Local Control	X	X	
	All Notes Off	X	X	
	Active Sense	X	X	
	Reset	X	X	

NOTES: NOTE 1: Recognized note numbers can be assigned by panel operation.

NOTE 2: Transmit channel # for each instrument can be changed to 1 — 16 by panel   operation.

Mode 1 : OMNI ON, POLY   Mode 2 : OMNI ON, MONO   O : Yes
Mode 3 : OMNI OFF, POLY   Mode 4: OMNI OFF, MONO   X : No

Drum Machines

Manufacturer
Roland
[Rhythm Machine]

Model
TR-505
Version 1.2   Date 2/17/86

Function		Transmitted	Recognized	Remarks
CHANNEL	Default	1 — 16	1 — 16	Memorized
	Changed	1 — 16	1 — 16	
MODE	Default	Mode 3	Mode 1	
	Messages		OMNI ON/OFF	
	Altered			
NOTE NUMBER		25 — 99	25 — 99	see note 1
	True Voice			
VELOCITY	Note On	O 9nH (v=4 —127)	O 9bH (v=1—127)	n = Inst CH, b = Basic CH
	Note Off	X 9nH (v=0)	X	see note 2
TOUCH	Key's	X	X	
	Chan's	X	X	
PITCH BENDER		X	X	
CONTROL CHANGE		X	X	
PROGRAM CHANGE		X	X	
	True #			
SYSTEM EXCLUSIVE		X	X	
SYSTEM COMMON	Song Pos	O	O*	*SYNC mode=MIDI
	Song Sel	0-5	0-5*	
	Tune	X	X	
SYSTEM REAL TIME	Clock	O	O*	*SYNC mode=MIDI
	Messages	O	O*	
AUX	Local Control	X	X	
	All Notes Off	X	X	
	Active Sense		X	
	Reset	X	X	

NOTES: NOTE 1: Recognized note numbers can be assigned by panel operation.

NOTE 2: Transmit channel # for each instrument can be changed to 1 — 16 by panel operation.

Mode 1 : OMNI ON, POLY   Mode 2 : OMNI ON, MONO   O : Yes
Mode 3 : OMNI OFF, POLY   Mode 4: OMNI OFF, MONO   X : No

Manufacturer
Roland
[Rhythm Machine]

Model
TR-707
Version 1.0   Date 11/9/84

Function		Transmitted	Recognized	Remarks
CHANNEL	Default	1 — 16	1 — 16	Memorized
	Changed	1 — 16	1 — 16	
MODE	Default	Mode 3	Mode 1	
	Messages	X	OMNI ON/OFF	
	Altered			
NOTE NUMBER	True Voice	35—51, 54, 56	35—51,54,56 *	* assigns to each rhythm voice (see notes)
VELOCITY	Note Cn	O 9nH (v=40—124)	O (v=1—127)	
	Note Off	X 9nH (v=0)	X	
TOUCH	Key's	X	X	
	Chan's	X	X	
PITCH BENDER		X	X	
CONTROL CHANGE		X	X	
PROGRAM CHANGE	True #	X	X	
SYSTEM EXCLUSIVE		O	O	For rhythm sequences
SYSTEM COMMON	Song Pos	O	O	
	Song Sel	0 — 3	0 — 3	
	Tune	X	X	
SYSTEM REAL TIME	Clock	O	O *	*SYNC mode = MIDI
	Messages	O	O*	
AUX	Local Control	X	X	*If received when SYNC mode = MIDI
	All Notes Off	X	X	
	Active Sense	O*	X	
	Reset	O*	X	

NOTES: Recognized note numbers can be assigned by panel operation. (35 — 98)

Mode 1 : OMNI ON, POLY   Mode 2 : OMNI ON, MONO   O : Yes
Mode 3 : OMNI OFF, POLY   Mode 4: OMNI OFF, MONO   X : No

| Manufacturer
Roland
[Rhythm Machine] | | Model
TR-727
Version 1.0 | Date 5/23/85 |

Function		Transmitted	Recognized	Remarks
CHANNEL	Default	1—16	1—16	memorized
	Changed	1—16	1—16	
MODE	Default	Mode 3	Mode 1	
	Messages	X	OMNI ON/OFF	
	Altered			
NOTE NUMBER		60—74 *	60—74 **	*see note 1 **see note 2
	True Voice			
VELOCITY	Note On	O 9nH (v=40—124)		
	Note Off	X 9nH (v=0)	X	
TOUCH	Key's	X	X	
	Chan's	X	X	
PITCH BENDER		X	X	
CONTROL CHANGE		X	X	
PROGRAM CHANGE		X	X	
	True #			
SYSTEM EXCLUSIVE		O	O	For rhythm sequences
SYSTEM COMMON	Song Pos	O	O	
	Song Sel	0 — 3	0 — 3	
	Tune	X	X	
SYSTEM REAL TIME	Clock	O	O*	* SYNC mode = MIDI
	Messages	O	O*	
AUX	Local Control	X	X	*If received when SYNC mode = MIDI
	All Notes Off	X	X	
	Active Sense	O*	X	
	Reset	O*	X	

NOTES: NOTE 1: If setting is A : 35—42, 45, 46, 48, 49, 51, 54, 56
If setting is B : 60—74

NOTE 2: Recognized note numbers can be assigned by panel operation. (35 — 98)

Mode 1 : OMNI ON, POLY   Mode 2 : OMNI ON, MONO   O : Yes
Mode 3 : OMNI OFF, POLY   Mode 4: OMNI OFF, MONO   X : No

Manufacturer	Model
Roland	**TR-909**
[Rhythm Machine]	Version 1.2 Date 12/13/83

Function		Transmitted	Recognized	Remarks
CHANNEL	Default	11	10	
	Changed	1—16	1—16	
MODE	Default	Mode 3	Mode 1	
	Messages	OMNI OFF, POLY	OMNI ON/OFF, POLY, MONO	
	Altered			
NOTE NUMBER		36-51	35—51	assigns to each rhythm voice
	True Voice			
VELOCITY	Note On	O 9nH (v=64—96)	O	
	Note Off	X 9nH (v=0)	X	
TOUCH	Key's	X	X	
	Chan's	X	X	
PITCH BENDER		X	X	
CONTROL CHANGE		X	X	
PROGRAM CHANGE		X	X	
	True #			
SYSTEM EXCLUSIVE		O	O	for rhythm sequences
SYSTEM COMMON	Song Pos	O	O	
	Song Sel	0-7	0-7	
	Tune	X	X	
SYSTEM REAL TIME	Clock	O	O*	MIDI mode enable
	Messages	O	O	
AUX	Local Control	X	X	* if received
	All Notes Off	X	X	
	Active Sense	X	X	
	Reset	O*	O	

NOTES:

Mode 1 : OMNI ON, POLY	Mode 2 : OMNI ON, MONO	O : Yes
Mode 3 : OMNI OFF, POLY	Mode 4: OMNI OFF, MONO	X : No

Drum Machines

Yamaha
[Drum Machine]

Model
RX11
Version —   Date —

Function		Transmitted	Recognized	Remarks
CHANNEL	Default	1	1	
	Changed	1-16	1-16	
MODE	Default	Mode 1	Mode 1	honors Modes 1,3
	Messages			
	Altered			
NOTE NUMBER		36-99	36-99	
	True Voice			
VELOCITY	Note On	O	O	
	Note Off	X	X	
TOUCH	Key's	X	X	
	Chan's	X	X	
PITCH BENDER		X	X	
CONTROL CHANGE	data entry 6	O	X	
PROGRAM CHANGE		X	X	
	True #			
SYSTEM EXCLUSIVE		O	O	data dumps
SYSTEM COMMON	Song Pos	X	X	
	Song Sel	0-9	0-9	
	Tune	X	X	
SYSTEM REAL TIME	Clock	O	O	
	Messages	Start,Stop,Continue	Start, Stop, Continue	
AUX	Local Control	X	X	
	All Notes Off	X	X	
	Active Sense	X	X	
	Reset	X	X	

NOTES:

Mode 1 : OMNI ON, POLY   Mode 2 : OMNI ON, MONO   O : Yes
Mode 3 : OMNI OFF, POLY   Mode 4: OMNI OFF, MONO   X : No

Manufacturer	Model
Yamaha	**RX21L**
[Digital Rhythm Programmer]	Version 1.0 Date 10/16/85

Function		Transmitted	Recognized	Remarks
CHANNEL	Default	X	1 — 16	memorized
	Changed	X	1 — 16	
MODE	Default	X	Mode 3	
	Messages	X	X	
	Altered			
NOTE NUMBER	True Voice	X	64 — 79	only recognized in CH INFO AVAIL mode
VELOCITY	Note On	X	O	
	Note Off	X	X	
TOUCH	Key's	X	X	
	Chan's	X	X	
PITCH BENDER		X	X	
CONTROL CHANGE		X	X	
PROGRAM CHANGE		X	X	
	True #		X	
SYSTEM EXCLUSIVE		O	O	see note 2
SYSTEM COMMON	Song Pos	X	O	
	Song Sel	0 — 3	0 — 3	
	Tune	X	X	
SYSTEM REAL TIME	Clock	O	O*	* in MIDI mode
	Messages	O	O	
AUX	Local Control	X	X	
	All Notes Off	X	X	
	Active Sense	X	X	
	Reset	X	X	

NOTES: Note 1: All messages except System Exclusive are bypassed to MIDI OUT.

      Note 2: Pattern, Song (only in SYS INFO AVAIL mode).

Mode 1 : OMNI ON, POLY	Mode 2 : OMNI ON, MONO	O : Yes
Mode 3 : OMNI OFF, POLY	Mode 4: OMNI OFF, MONO	X : No

Manufacturer
Emu
[Drum Machine]

Model
Drumulator
Version —   Date —

Function		Transmitted	Recognized	Remarks
CHANNEL	Default	N/A	1	doesn't transmit any MIDI messages
	Changed		1 — 16	
MODE	Default	N/A	Mode 3	
	Messages		X	
	Altered			
NOTE NUMBER		N/A	35 — 60	
	True Voice			
VELOCITY	Note On	N/A	O	
	Note Off		X	
TOUCH	Key's	N/A	X	
	Chan's		X	
PITCH BENDER		N/A	X	
CONTROL CHANGE		N/A	X	
PROGRAM CHANGE	True #	N/A	X	
SYSTEM EXCLUSIVE		N/A	X	
SYSTEM COMMON	Song Pos	N/A	*	*not available at printing
	Song Sel		*	
	Tune		X	
SYSTEM REAL TIME	Clock	N/A	O	*not available at printing
	Messages		*	
AUX	Local Control	N/A	X	*not available at printing
	All Notes Off		X	
	Active Sense		*	
	Reset		X	

NOTES: N/A : not applicable

Mode 1 : OMNI ON, POLY   Mode 2 : OMNI ON, MONO   O : Yes
Mode 3 : OMNI OFF, POLY   Mode 4: OMNI OFF, MONO   X : No

Manufacturer Emu [Sampling Drum Machine]		Model SP12 Version — Date —		

Function		Transmitted	Recognized	Remarks
CHANNEL	Default	N/A	1	SP12 doesn't transmit any MIDI channel messages
	Changed		1 — 16	
MODE	Default	N/A	Mode 1, 3	Honors Modes 1, 3
	Messages		OMNI ON/OFF, POLY	
	Altered			
NOTE NUMBER		N/A	12 — 59	12 — 43 = sound select
	True Voice			44 — 59 = pitch select
VELOCITY	Note On	N/A	O	
	Note Off		X	
TOUCH	Key's	N/A	X	
	Chan's		X	
PITCH BENDER		N/A	X	
CONTROL CHANGE		N/A	X	
PROGRAM CHANGE	True #	N/A	X	
SYSTEM EXCLUSIVE		O	O	data dumps
SYSTEM COMMON	Song Pos	X	X	
	Song Sel	X	X	
	Tune	X	X	
SYSTEM REAL TIME	Clock	O	O	
	Messages	Start, Stop	Start, Stop	
AUX	Local Control	X	X	
	All Notes Off	X	O (123-127)	
	Active Sense	X	X	
	Reset	X	X	
NOTES:				

Mode 1 : OMNI ON, POLY   Mode 2 : OMNI ON, MONO   O : Yes
Mode 3 : OMNI OFF, POLY   Mode 4: OMNI OFF, MONO   X : No

Drum Machines

Manufacturer
Sequential
[MIDI Drum Machine]

Model
Drum Traks
Version 0.5/0.4   Date 1/84

Function		Transmitted	Recognized	Remarks
CHANNEL	Default	1-16	1-16	memorized
	Changed	1-16	1-16	
MODE	Default	Mode 1	1	honors Modes 1,3
	Messages	X	OMNI ON/OFF	
	Altered			
NOTE NUMBER		35-84	35-84	Keys select sounds and tuning
	True Voice			
VELOCITY	Note On	O	O	
	Note Off	X	X	
TOUCH	Key's	X	X	
	Chan's	X	X	
PITCH BENDER		X	O*	Volumes
CONTROL CHANGE	mod 1	X	O*	Tunings *see notes
PROGRAM CHANGE		X	X	
	True #			
SYSTEM EXCLUSIVE		O	O	see note 2
SYSTEM COMMON	Song Pos	X	X	
	Song Sel	0-99	0-99	
	Tune	X	X	
SYSTEM REAL TIME	Clock	O	O	
	Messages	Start, Stop	Start, Stop, Continue	
AUX	Local Control	X	X	
	All Notes Off	X	X	
	Active Sense	X	X	
	Reset	X	X	

NOTES: Note 1: Pitch Bender and Control Change messages recognized by version 5 only.

Note 2: data dumps, pattern markers.

Mode 1 : OMNI ON, POLY   Mode 2 : OMNI ON, MONO   O : Yes
Mode 3 : OMNI OFF, POLY   Mode 4: OMNI OFF, MONO   X : No

Manufacturer	Model
Sequential	**Tom**
[MIDI Drum Machine]	Version — Date 3/85

Function		Transmitted	Recognized	Remarks
CHANNEL	Default	1-16	1-16	memorized
	Changed	1-16	1-16	
MODE	Default	1	1	Honors Modes 1,3,4
	Messages		OMNI ON/OFF, POLY, MONO	
	Altered			
NOTE NUMBER		35-60	35-60	
	True Voice			
VELOCITY	Note On	O	O	
	Note Off	X	X	
TOUCH	Key's	X	X	
	Chan's	X	X	
PITCH BENDER		X	O	Tuning
CONTROL CHANGE	mod 1	X	O	Volume or Panning
PROGRAM CHANGE		0-99	0-99	
	True #			
SYSTEM EXCLUSIVE		O	O	data dumps
SYSTEM COMMON	Song Pos	X	X	
	Song Sel	O	O	
	Tune	X	X	
SYSTEM REAL TIME	Clock	O	O	
	Messages	Start, Stop, Continue	Start, Stop, Continue	
AUX	Local Control	X	X	
	All Notes Off	X	X	
	Active Sense	X	X	
	Reset	X	X	
NOTES:				

Mode 1 : OMNI ON, POLY	Mode 2 : OMNI ON, MONO	O : Yes
Mode 3 : OMNI OFF, POLY	Mode 4: OMNI OFF, MONO	X : No

Drum Machines

Manufacturer	Model
Siel	MDP 40
[Drum Machine]	Version 1.0 Date 2/25/86

Function		Transmitted	Recognized	Remarks
CHANNEL	Default	1	1	
	Changed	1-16	1-16	
MODE	Default	Mode 3	Mode 1	honors Mode 1, 3
	Messages	X	X	
	Altered			
NOTE NUMBER		36 - 48	36 - 48	drum voices
	True Voice			
VELOCITY	Note On	X	X	
	Note Off	X	X	
TOUCH	Key's	X	X	
	Chan's	X	X	
PITCH BENDER		X	X	
CONTROL CHANGE		X	X	
PROGRAM CHANGE		1-46	1-46	1-40 Rhythms
	True #			41-46 Switches
SYSTEM EXCLUSIVE		X	X	
SYSTEM COMMON	Song Pos	X	X	
	Song Sel	X	X	
	Tune	X	X	
SYSTEM REAL TIME	Clock	O	O	
	Messages	O	O	
AUX	Local Control	X	X	
	All Notes Off	X	X	
	Active Sense	X	X	
	Reset	X	X	
NOTES:				

Mode 1 : OMNI ON, POLY   Mode 2 : OMNI ON, MONO   O : Yes
Mode 3 : OMNI OFF, POLY   Mode 4: OMNI OFF, MONO   X : No

Manufacturer **Alesis** [Digital Audio Effect Processor]		Model **MIDIFex** Version — Date —		

Function		Transmitted	Recognized	Remarks
CHANNEL	Default	N/A	1	
	Changed		1—16	
MODE	Default	N/A	3	
	Messages		X	
	Altered			
NOTE NUMBER	True Voice	N/A	N/A	
VELOCITY	Note On	N/A	N/A	
	Note Off			
TOUCH	Key's	N/A	N/A	
	Chan's			
PITCH BENDER		N/A	N/A	
CONTROL CHANGE		N/A	N/A	
PROGRAM CHANGE	True #	N/A	0-64*	*64 silences effect
SYSTEM EXCLUSIVE		N/A	N/A	
SYSTEM COMMON	Song Pos	N/A	N/A	
	Song Sel			
	Tune			
SYSTEM REAL TIME	Clock	N/A	N/A	
	Messages			
AUX	Local Control	N/A	N/A	
	All Notes Off			
	Active Sense			
	Reset			
NOTES: N/A : Not Applicable				

Mode 1 : OMNI ON, POLY   Mode 2 : OMNI ON, MONO   O : Yes
Mode 3 : OMNI OFF, POLY   Mode 4: OMNI OFF, MONO   X : No

Manufacturer	Model
ART	**DR1**
[Digital Audio Effects Processor]	Version 1.2 Date —

Function		Transmitted	Recognized	Remarks
CHANNEL	Default	X	1 — 16	note 1
	Changed	X	1 — 16	
MODE	Default	X	Mode 1,3	note 1
	Messages	X	OMNI ON/ OFF	
	Altered			
NOTE NUMBER		X	0 — 127	note 2
	True Voice			
VELOCITY	Note On	X	O	Ingores Note On v=0
	Note Off	X	O	note 2
TOUCH	Key's	X	O	ignores key number
	Chan's	X	O	note 2
PITCH BENDER		X	O	note 2
CONTROL CHANGE		X	O	note 2
PROGRAM CHANGE		X	0 — 127	assignable to any DR1 preset
	True #			
SYSTEM EXCLUSIVE		O	O	
SYSTEM COMMON	Song Pos	X	X	
	Song Sel	X	X	
	Tune	X	X	
SYSTEM REAL TIME	Clock	X	X	
	Messages	X	X	
AUX	Local Control	X	X	Reset causes DR1 to wait for next valid status
	All Notes Off	X	X	
	Active Sense	X	X	
	Reset	X	O	

NOTES: 1: Factory default is channel 1 OMNI ON. Current setting is saved in non-volatile ram and not changed when DR1 is powered on.

2: May be used for Performance MIDI control of DR 1 values. DR 1 recognizes controllers 1, 2, 3, 4, 5, 6, 8, 10, 11, 64, 65, 66, 67

Mode 1 : OMNI ON, POLY	Mode 2 : OMNI ON, MONO	O : Yes
Mode 3 : OMNI OFF, POLY	Mode 4: OMNI OFF, MONO	X : No

Manufacturer	Model		
Korg	**DVP-1**		
[Digital Voice Processor]	Version 1.0 Date 7/14/86		

Function		Transmitted	Recognized	Remarks
CHANNEL	Default	X	1 — 16	memorized
	Changed	X	1 — 16	
MODE	Default	X	Mode 1, 3	
	Messages	X	OMNI ON/OFF	
	Altered			
NOTE NUMBER		X	0 — 127	see note1
	True Voice		24 — 84	
VELOCITY	Note On	X	X	
	Note Off	X	X	
TOUCH	Key's	X	X	
	Chan's	X	X	
PITCH BENDER		X	OX	8 bit resolution
CONTROL CHANGE	DCO mod 1	X	OX	control number for freeze switch is set by parameter 88
	DCA mod 2	X	OX	
	volume 7	X	OX	
	freeze switch 64	X	OX	
	portamento 65	X	OX	
	freeze switch 69	X	OX	
PROGRAM CHANGE		X	0 — 127	enabled/disabled by parameter 83
	True #		0 — 63	
SYSTEM EXCLUSIVE		OX	OX	Program data
SYSTEM COMMON	Song Pos	X	X	
	Song Sel	X	X	
	Tune	X	X	
SYSTEM REAL TIME	Clock	X	X	
	Messages	X	X	
AUX	Local Control	X	X	
	All Notes Off	X	OX (123 — 127)	
	Active Sense	X	O	
	Reset	X	X	

NOTES: NOTE 1: set by parameters 86 and 87 (key window).

NOTE 2: OX means function can be enabled or disabled by value of parameter 83.

NOTE 3: recognized messages change according to mode.

Mode 1 : OMNI ON, POLY	Mode 2 : OMNI ON, MONO	O : Yes
Mode 3 : OMNI OFF, POLY	Mode 4: OMNI OFF, MONO	X : No

Manufacturer	Model
Korg	**SDD-2000**
[Sampling Digital Delay]	Version 1.0 Date 7/14/86

Function		Transmitted	Recognized	Remarks
CHANNEL	Default	N/A	1 — 16	memorized
	Changed		1 — 16	
MODE	Default	N/A	Mode 2	
	Messages		OMNI ON/OFF	
	Altered			
NOTE NUMBER		N/A	24 — 107	
	True Voice			
VELOCITY	Note On	N/A	O	
	Note Off		X	
TOUCH	Key's	N/A	X	
	Chan's		X	
PITCH BENDER		N/A	O	+/- 3 steps
CONTROL CHANGE	OSC 1	N/A	O	
PROGRAM CHANGE		N/A	0 — 127	
	True #		0 — 63	
SYSTEM EXCLUSIVE		N/A	O	program data only
SYSTEM COMMON	Song Pos	N/A	X	
	Song Sel		X	
	Tune		X	
SYSTEM REAL TIME	Clock	N/A	O	
	Messages		X	
AUX	Local Control	N/A	X	
	All Notes Off		O	
	Active Sense			
	Reset		X	

NOTES: N/A: Not Applicable

Powers up OMNI ON
Changes to OMNI OFF after checking or changing the receive channel.

Mode 1 : OMNI ON, POLY	Mode 2 : OMNI ON, MONO	O : Yes
Mode 3 : OMNI OFF, POLY	Mode 4: OMNI OFF, MONO	X : No

Manufacturer	Model
Lexicon	PCM 70
[Digital Effects Processor]	Version 1.00 Date 8/86

Function		Transmitted	Recognized	Remarks
CHANNEL	Default	1-16	1-16	saved in non-volatile memory
	Changed	1-16	1-16	
MODE	Default	X	1,3	Saved in non-volatile memory
	Messages	X	OMNI ON/OFF	
	Altered			
NOTE NUMBER		X	0-127	see note 1
	True Voice			
VELOCITY	Note On	X	O	see note 1
	Note Off	X	X	
TOUCH	Key's	X	X	see note 1
	Chan's	X	O	
PITCH BENDER		X	O	default value = 40h
CONTROL CHANGE	0-31	X	O	see note 1
	64-96	X	O	
PROGRAM CHANGE		0-119 see note 3	0-127 see note 2	
	True #			
SYSTEM EXCLUSIVE		X	X	
SYSTEM COMMON	Song Pos	X	X	
	Song Sel	X	X	
	Tune	X	X	
SYSTEM REAL TIME	Clock	X	X	
	Messages	X	X	
AUX	Local Control	X	X	
	All Notes Off	X	X	
	Active Sense		X	
	Reset	X	X	

NOTES: Note 1: used as patch source, power on default value =0
Note 2: Two Modes
      Fixed: 00-49 =Registers 0.0-4.9
           50-119 = Registers 0.0-6.9
     Table   0-127 = Programmed to correspond to any program
                register
Note 3: Program changes are always transmitted in FIXED format

Mode 1 : OMNI ON, POLY	Mode 2 : OMNI ON, MONO	O : Yes
Mode 3 : OMNI OFF, POLY	Mode 4: OMNI OFF, MONO	X : No

Audio Processors

Manufacturer		Model
Roland		**SDE-2500**
[Digital Delay]		Version 1.0 Date 3/2/85

Function		Transmitted	Recognized	Remarks
CHANNEL	Default	X	1—16	memorized
	Changed	X	1—16	
MODE	Default	X	Mode1,3	memorized
	Messages	X	OMNI ON/OFF	
	Altered			
NOTE NUMBER		X	X	
	True Voice		X	
VELOCITY	Note On	X	X	
	Note Off	X	X	
TOUCH	Key's	X	X	
	Chan's	X	X	
PITCH BENDER		X	X	
CONTROL CHANGE		X	X	
PROGRAM CHANGE		X	0 — 127	
	True #			
SYSTEM EXCLUSIVE		X	O	
SYSTEM COMMON	Song Pos	X	X	
	Song Sel	X	X	
	Tune	X	X	
SYSTEM REAL TIME	Clock	X	X	
	Messages	X	X	
AUX	Local Control	X	X	
	All Notes Off	X	X	
	Active Sense	X	X	
	Reset	X	X	

NOTES:

Mode 1 : OMNI ON, POLY   Mode 2 : OMNI ON, MONO   O : Yes
Mode 3 : OMNI OFF, POLY   Mode 4: OMNI OFF, MONO   X : No

FERRO TECHNOLOGIES

Manufacturer		Model	
Yamaha		**SPX90**	
[Digital Sound Processor]		Version 1.0 Date 10/5/85	

Function		Transmitted	Recognized	Remarks
CHANNEL	Default	N/A	1 — 16	memorized
	Changed		1 — 16	
MODE	Default	N/A	Mode 1, 3	memorized
	Messages		X	
	Altered			
NOTE NUMBER		N/A	0 — 127	pitch change and FREEZE B only
	True Voice			
VELOCITY	Note On	N/A	X	
	Note Off		X	
TOUCH	Key's	N/A	X	
	Chan's		X	
PITCH BENDER		N/A	X	
CONTROL CHANGE		N/A	X	
PROGRAM CHANGE		N/A	0 — 127	
	True #		1-90	
SYSTEM EXCLUSIVE		N/A	O	
SYSTEM COMMON	Song Pos	N/A	X	
	Song Sel		X	
	Tune		X	
SYSTEM REAL TIME	Clock	N/A	X	
	Messages		X	
AUX	Local Control	N/A	X	
	All Notes Off		X	
	Active Sense		X	
	Reset		X	

NOTES: N/A : Not Applicable

Mode 1 : OMNI ON, POLY	Mode 2 : OMNI ON, MONO	O : Yes
Mode 3 : OMNI OFF, POLY	Mode 4: OMNI OFF, MONO	X : No

Manufacturer	Model
Alesis	**MIDI Verb**
[MIDI Controlled Digital Reverb]	Version — Date —

Function		Transmitted	Recognized	Remarks
CHANNEL	Default	N/A	1	
	Changed		1 — 16	
MODE	Default	N/A	3	
	Messages		OMNI OFF, POLY	
	Altered			
NOTE NUMBER		N/A	N/A	
	True Voice			
VELOCITY	Note On	N/A	N/A	
	Note Off			
TOUCH	Key's	N/A	N/A	
	Chan's			
PITCH BENDER		N/A	N/A	
CONTROL CHANGE			N/A	
PROGRAM CHANGE		N/A	0 — 64*	*64 silences reverb
	True #			
SYSTEM EXCLUSIVE		N/A	N/A	
SYSTEM COMMON	Song Pos	N/A	N/A	
	Song Sel			
	Tune			
SYSTEM REAL TIME	Clock	N/A	N/A	
	Messages			
AUX	Local Control	N/A	N/A	
	All Notes Off			
	Active Sense			
	Reset			

NOTES: N/A: Not Applicable

Mode 1 : OMNI ON, POLY   Mode 2 : OMNI ON, MONO   O : Yes
Mode 3 : OMNI OFF, POLY   Mode 4: OMNI OFF, MONO   X : No

Manufacturer	Model
Ibanez	**SDR1000**
[Stereo Digital Reverberator]	Version 1.0 Date 4/1/86

Function		Transmitted	Recognized	Remarks
CHANNEL	Default	N/A	1 — 16	memorized
	Changed		1 — 16	
MODE	Default	N/A	Mode 1, 3	memorized
	Messages		X	
	Altered		X	
NOTE NUMBER		N/A	X	
	True Voice			
VELOCITY	Note On	N/A	X	
	Note Off			
TOUCH	Key's	N/A	X	
	Chan's		X	
PITCH BENDER		N/A	X	
CONTROL CHANGE		N/A	X	
PROGRAM CHANGE		N/A	0 — 127	
	True #			
SYSTEM EXCLUSIVE		N/A	X	
SYSTEM COMMON	Song Pos	N/A	X	
	Song Sel		X	
	Tune		X	
SYSTEM REAL TIME	Clock	N/A	X	
	Messages		X	
AUX	Local Control	N/A	X	
	All Notes Off		X	
	Active Sense		X	
	Reset		X	

NOTES: N/A: Not Applicable

* Program: 0 — 127
* Memory: 00 — 99

Mode 1 : OMNI ON, POLY	Mode 2 : OMNI ON, MONO	O : Yes
Mode 3 : OMNI OFF, POLY	Mode 4: OMNI OFF, MONO	X : No

Audio Processors

Manufacturer	Model
Roland	**SRV-2000**
[Digital Reverb]	Version 1.0 Date 3/30/85

Function		Transmitted	Recognized	Remarks
CHANNEL	Default	X	1—16	memorized
	Changed	X	1—16	
MODE	Default	X	Mode 1,3	memorized
	Messages	X	OMNI ON/OFF	
	Altered			
NOTE NUMBER		X	X	
	True Voice		X	
VELOCITY	Note On	X	X	
	Note Off	X	X	
TOUCH	Key's	X	X	
	Chan's	X	X	
PITCH BENDER		X	X	
CONTROL CHANGE		X	X	
PROGRAM CHANGE		X	0 — 127	
	True #			
SYSTEM EXCLUSIVE		X	O	parameters
SYSTEM COMMON	Song Pos	X	X	
	Song Sel	X	X	
	Tune	X	X	
SYSTEM REAL TIME	Clock	X	X	
	Messages	X	X	
AUX	Local Control	X	X	
	All Notes Off	X	X	
	Active Sense	X	X	
	Reset	X	X	
NOTES:				

Mode 1 : OMNI ON, POLY   Mode 2 : OMNI ON, MONO   O : Yes
Mode 3 : OMNI OFF, POLY   Mode 4: OMNI OFF, MONO   X : No

Function		Transmitted	Recognized	Remarks
CHANNEL	Default	N/A	1 — 16	memorized
	Changed		1 — 16	
MODE	Default	N/A	Mode 1,3	memorized
	Messages		X	
	Altered			
NOTE NUMBER	True Voice	N/A	X	
VELOCITY	Note On	N/A	X	
	Note Off		X	
TOUCH	Key's	N/A	X	
	Chan's		X	
PITCH BENDER		N/A	X	
CONTROL CHANGE		N/A	X	
PROGRAM CHANGE	True #	N/A	0-127	
			1-90	
SYSTEM EXCLUSIVE		N/A	X	
SYSTEM COMMON	Song Pos	N/A	X	
	Song Sel		X	
	Tune		X	
SYSTEM REAL TIME	Clock	N/A	X	
	Messages		X	
AUX	Local Control	N/A	X	
	All Notes Off		X	
	Active Sense		X	
	Reset		X	

Manufacturer: **Yamaha** [Digital Reverberator]
Model: **REV7** Version 1.0 Date 4/23/85

NOTES: N/A : Not Applicable

Mode 1 : OMNI ON, POLY Mode 2 : OMNI ON, MONO O : Yes
Mode 3 : OMNI OFF, POLY Mode 4: OMNI OFF, MONO X : No

Audio Processors

Manufacturer	Model
Akai	MPX-820
[MIDI Programmable Audio Mixer]	Version 1.0 Date 7/1/86

Function		Transmitted	Recognized	Remarks
CHANNEL	Default	X	1 — 16	Memorized
	Changed	X	1 — 16	
MODE	Default	X	Mode 3	
	Messages	X	X	
	Altered			
NOTE NUMBER		X	X	
	True Voice			
VELOCITY	Note On	X	X	
	Note Off	X	X	
TOUCH	Key's	X	X	
	Chan's	X	X	
PITCH BENDER		X	X	
CONTROL CHANGE		X	X	
PROGRAM CHANGE		X	0 — 98	
	True #			
SYSTEM EXCLUSIVE		O	O	ID:47
SYSTEM COMMON	Song Pos	X	X	
	Song Sel	X	X	
	Tune	X	X	
SYSTEM REAL TIME	Clock	X	X	
	Messages	X	X	
AUX	Local Control	X	X	
	All Notes Off	X	X	
	Active Sense	X	X	
	Reset	X	X	

NOTES:

Mode 1 : OMNI ON, POLY	Mode 2 : OMNI ON, MONO	O : Yes
Mode 3 : OMNI OFF, POLY	Mode 4: OMNI OFF, MONO	X : No

Manufacturer J L Cooper [Studio Muting Automation Unit]		Model MIDI Mute Version — Date —		

Function		Transmitted	Recognized	Remarks
CHANNEL	Default	1 — 16	1 — 16	
	Changed			
MODE	Default	Mode 3	Mode 3	
	Messages			
	Altered			
NOTE NUMBER		36 — 60	36 — 60	
	True Voice			
VELOCITY	Note On	O	O	
	Note Off	X	X	
TOUCH	Key's	X	X	
	Chan's			
PITCH BENDER		X	X	
CONTROL CHANGE		X	X	
PROGRAM CHANGE		X	X	
	True #			
SYSTEM EXCLUSIVE		O	O	System communication
SYSTEM COMMON	Song Pos			
	Song Sel	X	X	
	Tune			
SYSTEM REAL TIME	Clock	X	X	
	Messages			
AUX	Local Control			
	All Notes Off	X	X	
	Active Sense			
	Reset			

NOTES: Studio Muting Automation Unit uses MIDI note commands to generate/detect mute movements.

Mode 1 : OMNI ON, POLY	Mode 2 : OMNI ON, MONO	O : Yes
Mode 3 : OMNI OFF, POLY	Mode 4: OMNI OFF, MONO	X : No

Manufacturer	Model
J L Cooper	**Expression Plus**
[8 Channel MIDI Volume Controller]	Version — Date —

Function		Transmitted	Recognized	Remarks
CHANNEL	Default	1 — 16	1 — 16	
	Changed			
MODE	Default		Mode 3	
	Messages	N/A		
	Altered			
NOTE NUMBER		N/A	24 — 96	
	True Voice			
VELOCITY	Note On	X	O	
	Note Off		X	
TOUCH	Key's	X	X	
	Chan's	O	O	
PITCH BENDER		X	X	
CONTROL CHANGE	volume 7	O	O	
PROGRAM CHANGE		X	1 — 64	
	True #			
SYSTEM EXCLUSIVE		O	O	Patch Dump
SYSTEM COMMON	Song Pos			
	Song Sel	X	X	
	Tune			
SYSTEM REAL TIME	Clock	X	X	
	Messages			
AUX	Local Control			
	All Notes Off	X	X	
	Active Sense			
	Reset			

NOTES: N/A: Not Applicable

     Transmitted: Converts pedal movement to volume and/or after touch.
     Recognized: Selects note velocity, volume or after touch to control gain of 8 VCA's.

Mode 1 : OMNI ON, POLY	Mode 2 : OMNI ON, MONO	O : Yes
Mode 3 : OMNI OFF, POLY	Mode 4: OMNI OFF, MONO	X : No

Clarity — MIDI/XLV

Manufacturer: **Clarity** [Studio Interfacing Unit]
Model: **MIDI/XLV** Version 1.00 Date —

Function		Transmitted	Recognized	Remarks
CHANNEL	Default	1—16	1—16	Saved in non–volatile memory
	Changed	1—16	1—16	
MODE	Default	X	Mode 3	
	Messages	X		
	Altered			
NOTE NUMBER		X	0 — 127	See note 1
	True Voice	X		
VELOCITY	Note On	X	O	See note 1
	Note Off	X	O	
TOUCH	Key's	X	O	See note 1
	Chan's	X	O	
PITCH BENDER		X	O	Default value = 40H
CONTROL CHANGE		26 — 31	0 — 95	See note 1, 2
PROGRAM CHANGE		X	0 — 127	
	True #			
SYSTEM EXCLUSIVE		O	O	Id : 1F H
SYSTEM COMMON	Song Pos	X	X	
	Song Sel	X	X	
	Tune	X	X	
SYSTEM REAL TIME	Clock	X	X	
	Messages	X	X	
AUX	Local Control	X	X	
	All Notes Off	X	X	
	Active Sense	X	X	
	Reset	X	X	

NOTES: Note 1: Used as a patch source to digital LARC output and/or analog control voltage outputs. Power–on default value = 0.
Note 2: Controls 33 — 42 are assigned special functions.

Mode 1 : OMNI ON, POLY   Mode 2 : OMNI ON, MONO   O : Yes
Mode 3 : OMNI OFF, POLY Mode 4 : OMNI OFF, MONO X : No

Hinton — MIDIC/AMS DMX 15-80s

Manufacturer: **Hinton** [MIDI Effects Interface]
Model: **MIDIC/AMS DMX 15-80s** Version — Date 12/85

Function		Transmitted	Recognized	Remarks
CHANNEL	Default	N/A	1	
	Changed	N/A	1—16	
MODE	Default	N/A	Mode 2	honors modes 2,4
	Messages		OMNI ON/OFF	
	Altered			
NOTE NUMBER		N/A	0 — 127	
	True Voice		48 — 73	
VELOCITY	Note On	N/A	X	
	Note Off	N/A	X	
TOUCH	Key's	N/A	X	
	Chan's		X	
PITCH BENDER		N/A	O	7 bit resolution
CONTROL CHANGE		N/A	X	
PROGRAM CHANGE		N/A	0 — 8	sets operating modes of AMS DMX 15–80s
	True #			
SYSTEM EXCLUSIVE		N/A	X	
SYSTEM COMMON	Song Pos	N/A	X	
	Song Sel		X	
	Tune		X	
SYSTEM REAL TIME	Clock	N/A	X	
	Messages		X	
AUX	Local Control	N/A	X	
	All Notes Off		O (123 — 127)	
	Active Sense		X	
	Reset		X	

NOTES: Unit is a MIDI interface for AMS DMX 15—80s digital effects processor
N/A: Not Applicalbe

Mode 1 : OMNI ON, POLY   Mode 2 : OMNI ON, MONO   O : Yes
Mode 3 : OMNI OFF, POLY Mode 4 : OMNI OFF, MONO X : No

Hinton — MIDIC/Rev 1

Manufacturer: Hinton [MIDI Effects Interface]
Model: MIDIC/Rev 1   Version —   Date 12/85

Function		Transmitted	Recognized	Remarks
CHANNEL	Default	N/A	1	
	Changed		1—16	
MODE	Default	N/A	Mode 3	
	Messages		OMNI ON/OFF	
	Altered			
NOTE NUMBER		N/A	N/A	
	True Voice			
VELOCITY	Note On	N/A	N/A	
	Note Off			
TOUCH	Key's	N/A	X	Flange/chorus depth note 1
	Chan's		O	
PITCH BENDER		N/A	N/A	
CONTROL CHANGE	mod 1	N/A	O	modulation speed
	data entry 6		O	reverb time
	volume 7		O	master output note 1
PROGRAM CHANGE		N/A	0-89	
	True #			
SYSTEM EXCLUSIVE		N/A	O	
SYSTEM COMMON	Song Pos	N/A	N/A	
	Song Sel			
	Tune			
SYSTEM REAL TIME	Clock	N/A	N/A	
	Messages			
AUX	Local Control	N/A	N/A	
	All Notes Off			
	Active Sense			
	Reset			

NOTES: This unit is a MIDI interface for the Yamaha Rev 1 digital reverb.
Note 1: proposed enhancements (8/86)
N/A: Not Applicable

Mode 1: OMNI ON, POLY   Mode 2: OMNI ON, MONO
Mode 3: OMNI OFF, POLY   Mode 4: OMNI OFF, MONO
O: Yes   X: No

J L Cooper — QMI

Manufacturer: J L Cooper [Quantec Program Change Unit]
Model: QMI   Version —   Date —

Function		Transmitted	Recognized	Remarks
CHANNEL	Default	N/A	1—16	
	Changed			
MODE	Default	N/A	Mode 3	
	Messages			
	Altered			
NOTE NUMBER		N/A	X	
	True Voice			
VELOCITY	Note On	N/A	X	
	Note Off			
TOUCH	Key's	N/A	X	
	Chan's			
PITCH BENDER		N/A	X	
CONTROL CHANGE		N/A	X	
PROGRAM CHANGE		N/A	1—32	
	True #			
SYSTEM EXCLUSIVE		N/A	X	
SYSTEM COMMON	Song Pos	N/A	X	
	Song Sel			
	Tune			
SYSTEM REAL TIME	Clock	N/A	X	
	Messages			
AUX	Local Control	N/A	X	
	All Notes Off			
	Active Sense			
	Reset			

NOTES: N/A: Not Applicable
Midi program change to Quantec Converter.

Mode 1: OMNI ON, POLY   Mode 2: OMNI ON, MONO
Mode 3: OMNI OFF, POLY   Mode 4: OMNI OFF, MONO
O: Yes   X: No

MIDI Implementation Chart — MH-01M

Manufacturer: **Passport** [MIDI/Macintosh Interface]
Model: **MH-01M** Version 1.0 Date 8/12/86

Function		Transmitted	Recognized	Remarks
CHANNEL	Default	1 — 16	1 — 16	
	Changed			
MODE	Default	N/A	N/A	
	Messages	OMNI ON/OFF, POLY, MONO	OMNI ON/OFF, POLY, MONO	
	Altered			
NOTE NUMBER		0 — 127	0 — 127	
	True Voice		0 — 127	
VELOCITY	Note On	O	O	
	Note Off	O	O	
TOUCH	Key's	O	O	
	Chan's	O	O	
PITCH BENDER		O	O	
CONTROL CHANGE	All:	O	O	
PROGRAM CHANGE		O	O	
	True #			
SYSTEM EXCLUSIVE		O	O	
SYSTEM COMMON	Song Pos	O	O	
	Song Sel	O	O	
	Tune	O	O	
SYSTEM REAL TIME	Clock	O	O	
	Messages	O	O	
AUX	Local Control	O	O	
	All Notes Off	O	O	
	Active Sense	O	O	
	Reset	O	O	

NOTES: N/A: Not Applicable

The interface described above simply passes all incoming data to the host computer and transmits all data that is sent by the host. The software that is running on the host computer controls all other aspects of MIDI operation.

Mode 1: OMNI ON, POLY Mode 2: OMNI ON, MONO O: Yes
Mode 3: OMNI OFF, POLY Mode 4: OMNI OFF, MONO X: No

MIDI Implementation Chart — MH-01X

Manufacturer: **Passport** [MIDI Pro Interface]
Model: **MH-01X** Version 1.0 — 1.1 Date 8/12/86

Function		Transmitted	Recognized	Remarks
CHANNEL	Default	1 - 16	1 - 16	
	Changed			
MODE	Default	N/A	N/A	
	Messages	OMNI ON/OFF, POLY, MONO	OMNI ON/OFF, POLY, MONO	
	Altered			
NOTE NUMBER		0 — 127	0 — 127	
	True Voice			
VELOCITY	Note On	O	O	
	Note Off	O	O	
TOUCH	Key's	O	O	
	Chan's	O	O	
PITCH BENDER		O	O	
CONTROL CHANGE	All:	O	O	
PROGRAM CHANGE		O	O	
	True #			
SYSTEM EXCLUSIVE		O	O	
SYSTEM COMMON	Song Pos	O	O	
	Song Sel	O	O	
	Tune	O	O	
SYSTEM REAL TIME	Clock	O	O	
	Messages	O	O	
AUX	Local Control	O	O	
	All Notes Off	O	O	
	Active Sense	O	O	
	Reset	O	X	

NOTES: N/A: Not Applicable

The MIDI PRO Interface simply passes all MIDI data received (except Real—Time and Reset) to the host computer and transmits all data that is sent by the host. Real—Time messages can be generated and/or recognized by the MIDI PRO itself, depending on its mode of operation. Special System Exclusive messages are used between the interface and the host computer. (See the MIDI PRO spec. for complete details.) The software that is running on the host computer controls all other aspects of MIDI operation.

Mode 1: OMNI ON, POLY Mode 2: OMNI ON, MONO O: Yes
Mode 3: OMNI OFF, POLY Mode 4: OMNI OFF, MONO X: No

Passport [MIDI/Apple II Interface] — Model MH-01A/MH-02A, Version 1.0, Date 8/12/86

Manufacturer: Passport

Function		Transmitted	Recognized	Remarks
CHANNEL	Default	1 - 16	1 - 16	
	Changed			
MODE	Default	N/A	N/A	
	Messages	OMNI ON/OFF, POLY, MONO	OMNI ON/OFF, POLY, MONO	
	Altered			
NOTE NUMBER		0 — 127	0 — 127	
	True Voice			
VELOCITY	Note On	O	O	
	Note Off	O	O	
TOUCH	Key's	O	O	
	Chan's	O	O	
PITCH BENDER		O	O	
CONTROL CHANGE	All:	O	O	
PROGRAM CHANGE		O	O	
	True #			
SYSTEM EXCLUSIVE		O	O	
SYSTEM COMMON	Song Pos	O	O	
	Song Sel	O	O	
	Tune	O	O	
SYSTEM REAL TIME	Clock	O	O	
	Messages	O	O	
AUX	Local Control	O	O	
	All Notes Off	O	O	
	Active Sense	O	O	
	Reset	O	O	

NOTES: N/A: Not Applicable

The interface described above simply pass all incoming data to the host computer and transmit all data that is sent by the host. The software that is running on the host computer controlls all other aspects of MIDI operation.

Mode 1 : OMNI ON, POLY	Mode 2 : OMNI ON, MONO	O : Yes
Mode 3 : OMNI OFF, POLY	Mode 4 : OMNI OFF, MONO	X : No

Passport [MIDI/Commodore Interface] — Model MH-01C/MH-02C, Version 1.0, Date 8/12/86

Manufacturer: Passport

Function		Transmitted	Recognized	Remarks
CHANNEL	Default	1 - 16	1 - 16	
	Changed			
MODE	Default	N/A	N/A	
	Messages	OMNI ON/OFF, POLY, MONO	OMNI ON/OFF, POLY, MONO	
	Altered			
NOTE NUMBER		0 — 127	0 — 127	
	True Voice			
VELOCITY	Note On	O	O	
	Note Off	O	O	
TOUCH	Key's	O	O	
	Chan's	O	O	
PITCH BENDER		O	O	
CONTROL CHANGE	All:	O	O	
PROGRAM CHANGE		O	O	
	True #			
SYSTEM EXCLUSIVE		O	O	
SYSTEM COMMON	Song Pos	O	O	
	Song Sel	O	O	
	Tune	O	O	
SYSTEM REAL TIME	Clock	O	O	
	Messages	O	O	
AUX	Local Control	O	O	
	All Notes Off	O	O	
	Active Sense	O	O	
	Reset	O	O	

NOTES: The interface described above simply pass all incoming data to the host computer and transmit all data that is sent by the host. The software that is running on the host computer controls all other aspects of MIDI operation.

Mode 1 : OMNI ON, POLY	Mode 2 : OMNI ON, MONO	O : Yes
Mode 3 : OMNI OFF, POLY	Mode 4 : OMNI OFF, MONO	X : No

Roland MD-8 (MIDI–DCB Converter) — Version 5, Date 7/21/84

Manufacturer: Roland Model: MD-8

Function		Transmitted	Recognized	Remarks
CHANNEL	Default	X	X	Transmit channel = receive channel
	Changed	1—16	1—16	
MODE	Default	Mode 3	Mode 1	
	Messages	OMNI OFF, POLY	OMNI ON/OFF, POLY	
	Altered		MONO→OMNI ON	
NOTE NUMBER		36—99	0—127	
	True Voice		24—87	
VELOCITY	Note On	X	X	
	Note Off	X 9nH (v=0)	X	
TOUCH	Key's	X	X	
	Chan's	X	X	
PITCH BENDER		X	X	
CONTROL CHANGE		X	X	
PROGRAM CHANGE		0—127	0—127	
	True #			
SYSTEM EXCLUSIVE		X	X	
SYSTEM COMMON	Song Pos	X	X	
	Song Sel	X	X	
	Tune	X	X	
SYSTEM REAL TIME	Clock	X	X	
	Messages	X	X	
AUX	Local Control	X	X	
	All Notes Off	O (123)	O (123-127)	
	Active Sense	X	X	
	Reset	X	X	

NOTES: When power—up, ALL Notes OFF, OMNI OFF, POLY ON are sent.
When the MIDI CH switch is turned, receiver's mode always changes to MODE 3 (OMNI OFF, POLY).

Mode 1 : OMNI ON, POLY   Mode 2 : OMNI ON, MONO
Mode 3 : OMNI OFF, POLY   Mode 4 : OMNI OFF, MONO
O : Yes
X : No

Roland MD-8 (MIDI–DCB Converter) — Version 4, Date —

Manufacturer: Roland Model: MD-8

Function		Transmitted	Recognized	Remarks
CHANNEL	Default	X	X	transmit channel = receive channel
	Changed	1—16	1—16	
MODE	Default	Mode 3	Mode 1	ver 1 OLD MIDI
	Messages	OMNI OFF, POLY	OMNI ON/OFF, POLY	
	Altered		MONO→OMNI ON	
NOTE NUMBER		36—99	0—127	
	True Voice		24—87	
VELOCITY	Note On	X	X	
	Note Off	X 9nH (v=0)	X	
TOUCH	Key's	X	X	
	Chan's	X	X	
PITCH BENDER		X	X	
CONTROL CHANGE		X	X	
PROGRAM CHANGE		0—127	0—127	
	True #			
SYSTEM EXCLUSIVE		X	X	
SYSTEM COMMON	Song Pos	X	X	
	Song Sel	X	X	
	Tune	X	X	
SYSTEM REAL TIME	Clock	X	X	
	Messages	X	X	
AUX	Local Control	X	X	
	All Notes Off	O (123)	O (123—127)*	* version 1 (125—127) versions 3, 4: (123—127)
	Active Sense	X	X	
	Reset	X	X	

NOTES: When power—up, the following mode messages are sent.
version 1   POLY ON
versions 3, 4   All Notes OFF, OMNI OFF, POLY ON

Mode 1 : OMNI ON, POLY   Mode 2 : OMNI ON, MONO
Mode 3 : OMNI OFF, POLY   Mode 4 : OMNI OFF, MONO
O : Yes
X : No

360 Systems — MIDI Merge +

Manufacturer: 360 Systems [MIDI Merger]
Model: MIDI Merge +
Version: — Date 7/27/86

Function		Transmitted	Recognized	Remarks
CHANNEL	Default	x	16	see notes
	Changed			
MODE	Default	x	x	
	Messages	x	x	
	Altered			
NOTE NUMBER	True Voice	0 — 127	x	see notes
VELOCITY	Note On	x	x	
	Note Off	x	x	
TOUCH	Key's	x	x	
	Chan's	x	x	
PITCH BENDER		x	x	
CONTROL CHANGE				
PROGRAM CHANGE	True #	x	x	
SYSTEM EXCLUSIVE		x	x	
SYSTEM COMMON	Song Pos	x	x	
	Song Sel	x	x	
	Tune			
SYSTEM REAL TIME	Clock	x	x	
	Messages			
AUX	Local Control	x	x	see notes
	All Notes Off	O		
	Active Sense	x	x	
	Reset	x		

NOTES: Any MIDI input is passed unless user has enabled filters.

All Notes Off and Note Off $90 x 00 (where x = 0—127 on MIDI chs 1—16) are sent when A.N.O. button is pushed.

Mode 1 : OMNI ON, POLY Mode 2 : OMNI ON, MONO
Mode 3 : OMNI OFF, POLY Mode 4 : OMNI OFF, MONO
O : Yes X : No

Siel — MCI

Manufacturer: Siel [MIDI/Computer Interface]
Model: MCI
Version: — Date —

Function		Transmitted	Recognized	Remarks
CHANNEL	Default	N/A	N/A	
	Changed			
MODE	Default	Mode 1	Mode 1	
	Messages	x	OMNI ON, POLY	
	Altered			
NOTE NUMBER	True Voice	36-96	36-96	
VELOCITY	Note On	O	O	
	Note Off	x	x	
TOUCH	Key's	x	x	
	Chan's	x	x	
PITCH BENDER		x	x	
CONTROL CHANGE	switch 86	O	O	
PROGRAM CHANGE	True #	0-94	0-94	
SYSTEM EXCLUSIVE		O	O	
SYSTEM COMMON	Song Pos	x	x	
	Song Sel	x	x	
	Tune	x	x	
SYSTEM REAL TIME	Clock	x	x	
	Messages	x	x	
AUX	Local Control	x	x	
	All Notes Off	x	O 123,125,127	
	Active Sense	x	x	
	Reset	x	x	

NOTES: Interface for Z-80, 6502, 6510 CPU-based computers

Mode 1 : OMNI ON, POLY Mode 2 : OMNI ON, MONO
Mode 3 : OMNI OFF, POLY Mode 4 : OMNI OFF, MONO
O : Yes X : No

360 Systems — MIDI Patcher +

Manufacturer: **360 Systems** [MIDI Matrix Switcher]
Model: **MIDI Patcher +**
Version — Date 7/27/86

Function		Transmitted	Recognized	Remarks
CHANNEL	Default	X	16	see notes
	Changed			
MODE	Default	X	X	
	Messages			
	Altered			
NOTE NUMBER		X	X	
	True Voice			
VELOCITY	Note On	X	X	
	Note Off	X	X	
TOUCH	Key's	X	X	
	Chan's	X	X	
PITCH BENDER		X	X	
CONTROL CHANGE		X	X	
PROGRAM CHANGE		X	0—7	see notes
	True #			
SYSTEM EXCLUSIVE		X	X	
SYSTEM COMMON	Song Pos	X	X	
	Song Sel			
	Tune			
SYSTEM REAL TIME	Clock	X	X	
	Messages			
AUX	Local Control	X		
	All Notes Off	O	X	see notes
	Active Sense	X		
	Reset	X		

NOTES: Any MIDI input is passed to the user selected patch outputs.
Responds to Program Change on MIDI channel 16 of MIDI input # 4 only.
All notes off sent when new patch setup is selected.

Mode 1 : OMNI ON, POLY Mode 2 : OMNI ON, MONO
Mode 3 : OMNI OFF, POLY Mode 4 : OMNI OFF, MONO
O : Yes
X : No

JL Cooper — Blender

Manufacturer: **J L Cooper** [2 X 1 MIDI Merge Box]
Model: **Blender**
Version — Date —

Function		Transmitted	Recognized	Remarks
CHANNEL	Default	N/A	N/A	
	Changed			
MODE	Default	N/A	N/A	
	Messages			
	Altered			
NOTE NUMBER		N/A	N/A	
	True Voice			
VELOCITY	Note On	N/A	N/A	
	Note Off	N/A	N/A	
TOUCH	Key's	N/A	N/A	
	Chan's			
PITCH BENDER		N/A	N/A	
CONTROL CHANGE		N/A	N/A	
PROGRAM CHANGE		N/A	N/A	
	True #			
SYSTEM EXCLUSIVE		N/A	N/A	
SYSTEM COMMON	Song Pos	N/A	N/A	
	Song Sel			
	Tune			
SYSTEM REAL TIME	Clock	N/A	N/A	
	Messages			
AUX	Local Control	O	N/A	Panic Button
	All Notes Off			
	Active Sense			
	Reset			

NOTES: N/A: Not Applicable
2 Midi In to Midi Out merge box with data filters.

Mode 1 : OMNI ON, POLY Mode 2 : OMNI ON, MONO
Mode 3 : OMNI OFF, POLY Mode 4 : OMNI OFF, MONO
O : Yes
X : No

Manufacturer
J L Cooper
[16 X 20 Progammable Switcher]

Model
MSB 16/20
Version —   Date —

Function		Transmitted	Recognized	Remarks
CHANNEL	Default	N/A	1—16	
	Changed		X	
MODE	Default	N/A	X	
	Messages			
	Altered			
NOTE NUMBER		N/A	X	
	True Voice			
VELOCITY	Note On	N/A	X	
	Note Off			
TOUCH	Key's	N/A	X	
	Chan's			
PITCH BENDER		N/A	X	
CONTROL CHANGE		N/A	X	
PROGRAM CHANGE	True #	X	1 - 64	
SYSTEM EXCLUSIVE		O	O	data dumps/ext. control
SYSTEM COMMON	Song Pos	N/A	N/A	
	Song Sel			
	Tune			
SYSTEM REAL TIME	Clock	N/A	N/A	
	Messages			
AUX	Local Control	N/A	N/A	
	All Notes Off			
	Active Sense			
	Reset			

NOTES: N/A: Not Applicable

16 in by 20 out programmable switch box.

Mode 1 : OMNI ON, POLY	Mode 2 : OMNI ON, MONO
Mode 3 : OMNI OFF, POLY	Mode 4 : OMNI OFF, MONO

O : Yes
X : No

Manufacturer
J L Cooper
[8 X 10 Manual Switcher]

Model
MSB 1
Version —   Date —

Function		Transmitted	Recognized	Remarks
CHANNEL	Default	X	X	
	Changed			
MODE	Default	X	X	
	Messages			
	Altered			
NOTE NUMBER		X	X	
	True Voice			
VELOCITY	Note On	X	X	
	Note Off			
TOUCH	Key's	X	X	
	Chan's			
PITCH BENDER		X	X	
CONTROL CHANGE		X	X	
PROGRAM CHANGE	True #	X	X	
SYSTEM EXCLUSIVE		X	X	
SYSTEM COMMON	Song Pos	X	X	
	Song Sel			
	Tune			
SYSTEM REAL TIME	Clock	X	X	
	Messages			
AUX	Local Control	X	X	
	All Notes Off			
	Active Sense			
	Reset			

NOTES: Recognized: Manual 8 in,10 out switcher

Mode 1 : OMNI ON, POLY	Mode 2 : OMNI ON, MONO
Mode 3 : OMNI OFF, POLY	Mode 4 : OMNI OFF, MONO

O : Yes
X : No

Manufacturer

J L Cooper

[MIDI Clock/Clock Pulse Converter]

Model

MIDI Sync I

Version —   Date —

Function		Transmitted	Recognized	Remarks
CHANNEL	Default	N/A	N/A	
	Changed			
MODE	Default	N/A	N/A	
	Messages			
	Altered			
NOTE NUMBER	True Voice	N/A	N/A	
VELOCITY	Note On	N/A	N/A	
	Note Off	N/A	N/A	
TOUCH	Key's	N/A	N/A	
	Chan's			
PITCH BENDER		N/A	N/A	
CONTROL CHANGE		N/A	N/A	
PROGRAM CHANGE	True #	N/A	N/A	
SYSTEM EXCLUSIVE		N/A	X	
SYSTEM COMMON	Song Pos	N/A	X	
	Song Sel			
	Tune			
SYSTEM REAL TIME	Clock	N/A	O	
	Messages		Start, Stop	
AUX	Local Control	N/A	N/A	
	All Notes Off			
	Active Sense			
	Reset			

NOTES: N/A: Not Applicable

Converts Midi Clocks to 5 volt clock pulses.

Mode 1: OMNI ON, POLY   Mode 2: OMNI ON, MONO
Mode 3: OMNI OFF, POLY   Mode 4: OMNI OFF, MONO

O: Yes
X: No

Manufacturer

J L Cooper

[Clock Pulse/MIDI Clock Converter]

Model

MIDI Sync II

Version —   Date —

Function		Transmitted	Recognized	Remarks
CHANNEL	Default	N/A	N/A	
	Changed			
MODE	Default	N/A	N/A	
	Messages			
	Altered			
NOTE NUMBER	True Voice	N/A	N/A	
VELOCITY	Note On	N/A	N/A	
	Note Off	N/A	N/A	
TOUCH	Key's	N/A	N/A	
	Chan's			
PITCH BENDER		N/A	N/A	
CONTROL CHANGE		N/A	N/A	
PROGRAM CHANGE	True #	N/A	N/A	
SYSTEM EXCLUSIVE		N/A	N/A	
SYSTEM COMMON	Song Pos	N/A	N/A	
	Song Sel	X		
	Tune			
SYSTEM REAL TIME	Clock	O	N/A	
	Messages	Start, Stop		
AUX	Local Control	N/A	N/A	
	All Notes Off	X		
	Active Sense			
	Reset			

NOTES: N/A: Not Applicable

Clock Pulse to Midi Clock Converter.

Mode 1: OMNI ON, POLY   Mode 2: OMNI ON, MONO
Mode 3: OMNI OFF, POLY   Mode 4: OMNI OFF, MONO

O: Yes
X: No

Korg KMS-30

Manufacturer: Korg [MIDI Synchronizer]
Model: KMS-30 Version 1.0 Date 7/14/86

Function		Transmitted	Recognized	Remarks
CHANNEL	Default	X	X	
	Changed	X	X	
MODE	Default	X	X	
	Messages	X	X	
	Altered			
NOTE NUMBER	True Voice	X	X	
VELOCITY	Note On	X	X	
	Note Off	X	X	
TOUCH	Key's	X	X	
	Chan's	X	X	
PITCH BENDER		X	X	
CONTROL CHANGE		X	X	
PROGRAM CHANGE	True #	X	X	
SYSTEM EXCLUSIVE		X	X	
SYSTEM COMMON	Song Pos	X	X	
	Song Sel	X	X	
	Tune	X	X	
SYSTEM REAL TIME	Clock	O	O	
	Messages	Start, Stop	Start, Stop	
AUX	Local Control	X	X	
	All Notes Off	X	X	
	Active Sense	X	X	
	Reset	X	X	

NOTES: Transmits and receives System Real Time messages only.
MIDI out becomes MIDI thru when master clock set to MIDI.

Mode 1 : OMNI ON, POLY Mode 2 : OMNI ON, MONO O : Yes
Mode 3 : OMNI OFF, POLY Mode 4 : OMNI OFF, MONO X : No

Fostex 4050

Manufacturer: Fostex [Auto Locator]
Model: 4050 Version — Date —

Function		Transmitted	Recognized	Remarks
CHANNEL	Default	X	X	Does not use basic channel
	Changed	X	X	
MODE	Default	X	X	
	Messages	X	X	
	Altered			
NOTE NUMBER	True Voice	X	X	* *
VELOCITY	Note On	X	X	* *
	Note Off	X	X	* *
TOUCH	Key's	X	X	* *
	Chan's	X	X	* *
PITCH BENDER		X	X	*
CONTROL CHANGE				*
PROGRAM CHANGE	True #	X	X	*
SYSTEM EXCLUSIVE		unavailable at printing	unavailable at printing	
SYSTEM COMMON	Song Pos	O	X	
	Song Sel	X	X	
	Tune	X	X	*
SYSTEM REAL TIME	Clock	O	X	
	Messages	O	X	
AUX	Local Control	X	X	
	All Notes Off	X	X	* * *
	Active Sense	X	X	
	Reset	X	X	

NOTES: * Message received is directly transmitted.
MIDI will not operate during tape dump mode.

Mode 1 : OMNI ON, POLY Mode 2 : OMNI ON, MONO O : Yes
Mode 3 : OMNI OFF, POLY Mode 4 : OMNI OFF, MONO X : No

Manufacturer: Roland [Sync Box] — Model: SBX-80   Version —   Date —

Function		Transmitted	Recognized	Remarks
CHANNEL	Default	X	X	
	Changed	X	X	
MODE	Default	X	X	
	Messages	X	X	
	Altered		X	
NOTE NUMBER	True Voice	X	X*	*see notes
VELOCITY	Note On	X	X*	*see notes
	Note Off	X	X*	
TOUCH	Key's	X	X*	*see notes
	Chan's	X	X*	
PITCH BENDER		X	X*	*see notes
CONTROL CHANGE		X	*	
PROGRAM CHANGE	True #	X	X*	*see notes
SYSTEM EXCLUSIVE		O**	O**	**TAPE mode only
SYSTEM COMMON	Song Pos	O**	X	**see notes
	Song Sel	O**	X	**PLAY mode only
	Tune	X	X*	
SYSTEM REAL TIME	Clock	O	X	
	Messages	O	X	
AUX	Local Control	X	X*	*see notes
	All Notes Off	X	X*	
	Active Sense		X	
	Reset	x	X*	

NOTES: Received messages (marked *) are transmitted to MIDI OUT. They are not recognized by the SBX-80.

Mode 1: OMNI ON, POLY   Mode 2: OMNI ON, MONO
Mode 3: OMNI OFF, POLY   Mode 4: OMNI OFF, MONO
O: Yes   X: No

Manufacturer: Roland [Sync Box] — Model: SBX-10   Version 1.0   Date 8/19/85

Function		Transmitted	Recognized	Remarks
CHANNEL	Default	X	X	
	Changed	X	X	
MODE	Default	X	X	
	Messages	X	X *	*not passed to MIDI OUT
	Altered			
NOTE NUMBER	True Voice	X	X	
VELOCITY	Note On	X	X	
	Note Off	X	X	
TOUCH	Key's	X	X	
	Chan's	X	X	
PITCH BENDER		X	X	
CONTROL CHANGE		X	X	
PROGRAM CHANGE	True #	X	X	
SYSTEM EXCLUSIVE		X	X	
SYSTEM COMMON	Song Pos	X	X	
	Song Sel	X	X	
	Tune	X	X	
SYSTEM REAL TIME	Clock	O*	O	only transmitted in MIDI MODE
	Messages	O*	O	
AUX	Local Control	X	X	
	All Notes Off	X	X	
	Active Sense	X	X	
	Reset	X	X	

NOTES: Except for Mode and System Real Time, messages received from MIDI IN are directly transmitted to MIDI OUT.

Mode 1: OMNI ON, POLY   Mode 2: OMNI ON, MONO
Mode 3: OMNI OFF, POLY   Mode 4: OMNI OFF, MONO
O: Yes   X: No

Axxess Unlimited, Inc.
[MIDI Processing Unit]
Model: Mapper Version: — Date: —

Function		Transmitted	Recognized	Remarks
CHANNEL	Default	N/A	N/A	Can filter/pass all Channel messages
	Changed			
MODE	Default	N/A	N/A	always filters Mode messages
	Messages			
	Altered			
NOTE NUMBER		O	O	
	True Voice			
VELOCITY	Note On	O	O	note 1
	Note Off	O	O	
TOUCH	Key's	OX	OX	note 1
	Chan's	O	O	
PITCH BENDER		OX	OX	note 1
CONTROL CHANGE	MSB 0-31	OX	OX	note 1
	LSB 32-63	OX	OX	
	Switch 64-121	OX	OX	
PROGRAM CHANGE		OX	OX	note 1
	True #			
SYSTEM EXCLUSIVE		OX	OX	
SYSTEM COMMON	Song Pos	N/A	N/A	
	Song Sel			
	Tune			
SYSTEM REAL TIME	Clock	N/A	N/A	
	Messages			
AUX	Local Control	N/A	N/A	
	All Notes Off			
	Active Sense			
	Reset			

NOTES: Note 1: The Mapper can map these messages to other data types. For example, Channel Pressure can be mapped to Pitch Bend. Check the manual for complete details.

N/A: Not Applicable

Mode 1 : OMNI ON, POLY Mode 2 : OMNI ON, MONO
Mode 3 : OMNI OFF, POLY Mode 4 : OMNI OFF, MONO

O : Yes X : No

Alesis
[Remote Program Change Device]
Model: MPX Version: — Date: —

Function		Transmitted	Recognized	Remarks
CHANNEL	Default	1	N/A	see notes
	Changed	1 — 16		
MODE	Default	Mode 3	N/A	
	Messages			
	Altered			
NOTE NUMBER		N/A	N/A	
	True Voice			
VELOCITY	Note On	N/A	N/A	
	Note Off			
TOUCH	Key's	N/A	N/A	
	Chan's	N/A	N/A	
PITCH BENDER		N/A	N/A	
CONTROL CHANGE				
PROGRAM CHANGE		0 — 64*	N/A	see notes
	True #			
SYSTEM EXCLUSIVE		N/A	N/A	
SYSTEM COMMON	Song Pos	N/A	N/A	
	Song Sel			
	Tune			
SYSTEM REAL TIME	Clock	N/A	N/A	
	Messages			
AUX	Local Control	N/A	N/A	
	All Notes Off			
	Active Sense			
	Reset			

NOTES: N/A: Not Applicable

In "burst mode" MPX transmits program change message on all channels

Mode 1 : OMNI ON, POLY Mode 2 : OMNI ON, MONO
Mode 3 : OMNI OFF, POLY Mode 4 : OMNI OFF, MONO

O : Yes X : No

J L Cooper — MIDI Link

Manufacturer: **J L Cooper** [Master Program Change Device]
Model: **MIDI Link** Version — Date —

Function		Transmitted	Recognized	Remarks
CHANNEL	Default	1—16	1—16	
	Changed			
MODE	Default	N/A	N/A	
	Messages	N/A	N/A	
	Altered			
NOTE NUMBER	True Voice	N/A	N/A	
VELOCITY	Note On	N/A	N/A	
	Note Off	N/A	N/A	
TOUCH	Key's	N/A	N/A	
	Chan's			
PITCH BENDER		N/A	N/A	
CONTROL CHANGE		N/A	N/A	
PROGRAM CHANGE		1—99	1—99	
	True #			
SYSTEM EXCLUSIVE		O	O	Patch Dump
SYSTEM COMMON	Song Pos			
	Song Sel	X	X	
	Tune			
SYSTEM REAL TIME	Clock			
	Messages	X	X	
AUX	Local Control			
	All Notes Off	X	X	
	Active Sense			
	Reset			

NOTES: N/A: Not Applicable
Uses program change commands to send sets of program change commands to selected equipment.

Mode 1 : OMNI ON, POLY   Mode 2 : OMNI ON, MONO   O : Yes
Mode 3 : OMNI OFF, POLY   Mode 4 : OMNI OFF, MONO   X : No

Roland — PG-300

Manufacturer: **Roland** [Programmer for JU-1, JU-2]
Model: **PG-300** Version 1.0 Date 12/11/85

Function		Transmitted	Recognized	Remarks
CHANNEL	Default	1	X	used as 'Unit #' in Exclusive messages
	Changed	1—16	X	
MODE	Default	X	X	
	Messages	X	X	
	Altered			
NOTE NUMBER	True Voice	X	X	
VELOCITY	Note On	X	X	
	Note Off	X	X	
TOUCH	Key's	X	X	
	Chan's	X	X	
PITCH BENDER		X	X	
CONTROL CHANGE		X		
PROGRAM CHANGE		X	X	
	True #		X	
SYSTEM EXCLUSIVE		O	X	Tone parameter
SYSTEM COMMON	Song Pos	X	X	
	Song Sel	X	X	
	Tune	X	X	
SYSTEM REAL TIME	Clock	X	X	
	Messages	X	X	
AUX	Local Control	X	X	
	All Notes Off	X	X	
	Active Sense	O	O	
	Reset	X	X	

NOTES: This unit transmits all received MIDI messages except Active Sense. It generates System Exclusive and Active Sensing messages.

Mode 1 : OMNI ON, POLY   Mode 2 : OMNI ON, MONO   O : Yes
Mode 3 : OMNI OFF, POLY   Mode 4 : OMNI OFF, MONO   X : No

MIDI Control Devices

Voyce LX-4

Manufacturer: Voyce [MIDI Controller] — Model: LX-4 — Version: — — Date: —

Function		Transmitted	Recognized	Remarks
CHANNEL	Default	1-4	1,2	see notes
	Changed			
MODE	Default	X	Mode 3	
	Messages	X	X	
	Altered			
NOTE NUMBER		0-127	0-127	LX-4 can shift zones up or down 2 octaves
	True Voice			
VELOCITY	Note On	O	O	* not available at printing
	Note Off	*	*	
TOUCH	Key's	*	*	* not available at printing
	Chan's	O	O	
PITCH BENDER		O	O	
CONTROL CHANGE	mod 1	O	O	
PROGRAM CHANGE		0-127	0-127	
	True #		1-128	
SYSTEM EXCLUSIVE		X	X	
SYSTEM COMMON	Song Pos	*	*	* not available at printing
	Song Sel	*	*	
	Tune			
SYSTEM REAL TIME	Clock	*	*	* not available at printing
	Messages	*	*	
AUX	Local Control	*	*	* not available at printing
	All Notes Off	*	*	
	Active Sense			
	Reset			

NOTES: The LX-4 routes signals from a master keyboard or controller (chans 1 and 2) to up to four slaves (chans 1-4) simultaneously. The master keyboard can be split into three zones. Independent program change messages can be sent to each slave. See manual for full details.

Mode 1 : OMNI ON, POLY   Mode 2 : OMNI ON, MONO
Mode 3 : OMNI OFF, POLY   Mode 4 : OMNI OFF, MONO
O : Yes   X : No

Yamaha MCS2

Manufacturer: Yamaha [MIDI Control Station] — Model: MCS2 — Version: 1.0 — Date: 9/25/85

Function		Transmitted	Recognized	Remarks
CHANNEL	Default	1 — 16 *	1-16	*memorized
	Changed	1 — 16	X	
MODE	Default	X	X	
	Messages	OMNI ON/OFF, POLY, MONO	OMNI ON/OFF, POLY, MONO	
	Altered			
NOTE NUMBER		X	0 — 127	
	True Voice			
VELOCITY	Note On	X	O	
	Note Off	X	O	
TOUCH	Key's	X	O	
	Chan's	X	O	
PITCH BENDER		O	O	7 bit resolution
CONTROL CHANGE	0—121	O	O	
PROGRAM CHANGE		0 — 63	0 —127	
	True #			
SYSTEM EXCLUSIVE		X	O*	* MIDI "IN/1" only
SYSTEM COMMON	Song Pos	X	O*	* MIDI "IN/1" only
	Song Sel	X	O*	
	Tune	O	O*	
SYSTEM REAL TIME	Clock	O	O*	* MIDI "IN/1" only
	Messages	O	O*	
AUX	Local Control	O	X	
	All Notes Off	X	X	* MIDI "IN/1" only
	Active Sense	O	O	
	Reset	O	O*	

NOTES: Received messages from MIDI IN/1 and MIDI IN/2 are only bypassed to MIDI OUT.

Mode 1 : OMNI ON, POLY   Mode 2 : OMNI ON, MONO
Mode 3 : OMNI OFF, POLY   Mode 4 : OMNI OFF, MONO
O : Yes   X : No

Channel Filter

Manufacturer: J L Cooper [MIDI Channel Filter]
Model: Channel Filter
Version: —
Date: —

Function		Transmitted	Recognized	Remarks
CHANNEL	Default	1	1—16	Filters all but selected channel data.
	Changed			
MODE	Default	Mode 3	Mode 3	
	Messages			
	Altered			
NOTE NUMBER	True Voice	N/A	N/A	
VELOCITY	Note On	N/A	N/A	
	Note Off			
TOUCH	Key's	N/A	N/A	
	Chan's			
PITCH BENDER		N/A	N/A	
CONTROL CHANGE		N/A	N/A	
PROGRAM CHANGE	True #	N/A	N/A	
SYSTEM EXCLUSIVE		N/A	N/A	
SYSTEM COMMON	Song Pos	N/A	N/A	
	Song Sel			
	Tune			
SYSTEM REAL TIME	Clock	N/A	N/A	
	Messages			
AUX	Local Control	N/A	N/A	
	All Notes Off			
	Active Sense			
	Reset			

NOTES: N/A: Not Applicable

Mode 1: OMNI ON, POLY Mode 2: OMNI ON, MONO
Mode 3: OMNI OFF, POLY Mode 4: OMNI OFF, MONO
O: Yes X: No

Channelizer

Manufacturer: J L Cooper [MIDI Channel Converter]
Model: Channelizer
Version: —
Date: —

Function		Transmitted	Recognized	Remarks
CHANNEL	Default	1—16	1—16	see notes
	Changed			
MODE	Default	Mode 3	Mode 1	
	Messages			
	Altered			
NOTE NUMBER	True Voice	N/A	N/A	
VELOCITY	Note On	N/A	N/A	
	Note Off			
TOUCH	Key's	N/A	N/A	
	Chan's			
PITCH BENDER		N/A	N/A	
CONTROL CHANGE		N/A	N/A	
PROGRAM CHANGE	True #	N/A	N/A	
SYSTEM EXCLUSIVE		N/A	N/A	
SYSTEM COMMON	Song Pos	N/A	N/A	
	Song Sel			
	Tune			
SYSTEM REAL TIME	Clock	N/A	N/A	
	Messages			
AUX	Local Control	N/A	N/A	
	All Notes Off			
	Active Sense			
	Reset			

NOTES: The Channelizer ignores channel in input and converts to selected channel on output.

Mode 1: OMNI ON, POLY Mode 2: OMNI ON, MONO
Mode 3: OMNI OFF, POLY Mode 4: OMNI OFF, MONO
O: Yes X: No

Channel Converters / Control Voltage Converters

Roland MPU-103

Manufacturer: Roland
Model: MPU-103
[MIDI Channel Filter/Converter]
Version 1.0   Date 3/6/85

Function		Transmitted	Recognized	Remarks
CHANNEL	Default	1—16	1—16	depends on FILTER and CONVERTER settings
	Changed	1—16	1—16	
MODE	Default	Mode 3	Mode 3	see notes
	Messages	O	N/A	
	Altered			
NOTE NUMBER		0—127	N/A	
	True Voice			
VELOCITY	Note On	O	N/A	
	Note Off	O	N/A	
TOUCH	Key's	O	N/A	see notes
	Chan's	O	N/A	see notes
PITCH BENDER		O	N/A	see notes
CONTROL CHANGE	0—121	O	N/A	see notes
PROGRAM CHANGE	True #	O	N/A	see notes
SYSTEM EXCLUSIVE		O	N/A	see notes
SYSTEM COMMON	Song Pos	O	N/A	see notes
	Song Sel	O	N/A	
	Tune	O	N/A	
SYSTEM REAL TIME	Clock	O	N/A	see note
	Messages	O	N/A	
AUX	Local Control	O	N/A	
	All Notes Off	O (123—127)	N/A	
	Active Sense	X		
	Reset	O		

NOTES: All received messages are transmitted when FUNCTION MODE is NORMAL. When FUNCTION MODE is set to KEY EVENT ONLY, only received Note Number and Velocity messages are transmitted.

Mode 1: OMNI ON, POLY   Mode 2: OMNI ON, MONO   O: Yes
Mode 3: OMNI OFF, POLY   Mode 4: OMNI OFF, MONO   X: No

J L Cooper CV Out

Manufacturer: J L Cooper
Model: CV Out
[MIDI to CV/Gate Converter]
Version —   Date —

Function		Transmitted	Recognized	Remarks
CHANNEL	Default	N/A	1—16	Set by dip switch
	Changed			
MODE	Default	N/A	Mode 3	Mono output may respond to high, low or last note
	Messages			
	Altered			
NOTE NUMBER		N/A	36 — 99	note 36 = 0 volts at 1 volt/octave
	True Voice			
VELOCITY	Note On	N/A	X	
	Note Off	N/A	X	
TOUCH	Key's	N/A	X	
	Chan's			
PITCH BENDER		N/A	X	
CONTROL CHANGE		N/A	X	
PROGRAM CHANGE	True #	N/A	X	
SYSTEM EXCLUSIVE		N/A	X	
SYSTEM COMMON	Song Pos	N/A	X	
	Song Sel			
	Tune			
SYSTEM REAL TIME	Clock	N/A	X	
	Messages			
AUX	Local Control			
	All Notes Off	N/A	X	
	Active Sense			
	Reset			

NOTES: N/A: Not Applicable
Midi to CV and gate converter, settable to positive or negative gate.

Mode 1: OMNI ON, POLY   Mode 2: OMNI ON, MONO   O: Yes
Mode 3: OMNI OFF, POLY   Mode 4: OMNI OFF, MONO   X: No

J L Cooper — CV In [CV/Gate to MIDI Converter]

Manufacturer: J L Cooper
Model: CV In
Version: — Date: —

Function		Transmitted	Recognized	Remarks
CHANNEL	Default	1 — 16	N/A	Dip switch
	Changed			
MODE	Default	Mode 4	N/A	
	Messages			
	Altered			
NOTE NUMBER		36 — 99	N/A	
	True Voice			
VELOCITY	Note On	X	N/A	
	Note Off			
TOUCH	Key's	X	N/A	
	Chan's			
PITCH BENDER		X	N/A	
CONTROL CHANGE		X	N/A	
PROGRAM CHANGE	True #	X	N/A	
SYSTEM EXCLUSIVE		X	N/A	
SYSTEM COMMON	Song Pos	X	N/A	
	Song Sel			
	Tune			
SYSTEM REAL TIME	Clock	X	N/A	
	Messages			
AUX	Local Control	X	N/A	
	All Notes Off			
	Active Sense			
	Reset			

NOTES: N/A: Not Applicable

CV/Gate to MIDI converter, positive or negative gate.

Mode 1 : OMNI ON, POLY   Mode 2 : OMNI OFF, POLY
Mode 3 : OMNI OFF, MONO   Mode 4 : OMNI OFF, MONO
O : Yes
X : No

J L Cooper — MIDI Interface [8 voice MIDI to CV/Gate Converter]

Manufacturer: J L Cooper
Model: MIDI Interface
Version: — Date: —

Function		Transmitted	Recognized	Remarks
CHANNEL	Default	N/A	1 — 16	
	Changed			
MODE	Default	N/A	Mode 3	*unavailable at printing
	Messages		*	
	Altered			
NOTE NUMBER		N/A	36 — 99	
	True Voice			
VELOCITY	Note On	N/A	O	
	Note Off		X	
TOUCH	Key's	N/A	X	
	Chan's		X	
PITCH BENDER		N/A	O	
CONTROL CHANGE		N/A	X	Modulation via internal LFO
PROGRAM CHANGE	True #	N/A	X	
SYSTEM EXCLUSIVE		N/A	X	
SYSTEM COMMON	Song Pos	N/A	X	
	Song Sel			
	Tune			
SYSTEM REAL TIME	Clock	N/A	X	
	Messages			
AUX	Local Control	N/A	X	
	All Notes Off		O	
	Active Sense			
	Reset		X	

NOTES: N/A: Not Applicable

Midi to CV/Gate converter with 8 voices.

Mode 1 : OMNI ON, POLY   Mode 2 : OMNI ON, MONO
Mode 3 : OMNI OFF, POLY   Mode 4 : OMNI OFF, MONO
O : Yes
X : No

Control Voltage Converters

J L Cooper — MIDI Wind Driver

Manufacturer: **J L Cooper** [CV/Gate to MIDI Converter]
Model: **MIDI Wind Driver** — Version — Date —

Function		Transmitted	Recognized	Remarks
CHANNEL	Default	1—16	N/A	Dip switch
	Changed	1—16		
MODE	Default	Mode 3	N/A	
	Messages			
	Altered			
NOTE NUMBER		36—99	N/A	
	True Voice			
VELOCITY	Note On	O	N/A	
	Note Off	X		
TOUCH	Key's	X	N/A	Via CV input
	Chan's	O		
PITCH BENDER		O	N/A	Via CV input
CONTROL CHANGE		X		
PROGRAM CHANGE		X	N/A	
	True #			
SYSTEM EXCLUSIVE		X	N/A	
SYSTEM COMMON	Song Pos		N/A	
	Song Sel	X		
	Tune			
SYSTEM REAL TIME	Clock	X		
	Messages		N/A	
AUX	Local Control		N/A	
	All Notes Off	X		
	Active Sense			
	Reset			

NOTES: N/A: Not Applicable.

CV/Gate to MIDI Box.

Mode 1: OMNI ON, POLY   Mode 2: OMNI ON, MONO
Mode 3: OMNI OFF, POLY   Mode 4: OMNI OFF, MONO
O: Yes   X: No

Roland — MPU-101

Manufacturer: **Roland** [MIDI to CV Interface]
Model: **MPU-101** — Version 1.0 — Date 3/2/85

Function		Transmitted	Recognized	Remarks
CHANNEL	Default	1—16	1—16	Set by MIDI—CHANNEL switch
	Changed	1—16	X	
MODE	Default	X	Mode 4 , 3	Set by OPERATION MODE switch:M=4 P, S=3
	Messages	X	X	
	Altered			
NOTE NUMBER		0—127	0—127	see notes
	True Voice			
VELOCITY	Note On	O	O*	* not recognized when MODE = T (see notes)
	Note Off	O	X	
TOUCH	Key's	O*	X	* received in basic channel (see notes)
	Chan's	O*	O	
PITCH BENDER		O*	O	* received in basic channel (see notes)
CONTROL CHANGE	mod 1	O*	O	* received in basic channel
	volume 7	O*	O	see notes
	hold 64	O*	O	
PROGRAM CHANGE		O*	X	* received in basic channel (see notes)
	True #		X	
SYSTEM EXCLUSIVE		O	X	transmits received message (see
SYSTEM COMMON	Song Pos	X	X	
	Song Sel	X	X	
	Tune	X	X	
SYSTEM REAL TIME	Clock	X	O	MODE = T only
	Messages	X	O	see notes
AUX	Local Control	X	X	
	All Notes Off	O	X	
	Active Sense	X	X	
	Reset	X	X	

NOTES: The MPU-101 has four OPERATION MODES — M: MONO, P: POLY, S: SPECIAL, T: TRIGGER

In the TRIGGER MODE, only System Real Time messages are recognized. No messages are transmitted.

In the MONO MODE, no messages are transmitted.

Mode 1: OMNI ON, POLY   Mode 2: OMNI ON, MONO
Mode 3: OMNI OFF, POLY   Mode 4: OMNI OFF, MONO
O: Yes
X: No

Manufacturer **Roland** [CV-MIDI Converter]

Model **OP-8M** Version 1.2 Date —

Function		Transmitted	Recognized	Remarks
CHANNEL	Default	X	N/A	Transmitter only
	Changed	1—16		
MODE	Default	Mode 3	N/A	
	Messages	OMNI OFF, POLY		
	Altered			
NOTE NUMBER	True Voice	0 — 127	N/A	
VELOCITY	Note On	O	N/A	
	Note Off	X 9nH (v=0)		
TOUCH	Key's	X	N/A	
	Chan's	X		
PITCH BENDER		X	N/A	
CONTROL CHANGE		X	N/A	
PROGRAM CHANGE	True #	0—126	N/A	
SYSTEM EXCLUSIVE		X	N/A	
SYSTEM COMMON	Song Pos	X	N/A	
	Song Sel	X		
	Tune	X		
SYSTEM REAL TIME	Clock	X	N/A	
	Messages	X		
AUX	Local Control	X	N/A	
	All Notes Off	X		
	Active Sense	X		
	Reset	X		

NOTES: When powered up, MONO, OMNI OFF, POLY are sent in ch—16, then in ch—15...ch—1.

Trnasmitter only.

Mode 1 : OMNI ON, POLY   Mode 2 : OMNI ON, MONO   O : Yes
Mode 3 : OMNI OFF, POLY Mode 4 : OMNI OFF, MONO X : No

Manufacturer **IDP** [Intelligent 6 Channel Dimmer Pack]

Model **IDP 612** Version 1.00 Date 7/25/86

Function		Transmitted	Recognized	Remarks
CHANNEL	Default	1—16	1—16	memorized
	Changed	1—16	1—16	
MODE	Default	X	Mode 1, 3	memorized
	Messages	X	OMNI ON/OFF	
	Altered	X	X	
NOTE NUMBER	True Voice	X	0 — 127	Light number for Bump Buttons.
VELOCITY	Note On	X	O	Intensity for Bump Buttons.
	Note Off	X	O	
TOUCH	Key's	X	X	
	Chan's	X	X	
PITCH BENDER		X	O	Grand Master Programmable
CONTROL CHANGE	fader 1	X	O	Programmable
PROGRAM CHANGE	True #	X	0 — 127	Scene number.
SYSTEM EXCLUSIVE		O	O	
SYSTEM COMMON	Song Pos	X	X	
	Song Sel	X	X	
	Tune	X	X	
SYSTEM REAL TIME	Clock	X	X	
	Messages	X	X	
AUX	Local Control	X	X	
	All Notes Off	X	O*	*Does not turn off lights.
	Active Sense	X	O	
	Reset	X	O	

NOTES: The IDP 612 is a 7200 Watt 6 channel lighting controller that can be controlled by MIDI messages.

Mode 1 : OMNI ON, POLY   Mode 2 : OMNI ON, MONO   O : Yes
Mode 3 : OMNI OFF, POLY Mode 4 : OMNI OFF, MONO X : No

J L Cooper — MLC-1

Manufacturer: **J L Cooper** [Lighting Controller]
Model: **MLC-1**
Version — Date —

Function		Transmitted	Recognized	Remarks
CHANNEL	Default	1 — 16	1 — 16	Dip switch
	Changed			
MODE	Default	Mode 3	Mode 3	
	Messages			
	Altered			
NOTE NUMBER		36 — 60	36 — 60	
	True Voice			
VELOCITY	Note On	O	O	
	Note Off	X	X	
TOUCH	Key's	X	X	
	Chan's			
PITCH BENDER		X	X	
CONTROL CHANGE		X	X	
PROGRAM CHANGE		X	X	
	True #			
SYSTEM EXCLUSIVE		O	O	System communication
SYSTEM COMMON	Song Pos	X	X	
	Song Sel			
	Tune			
SYSTEM REAL TIME	Clock	X	X	
	Messages			
AUX	Local Control	X	X	
	All Notes Off			
	Active Sense			
	Reset			

NOTES: Converts lighting fader movements to note commands

Mode 1 : OMNI ON, POLY   Mode 2 : OMNI ON, MONO
Mode 3 : OMNI OFF, POLY   Mode 4 : OMNI OFF, MONO
O : Yes   X : No

J L Cooper — MIDI Disk

Manufacturer: **J L Cooper** [SysEx Data Dump Storage Unit]
Model: **MIDI Disk**
Version — Date —

Function		Transmitted	Recognized	Remarks
CHANNEL	Default	N/A	N/A	
	Changed			
MODE	Default	N/A	N/A	
	Messages			
	Altered			
NOTE NUMBER		N/A	N/A	
	True Voice			
VELOCITY	Note On	N/A	N/A	
	Note Off			
TOUCH	Key's	N/A	N/A	
	Chan's			
PITCH BENDER		N/A	N/A	
CONTROL CHANGE		N/A	N/A	
PROGRAM CHANGE		N/A	N/A	
	True #			
SYSTEM EXCLUSIVE		O	N/A	
SYSTEM COMMON	Song Pos	N/A	N/A	
	Song Sel			
	Tune			
SYSTEM REAL TIME	Clock	N/A	N/A	
	Messages			
AUX	Local Control	N/A	N/A	
	All Notes Off			
	Active Sense			
	Reset			

NOTES: N/A: Not Applicable

Off-line MIDI System Exclusive data dump storage on diskette

Mode 1 : OMNI ON, POLY   Mode 2 : OMNI ON, MONO
Mode 3 : OMNI OFF, POLY   Mode 4 : OMNI OFF, MONO
O : Yes   X : No

Korg MEX-8000

Manufacturer: **Korg** [Memory Expander]
Model: **MEX-8000**
Version 1.0   Date 7/14/86

Function		Transmitted	Recognized	Remarks
CHANNEL	Default	1—16	1—16	
	Changed	1—16	1—16	
MODE	Default	Mode 3	Mode 3	
	Messages	X	X	
	Altered			
NOTE NUMBER				
	True Voice	X	X	
VELOCITY	Note On	X	X	
	Note Off	X	X	
TOUCH	Key's	X	X	
	Chan's	X	X	
PITCH BENDER		X	X	
CONTROL CHANGE		X	X	
PROGRAM CHANGE	True #	0—63	X	
SYSTEM EXCLUSIVE		O	O	Data dump/load
SYSTEM COMMON	Song Pos	X	X	
	Song Sel	X	X	
	Tune	X	X	
SYSTEM REAL TIME	Clock	X	X	
	Messages	X	X	
AUX	Local Control	X	X	
	All Notes Off	X	X	
	Active Sense	X	X	
	Reset	X	X	

NOTES: MEX 8000 is a data dump storage unit for Korg DW-8000, EX-8000, DW-6000, DVP-1, Poly-800 II, EX-800, Poly-800 + MDK synthesizers.

Recognized data (transmit/receive) will be selected by DEVICE switch setting.

Mode 1: OMNI ON, POLY	Mode 2: OMNI ON, MONO	O : Yes
Mode 3: OMNI OFF, POLY	Mode 4: OMNI OFF, MONO	X : No

Roland MKS-900

Manufacturer: **Roland** [MIDI Signal Indicator]
Model: **MKS-900**
Version 1.0   Date 3/4/85

Function		Transmitted	Recognized	Remarks
CHANNEL	Default	N/A	1—16	
	Changed	1—16	1—16	
MODE	Default	N/A	Mode 1, 3	
	Messages	O	X	
	Altered			
NOTE NUMBER		0—127 *	0—127	In TUNE mode only note number 69(A) is sent
	True Voice		21—108	
VELOCITY	Note On	O	X	see notes
	Note Off	O	X	
TOUCH	Key's	O	X	see notes
	Chan's	O	X	
PITCH BENDER		O	X	see notes
CONTROL CHANGE	0—63	O	X	see notes
	hold 64	O	O	
	65—121		X	
PROGRAM CHANGE	True #	O	0—127 / 0—127	see notes
SYSTEM EXCLUSIVE		O	X	
SYSTEM COMMON	Song Pos	O	X	see notes
	Song Sel	O	X	
	Tune	O	X	
SYSTEM REAL TIME	Clock	O	X	see notes
	Messages	O	X	
AUX	Local Control	O	X	see notes
	All Notes Off	O	O	
	Active Sense	O	O	
	Reset	O	X	

NOTES: MKS-900 has three modes. In the "1-16" mode, only messages received on the selected channels are transmitted. In the ALL mode, messages received on any channels are transmitted. In the TUNE mode only Note Number 69, Tune, All Notes Off, and Active Sense are transmitted.

All recognized messages, except Active Sense, are displayed.

Mode 1: OMNI ON, POLY	Mode 2: OMNI ON, MONO	O : Yes
Mode 3: OMNI OFF, POLY	Mode 4: OMNI OFF, MONO	X : No

Mimetics — Soundscape

Manufacturer: Mimetics [Tape Deck]
Model: Soundscape — Version 1 — Date —

Function		Transmitted	Recognized	Remarks
CHANNEL	Default	1*	1*	see note 1
	Changed	1—16	1—16	
MODE	Default	Mode 3	Mode 3	
	Messages	X	X	
	Altered			
NOTE NUMBER		0—127	0—127	see note 1
	True Voice			
VELOCITY	Note On	O 9nH (v≠0)	O	
	Note Off	O	O	see note 1
TOUCH	Key's	O	O	see note 1
	Chan's	O	O	see note 1
PITCH BENDER		O	O	see note 1
CONTROL CHANGE		0—121		
PROGRAM CHANGE		0—127	0—127	see note 1
	True #			
SYSTEM EXCLUSIVE		X	X	
SYSTEM COMMON	Song Pos	X	O	
	Song Sel	X	X	
	Tune	X	X	
SYSTEM REAL TIME	Clock	X	O	
	Messages	X	O	
AUX	Local Control	X	X	
	All Notes Off	X	X	
	Active Sense	X	X	
	Reset	X	X	

NOTES: NOTE 1: From/to any module in patch panel. Selectable enable/disable filter on each track.

Software module for Commodore Amiga

| Mode 1 : OMNI ON, POLY | Mode 2 : OMNI ON, MONO | O : Yes |
| Mode 3 : OMNI OFF, POLY | Mode 4 : OMNI OFF, MONO | X : No |

Dr T's Music Software — KCS

Manufacturer: Dr T's Music Software [Keyboard Controlled Sequencer]
Model: KCS — Version — Date —

Function		Transmitted	Recognized	Remarks
CHANNEL	Default	1—16	1—16	
	Changed			
MODE	Default	O	N/A	
	Messages			
	Altered			
NOTE NUMBER		0—127	0—127	
	True Voice			
VELOCITY	Note On	O	O	
	Note Off	O	O	
TOUCH	Key's	X	X	
	Chan's	O	O	
PITCH BENDER		O	O	
CONTROL CHANGE		O	O	
PROGRAM CHANGE		0—127	0—127	
	True #			
SYSTEM EXCLUSIVE		O	X	
SYSTEM COMMON	Song Pos	O	O*	*only C128 and Atari software
	Song Sel	O	X	
	Tune	O	X	
SYSTEM REAL TIME	Clock	O	O	
	Messages	O	O	
AUX	Local Control	O	N/A	
	All Notes Off	O		
	Active Sense	O	X	
	Reset	O		

NOTES: Any MIDI message, including System Exclusive, can be sent using the STEP ENTRY mode of data input.

N/A: Not Applicable

| Mode 1 : OMNI ON, POLY | Mode 2 : OMNI ON, MONO | O : Yes |
| Mode 3 : OMNI OFF, POLY | Mode 4 : OMNI OFF, MONO | X : No |

Software

Mimetics Soundscape (Internal Synth)

Manufacturer: Mimetics [Internal Synth]
Model: Soundscape
Version 1 — Date —

Function		Transmitted	Recognized	Remarks
CHANNEL	Default	X	1—16	
	Changed	X	X	
MODE	Default	X	Mode 3	
	Messages	X	X	
	Altered			
NOTE NUMBER		X	0—127	
	True Voice		0—120	
VELOCITY	Note On	X	O	
	Note Off	X	O	
TOUCH	Key's	X	X	
	Chan's	X	X	
PITCH BENDER		X	O	0-12 semitones
CONTROL CHANGE	0—63		64—121	unavailable at printing
PROGRAM CHANGE		X	X	
	True #			
SYSTEM EXCLUSIVE		X	X	
SYSTEM COMMON	Song Pos	X	X	
	Song Sel	X	X	
	Tune	X	X	
SYSTEM REAL TIME	Clock	X	X	
	Messages	X	X	
AUX	Local Control	X	X	
	All Notes Off	X	X	
	Active Sense	X	X	
	Reset	X	X	

NOTES: Software module for Commodore Amiga

Mode 1: OMNI ON, POLY   Mode 2: OMNI ON, MONO
Mode 3: OMNI OFF, POLY Mode 4: OMNI OFF, MONO
O: Yes   X: No

Mimetics Soundscape (Player Piano)

Manufacturer: Mimetics [Player Piano]
Model: Soundscape
Version 1 — Date —

Function		Transmitted	Recognized	Remarks
CHANNEL	Default	X	1, 2	
	Changed	X	1—16	
MODE	Default	X	Mode 3	
	Messages	X	X	
	Altered			
NOTE NUMBER		X	0—127	
	True Voice			
VELOCITY	Note On	X	O	
	Note Off	X	O	
TOUCH	Key's	X	X	
	Chan's	X	X	
PITCH BENDER		X	X	
CONTROL CHANGE		X	*	*unavailable at printing
PROGRAM CHANGE		X	X	
	True #			
SYSTEM EXCLUSIVE		X	X	
SYSTEM COMMON	Song Pos	X	X	
	Song Sel	X	X	
	Tune	X	X	
SYSTEM REAL TIME	Clock	X	X	
	Messages	X	X	
AUX	Local Control	X	X	
	All Notes Off	X	X	
	Active Sense	X	X	
	Reset	X	X	

NOTES: Software module for Commodore Amiga

Mode 1: OMNI ON, POLY   Mode 2: OMNI ON, MONO
Mode 3: OMNI OFF, POLY Mode 4: OMNI OFF, MONO
O: Yes   X: No

Mimetics [Clock] — Soundscape

Manufacturer: **Mimetics** [Clock]
Model: **Soundscape** Version 1
Date —

Function		Transmitted	Recognized	Remarks
CHANNEL	Default	x	x	
	Changed	x	x	
MODE	Default	x	x	
	Messages	x	x	
	Altered			
NOTE NUMBER		x	x	
	True Voice		x	
VELOCITY	Note On	x	x	
	Note Off	x	x	
TOUCH	Key's	x	x	
	Chan's	x	x	
PITCH BENDER		x	x	
CONTROL CHANGE	tempo coarse 1	o	o	Tempo coarse (0—254, CPS)
	tempo fine 2	x		
PROGRAM CHANGE		x	x	
	True #		x	
SYSTEM EXCLUSIVE		x	x	
SYSTEM COMMON	Song Pos	o	o	
	Song Sel	x	x	
	Tune	x	x	
SYSTEM REAL TIME	Clock	o	o	
	Messages	o	o	
AUX	Local Control	x	x	
	All Notes Off	x	x	
	Active Sense	x	x	
	Reset	x	x	

NOTES: Software module for Commodore Amiga

Mode 1 : OMNI ON, POLY Mode 2 : OMNI ON, MONO
Mode 3 : OMNI OFF, POLY Mode 4 : OMNI OFF, MONO
O : Yes X : No

Mimetics [MIDI Mixer] — Soundscape

Manufacturer: **Mimetics** [MIDI Mixer]
Model: **Soundscape** Version 1
Date —

Function		Transmitted	Recognized	Remarks
CHANNEL	Default	1—16	1—16	
	Changed	x	x	
MODE	Default	x	x	
	Messages		x	
	Altered			
NOTE NUMBER		0—127	0—127	
	True Voice		0—127	
VELOCITY	Note On	o	o	
	Note Off	o	o	
TOUCH	Key's	o	o	
	Chan's	o	o	
PITCH BENDER		o	o	
CONTROL CHANGE		*	*	*unavailable at printing
PROGRAM CHANGE		o	o	
	True #			
SYSTEM EXCLUSIVE		x	x	
SYSTEM COMMON	Song Pos	o	o	
	Song Sel	o	o	
	Tune	o	o	
SYSTEM REAL TIME	Clock	o	o	
	Messages	o	o	
AUX	Local Control	o	o	
	All Notes Off	o	o	
	Active Sense	o	o	
	Reset	o	o	

NOTES: No interpretation of any MIDI data

Software module for Commodore Amiga

Mode 1 : OMNI ON, POLY Mode 2 : OMNI ON, MONO
Mode 3 : OMNI OFF, POLY Mode 4 : OMNI OFF, MONO
O : Yes X : No

Manufacturer
Passport
[Music Editing/Playback Software]

Model
Music Shop
Version 1.0 — 1.1   Date 8/12/86

Function		Transmitted	Recognized	Remarks
CHANNEL	Default	1	1 — 16	
	Changed	1 — 16	1 — 16	
MODE	Default	Mode 1	Mode 1	
	Messages	X	X	
	Altered			
NOTE NUMBER	True Voice	32 — 98	32 — 98	
VELOCITY	Note On	X	X	Note On sent with velocity = 64
	Note Off	X	X	
TOUCH	Key's	X	X	
	Chan's	X	X	
PITCH BENDER		X	X	
CONTROL CHANGE		X	X	
PROGRAM CHANGE	True #	0 — 127	0 — 127	
			1 — 128	
SYSTEM EXCLUSIVE		X	X	
SYSTEM COMMON	Song Pos	X	X	
	Song Sel	X	X	
	Tune	X	X	
SYSTEM REAL TIME	Clock	O	X	
	Messages	O	X	
AUX	Local Control	X	X	* Only one Active Sensing message is sent when playback is stopped.
	All Notes Off	X	X	
	Active Sense	O*	X	
	Reset	X	X	

NOTES:

Mode 1 : OMNI ON, POLY	Mode 2 : OMNI ON, MONO	O : Yes
Mode 3 : OMNI OFF, PO_Y	Mode 4 : OMNI OFF, MONO	X : No

Manufacturer
Passport
[Sequencing & Editing Software]

Model
Master Tracks
Version 1.0 — 1.8   Date 7/1/86

Function		Transmitted	Recognized	Remarks
CHANNEL	Default	1	1 — 16	
	Changed	1 — 16	1 — 16	
MODE	Default	Mode 3	Mode 1	
	Messages	OMNI ON/OFF	N/A	Mode messages can be entered in Step editor for subsequent Playback
	Altered			
NOTE NUMBER	True Voice	0 — 127	0 — 127	
VELOCITY	Note On	O	O	
	Note Off	O	O	
TOUCH	Key's	O	O	
	Chan's	O	O	
PITCH BENDER		O	O	
CONTROL CHANGE	All:	O	O	Control Change messages are recorded as received and are transmitted on subsequent playback. Also, any control change message may be entered in step editing mode.
PROGRAM CHANGE	True #	0 — 127	0 — 127	Displayed value is 0—127 in step editor.
			1 — 128	
SYSTEM EXCLUSIVE		X	X	
SYSTEM COMMON	Song Pos	X	X	
	Song Sel	X	X	
	Tune	X	X	
SYSTEM REAL TIME	Clock	O	O	
	Messages	O	O	
AUX	Local Control	O*	X	* These messages can be entered in step editor and transmitted during subsequent Playback.
	All Notes Off	O*	X	
	Active Sense	X	X	
	Reset	X	X	

NOTES: N/A: Not Applicable

AUX messages are only sent when playback is completed or stopped in mid—play to ensure that all notes turn off on all instruments. Only 1 active sensing byte is sent at that time. If selected, Thru function will pass all messages except exclusive and Real—Time from IN to OUT.

Mode 1 : OMNI ON, POLY	Mode 2 : OMNI ON, MONO	O : Yes
Mode 3 : OMNI OFF, POLY	Mode 4 : OMNI OFF, MONO	X : No

Software

MIDI Implementation Chart

Manufacturer: Southworth Music
Model: Total Music — Version 1.1 — Date 6/8/86
[Macintosh Sequencer]

Function		Transmitted	Recognized	Remarks
CHANNEL	Default	1	1—16	
	Changed	1—16	1—16	
MODE	Default	Mode1	Mode 1	
	Messages	OMNI ON/OFF, POLY, MONO	OMNI ON/OFF, POLY, MONO	
	Altered			
NOTE NUMBER		0—127	0—127	
	True Voice			
VELOCITY	Note On	O	O	
	Note Off	O	O	
TOUCH	Key's	O	O	
	Chan's	O	O	
PITCH BENDER		O	O	
CONTROL CHANGE		O	O	
PROGRAM CHANGE		0—127	0—127	
	True #		1—128	
SYSTEM EXCLUSIVE		O	O	Not in real—time
SYSTEM COMMON	Song Pos	*	*	* unavailable at printing
	Song Sel	*	*	
	Tune	*		
SYSTEM REAL TIME	Clock	O	O	
	Messages	O	O	
AUX	Local Control	O	X	
	All Notes Off	O	X	
	Active Sense	X	X	
	Reset	X	X	
NOTES:				

Mode 1 : OMNI ON, POLY   Mode 2 : OMNI ON, MONO
Mode 3 : OMNI OFF, POLY   Mode 4 : OMNI OFF, MONO
O : Yes   X : No

Manufacturer: Passport
Model: Polywriter / Leadsheeter — Version 1.2 — 2.3 — Date 7/1/86
[Notation Transcription/Editing Software]

Function		Transmitted	Recognized	Remarks
CHANNEL	Default	1	1—16	
	Changed	1	1—16	
MODE	Default	Mode 1	Mode 1	
	Messages	X	X	
	Altered			
NOTE NUMBER		36—96	36—96	
	True Voice	36—96		
VELOCITY	Note On	X	X	Note on is transmitted w/velocity = 64
	Note Off	X	X	
TOUCH	Key's	X	X	
	Chan's	X	X	
PITCH BENDER		X	X	
CONTROL CHANGE		X	X	
PROGRAM CHANGE		X	X	
	True #			
SYSTEM EXCLUSIVE		X	X	
SYSTEM COMMON	Song Pos	X	X	
	Song Sel	X	X	
	Tune	X	X	
SYSTEM REAL TIME	Clock	X	O*	* see notes
	Messages	X	O*	
AUX	Local Control	X	X	
	All Notes Off	X	X	
	Active Sense	X	X	
	Reset	X	X	

NOTES: Versions 1.3 & 2.3 (Apple IIc) and version 2.2 (Apple IIe) will sync to MIDI Clocks and Real Time Commands. Version 2.x means version 1.x updated by Polywriter Utilities.

Mode 1 : OMNI ON, POLY   Mode 2 : OMNI ON, MONO
Mode 3 : OMNI OFF, POLY   Mode 4 : OMNI OFF, MONO
O : Yes   X : No

Forte Music — MIDI Mod

Manufacturer: **Forte Music** [Acoustic/Electric Piano MIDI Retro-Fit]
Model: **MIDI Mod**   Version 6.3   Date 8/15/86

Function		Transmitted	Recognized	Remarks
CHANNEL	Default	1, 2	X	Transmits on any two MIDI channels
	Changed	1—16	X	
MODE	Default	Mode 3	X	
	Messages	X		
	Altered			
NOTE NUMBER		0—127	X	
	True Voice			
VELOCITY	Note On	O	X	
	Note Off	X 9nH (v=0)	X	
TOUCH	Key's	X	X	
	Chan's			
PITCH BENDER		X	X	
CONTROL CHANGE	sustain 64	O	O	
PROGRAM CHANGE		X	X	
	True #			
SYSTEM EXCLUSIVE		X	X	
SYSTEM COMMON	Song Pos	X	X	
	Song Sel	X	X	
	Tune	X	X	
SYSTEM REAL TIME	Clock	X	X	
	Messages	X	X	
AUX	Local Control	X	X	
	All Notes Off	X	X	
	Active Sense	X	X	
	Reset	X	X	
NOTES:				

Mode 1: OMNI ON, POLY   Mode 2: OMNI ON, MONO
Mode 3: OMNI OFF, POLY   Mode 4: OMNI OFF, MONO
O: Yes   X: No

J L Cooper — MIDI Retro Fit

Manufacturer: **J L Cooper** [Linn Drum MIDI]
Model: **MIDI Retro Fit**   Version —   Date —

Function		Transmitted	Recognized	Remarks
CHANNEL	Default	1—16	1—16	
	Changed			
MODE	Default	Mode 3	Mode 3	
	Messages			
	Altered			
NOTE NUMBER		24—96	24—96	
	True Voice			Programmably Assignable
VELOCITY	Note On	X	X	
	Note Off	X	X	
TOUCH	Key's	X	X	
	Chan's			
PITCH BENDER		X	X	
CONTROL CHANGE		X	X	
PROGRAM CHANGE		X	X	
	True #			
SYSTEM EXCLUSIVE		O	O	Data Dump
SYSTEM COMMON	Song Pos	X	O	
	Song Sel	X	X	
	Tune	X	X	
SYSTEM REAL TIME	Clock	O	O	
	Messages	Start, Stop, Continue	Start, Stop, Continue	
AUX	Local Control			
	All Notes Off	X	X	
	Active Sense			
	Reset			
NOTES: MIDI modification for LinnDrums				

Mode 1: OMNI ON, POLY   Mode 2: OMNI ON, MONO
Mode 3: OMNI OFF, POLY   Mode 4: OMNI OFF, MONO
O: Yes   X: No

Modifications

Manufacturer
Forte Music
[Yamaha PF-10/PF 15 MIDI Retro-Fit]

Model
MIDI Mod
Version 8.0

Date 8/15/86

Function		Transmitted	Recognized	Remarks
CHANNEL	Default	1	1	
	Changed	1—16	1—16	Transmits on two channels when split
MODE	Default	Mode 3	Mode 3	
	Messages	X	X	
	Altered			
NOTE NUMBER		0 — 127	22 — 108	
	True Voice			
VELOCITY	Note On	O	O	
	Note Off	X 9nH (v=0)	X	
TOUCH	Key's	X	X	
	Chan's	X	X	
PITCH BENDER		X	X	
CONTROL CHANGE	sustain 64	O	O	
PROGRAM CHANGE		O 0 — 87	X	PF10 Midi—Mod transmits 0—75
	True #			
SYSTEM EXCLUSIVE		X	X	
SYSTEM COMMON	Song Pos	X	X	
	Song Sel	X	X	
	Tune	X	X	
SYSTEM REAL TIME	Clock	X	X	
	Messages	X	X	
AUX	Local Control	X	X	
	All Notes Off	X	X	
	Active Sense	X	X	
	Reset	X	X	
NOTES:				

Mode 1 : OMNI ON, POLY   Mode 2 : OMNI ON, MONO
Mode 3 : OMNI OFF, POLY   Mode 4 : OMNI OFF, MONO

O : Yes
X : No

525 687